MANAGEMENT OF THE
PUBLIC SCHOOL LOGISTICAL SYSTEM

MANAGEMENT OF THE PUBLIC SCHOOL LOGISTICAL SYSTEM

By

GEORGE W. HARRIS, JR., Ph.D.

Associate Professor of Educational
Leadership, College of Education
The University of Tennessee-Knoxville

CHARLES C THOMAS • PUBLISHER
Springfield • Illinois • U.S.A.

Published and Distributed Throughout the World by

CHARLES C THOMAS • PUBLISHER
2600 South First Street
Springfield, Illinois 62717

© *1985 by* CHARLES C THOMAS • PUBLISHER

ISBN 0-398-05100-3

Library of Congress Catalog Card Number: 84-24043

With THOMAS BOOKS *careful attention is given to all details of manufacturing and design. It is the Publisher's desire to present books that are satisfactory as to their physical qualities and artistic possibilities and appropriate for their particular use.* THOMAS BOOKS *will be true to those laws of quality that assure a good name and good will.*

Printed in the United States of America
SC-R-3

Library of Congress Cataloging in Publication Data

Harris, George W., Jr.
 Management of the public school logistical system.

  Bibliography: p.
  Includes index.
  1. School business administrators — United States.
 2. Public schools — United States — Business administration.
 I. Title.
 LB2823.5.H35   1985   371.2   84-24043
 ISBN 0-398-05100-3

ACKNOWLEDGEMENTS

To the ALMIGHTY, my family and all those that have made it possible, directly or indirectly, to construct this volume.

PREFACE

School district business managers are not usually viewed by their colleagues, or even by local community laypersons as logisticians. The school business manager is more or less identified as the person who holds the purse strings of the school district. Tasks involving budgetary matters, costs, personnel requirements, services and material items are many times taken for granted by educators and laypersons alike.

The task of providing administrative leadership to the school district's logistical program places the school business manager or Logistical Manager in a highly strategic position on the superintendent's central office team. Additional importance of logistical management is also realized in the everyday operation of the overall school district effort. Every segment of the school district must depend upon logistical support (with the instructional program demanding a "lion's share" of such support). Instruction (being the major task of the school district) must be logistically supported in order that its daily operations and its accomplishment of major and minor goals are attained.

Along with supporting the school district's instructional program, the logistical program must indeed support itself with those needs necessary to keep operational. Outside of finances little emphasis is given to the remaining segments of the school district's logistical effort, until a logistical service is reduced or terminated. The quality of a school district's logistical offerings will well determine the quality of the school system's instructional offering to the public.

This book has been developed to present the managerial format of the Logistical Manager, his/her position and (1) responsibility as a member of the superintendent's central office team; (2) an overall and specific view of school logistics; and (3) task mastership by the Logistical Manager.

This book has been planned for both the graduate student and the logistical practitioner. Guidance and awareness of school logistics can be gained through the presentation of sequential offerings that have been systemized to allow for the reader's chronological construction of the logistical process. The book has been divided into six parts which presents the overall logistical picture as it involves the public school district.

Part I (Logistical and Managerial Foundations) provides a concrete presentation of instruction and logistics. It also presents the responsibilities of the Logistical Manager to the superintendent's central office team, the entire school district and the specific individual school building operating within the district.

Part II (Logistical Limits and Objective Direction) presents the governmental statutory boundaries and directions for execution in the Logistical Manager's field of operations. In addition, Chapter IV illustrates the importance of the establishment of objectives and a planning process constructed to achieve those objectives.

Part III (The Control of Electronic Services) gives the reader the rationale for the importance of the computerization of the school district. Also, indication is made to the areas of the school district in which computer assistance can enhance daily operations.

Part IV (Managing The School District's Financial Nerve Center) placing considerable emphasis on the managing of school finances from the standpoint of budgeting, accounting, auditing, plus capital outlay projections and expenses.

Part V (Providing Specialists, Materiel and Protection) points to the logistical personnel management function where noncertificated specialists such as transportation, food, custodial, clerical, maintenance, and other service personnel are recruited, hired, trained and assigned to various positions throughout the school district. Part V also gives direction to the requisition and acquiring of supplies and equipment plus the warehousing management tasks involved in the storage of such items. Protection of the school district's property and personnel comes through the risk management program provided by the Logistical Manager and his/her team.

Part VI (Those Routine Yet Essential Tasks and Techniques of The School Logistician). Presentation is made here concerning the (1) Daily services of building operations and maintenance; (2) The school district transportation program; and (3) The food service program. Proper administration is needed to keep efficiency, economy and quality of operation continuous in these three program areas.

This book presents a panoramic view of the Logistical Manager and his/her logistical team's sphere of operation within the local public school district. Presentations are made concerning the various logistical service offerings to the school district's instructional program. Explanation is also made on how each service offering keeps the instructional program functioning. Emphasis is given throughout the book to provide that knowledge which is associated with the various logistical service segments. Higher levels of skill attainment in logistical service management has been delegated to advanced logistical courses in school business administration and logistics along with administrative internship activities. Training of this nature should be supervised by administrator training institutions with local school districts acting as field operation centers.

CONTENTS

MANAGEMENT OF THE
PUBLIC SCHOOL LOGISTICAL SYSTEM

PART ONE
LOGISTICAL AND MANAGERIAL FOUNDATIONS

CHAPTER I

TASK MASTERSHIP OF THE LOGISTICAL MANAGER

THE INSTRUCTIONAL FUNCTION
OF THE LOCAL SCHOOL DISTRICT

In most of our states (except for Hawaii which has a state system of education and the District of Columbia which is a federal district) local school districts have been given charge of four distinct legal powers to provide for a system of public education. Such powers that are granted by the state legislatures and delegated down to local school districts with their local boards of education are:

1. Permissive powers—Those powers granted to a local school district to allow, but not require certain privileges.

2. Mandatory powers—Powers granted to the local school district that must be followed to the letter as brought forth in the state statutes.

3. Discretionary powers—Those custom made powers delegated by the state to the local school board for their sole use. Such powers cannot be delegated by the local board to its administrative corps (superintendent, central office team, and principals).

4. Ministerial powers—Powers that have been delegated from the state to the local board of education with pronounced perimeters. The local board of education can in turn delegate such powers (again within perimetric boundaries) to its subordinate administrative corps.

The primary thrusts of permissive, mandatory, discretionary and ministerial powers are that of: (1) proper construction, (2) staff development, (3) instructional assistance, (4) instructional offerings, and (5) evaluation of the local district's instructional program. A local district's instructional format can be further divided into such categories as:

1. Elementary education
2. Middle school education
3. Secondary education
4. Vocational-industrial education
5. Special education
6. Career education
7. Gifted education

8. Community education
9. Alternative education
10. Televised and electronically assisted education
11. Computer education
12. Adult education

The construction of the local school district's instructional program must be within those guidelines prescribed by the state. It is the overall responsibility of the superintendent and/or designated member of the central office administrative team (depending upon district organization and/or the size of the local school district). Such a designated team member would be an assistant superintendent of instruction, or a director of instruction who would ensure that state requirements were being met. Construction of the instructional program or its various segments cannot be a one time effort. The curriculum must undergo frequent evaluations in order to identify needs for alterations or termination.

Whenever the process of construction of an area of the curriculum is at hand, there is a need for input by teachers, professional consultants and lay members of the community. Such input allows for: (1) direct participation, (2) knowledge of the daily instructional process, and (3) the attaining of student objectives as observed by the teaching staff. Professional consultants from publishing companies and teacher training institutions have the ability to provide a broader concept of the daily instructional process. The lay public is in a position to present the academic and social needs of the student population. This action can be met through assistance and interaction of school personnel by means of a proper curriculum.

Input from such internal and external groups as previously mentioned will provide the central office administrator(s) of instruction with the groundwork needed to construct decisions concerning the district's instructional program (or a segment thereof), and the goals to be reached by professional effort and child participation.

The development of the instructional staff to meet a devised curriculum is also a responsibility of the superintendent and/or the central office designee of instruction. In order to carry out the prescribed instructional program teachers must possess legal requirements (through certification), plus knowledge and teaching skills. Alteration(s) or the introduction of a new phase to the established curriculum will foster the need for teacher retraining. This can be attained through university classes, special academies and/or district level inservice. The development of meaningful inservice training is a responsibility of the central office administrator of instruction. Action of this type requires a need for coordination between: (1) the central office administrator of curriculum, (2) central office supervisors of instruction, and (3) building principals concerning the scope of such inservice training, and the general development of the instructional staff.

Central office supervisors and principals play a very dominant role in instructional assistance to the teaching staff. In addition to inservice and overall staff development, direct individualized evaluation of instruction is a must in order to ensure that building level, local district and state goals are met. Teacher assistance needs are to be provided by both the principal and the instructional supervisor whenever required. The approach of helper, not liquidator should be used to promote the improvement of instructional skills.

Course offerings should follow state guidelines and also meet the needs of the local school district. Again input to the central office administrator by the teaching staff, building principals, supervisory staff, professional consultants and community lay persons is a must.

Overall evaluation of the district's instructional program is needed on a yearly (academic year) basis in order to attain information concerning the reaching of established goals of the district's instructional program. A general evaluation should be conducted in addition to the individualized instructional evaluations by supervisory, building level administrators, and teachers. Overall evaluation of a particular segment of the curriculum can be attained through test results (classroom and standardized), job performance, college admission, military acceptance and success, etc.

It is apparent that the instructional process is the primary effort of the local school district and is a direct link between schools and the society they serve. Society demands that education take place in order to prepare its citizens to: (1) lead their daily lives, (2) contribute to the nation, and (3) maintain from generation to generation the perpetuation of national standards. Though the nation has fifty states and the District of Columbia, the instructional standard bearer (the public school system) promotes the previously mentioned universal ideals.

LOGISTICS AND THEIR FUNCTION
IN THE LOCAL SCHOOL DISTRICT

Discussion has been brought forth indicating instruction's primary status in the public school district. Emphasis will now be given to a secondary, but important thrust of logistics (which is the main support of the primary instructional program). The absence or severe reduction of the logistical program will impair and eventually terminate the instructional process.

The administration of the school district from the superintendent to that of the Logistical Manager at the central office level presents a dual role of

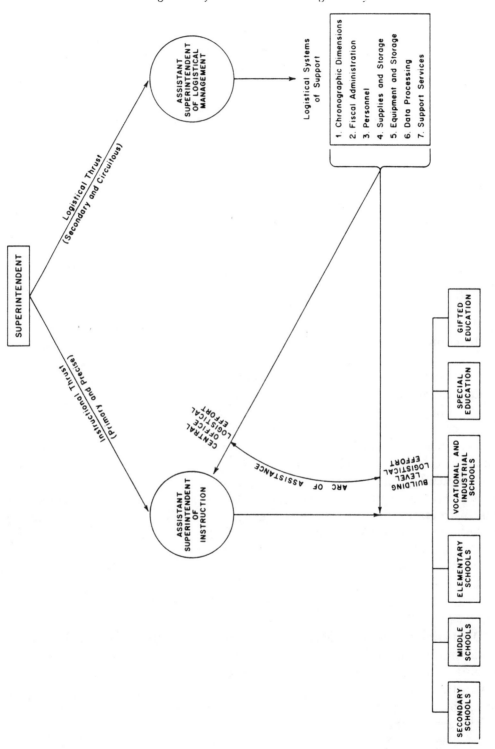

Figure 1. Central Office Logistical and Instructional Flow to Subordinate Building Level Units of Instruction.

both instruction and logistics (see Figure 1). However, the logistical thrust presents a breakdown of yet more specific segments of the main secondary effort. They are: (1) Chronographic Dimensions, (2) Finances, (3) Personnel, (4) Supplies and Storage, (5) Equipment and Storage, (6) Data Processing, and (7) Support Services. These specific segments or facilitating sources give strength to instruction. Administration of these specific sources are the responsibility of the Logistical Manager. A direct identification of these items of support are:

1. Chronographic Dimensions—Chronographic Dimension or time as used by the Logistical Manager. These dimensions are further subdivided into three categories which are essential to the heartbeat of the school district. They are:
   a. Time that has *ELAPSED*—Elapsed time can present the logistical manager with a history of *past* supporting ventures of the school district which can assist in present and future situations.
   b. Time that is *CURRENT*—The measurable period of enacting the instructional and logistical process *in progress* offers a pulsation that can readily be measured.
   c. Time that is *PROJECTED*—Planning for *future* operations of the school district is essential to perpetuate a synchronized flow from:
      (1) Calendar year to calendar year
      (2) Academic year to academic year
      (3) Fiscal year to fiscal year
      (4) Decade to decade
      (5) Generation to generation
      (6) Century to century
      (7) To infinity (see Figure 2)
2. Fiscal Administration—The fiscal business of the school district is the sole foundation of the instructional program. Proper and accurate operation of this source is the responsibility of the Logistical Manager. Without the presence of funds the instructional machine is at a standstill. Without the means of the budgetary process—quality and control of the instructional process are neutralized. Without the proper accounting of liquid and nonliquid assets, and auditing plus inventory procedures, crises and forthcoming terminations would be in order. Finances are the foundational rock upon which the house of public education is built.
3. Personnel—People are needed to support the instructional program whether directly (such as teachers, counselors, supervisors, administrators) or indirectly (those individuals serving as custodians, maintenance workers, clerical personnel, food service employees, bus drivers, etc.).

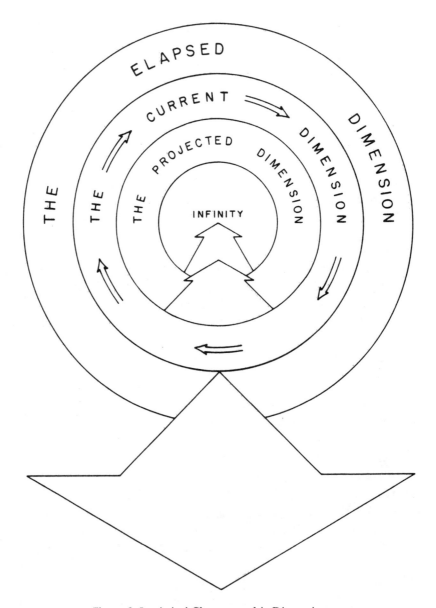

Figure 2. Logistical Chronographic Dimensions.

Personnel are recruited, hired and assigned according to:
a. Qualifications
b. Skills
c. Training
d. Experience
e. Job Requirements

f. Union and Organizational Contracts

g. Employment Record

Whether the employee is directly or indirectly related to instruction he or she contributes to the overall goal of educating the populace.

4. Supplies and Storage—There is a definite need for the consumable tools called supplies in the educational program. Supply items are categorized as instructional or noninstructional. For example, some instructional supply items are:

a. Pencils and Pens

b. Chalk

c. Books

d. Erasers

e. Paper

f. Paste

g. etc.

Noninstructional related supply items are that of:

a. Soap

b. Paper Products

c. Wax

d. Carpet Cleaner

e. Glass Cleaner

f. Postage Stamps

g. etc.

Supply items will have one or more of the following traits [1]:

a. It is consumed in use.

b. It loses its original shape or appearance with use.

c. It is expendable, that is, if lost or expended through fair wear and tear, it can be replaced.

d. Relatively inexpensive.

e. Loses its identity through infusion with another complex unit or substance.

There is a need for managing a warehousing program for the storage of various supplies items.

5. Equipment and Storage—Similar to supplies, however, equipment represents tools that are also essential to and assist in the educational process. [2]

Items of equipment can also be instructional or noninstructional related. Examples of instructional related equipment are as follows:

a. Desks

b. Chairs

c. Tables

d. Microscopes

  e. Industrial Arts Machinery

  f. Paper Cutter

  g. Other similar items

   Some noninstructional equipment items are:

  a. Furnace

  b. Air Conditioning Unit

  c. Public Address System

  d. Wash Basins

  e. Shower Stalls

  f. Drinking Fountain

  g. Vehicles

Equipment items are not consumed, but lose their value through the process of depreciation. School districts will sometimes sell depreciated equipment, or trade it in on new equipment. The following factors indicate the characteristics of equipment:

  a. Retains its original shape and appearance through use.

  b. It is not expendable. Can be repaired or replaced if damaged or worn out.

  c. Represents a monetary investment which makes it feasible and advisable to capitalize the item.

  d. Identity is not lost through infusion with a more complex unit or substance. [3]

With some equipment items being purchased in lots, they must be stored properly in warehousing units. This provides for safekeeping and a basis for proper inventory control.

6. Data Processing—Computerization is a necessity to the modern day public school program by providing for an enormous data bank and data processing center. To assist in providing flexibility to the school district, terminals should be installed in all school buildings (providing computer capabilities to building principals) and other departmental units outside of central office such as the transportation office, maintenance shop, central food preparation center, etc.

  The basic primary areas of data processing would be:

  a. Instruction

  b. Administration

  c. Internal and External Research

  d. Logistical Management

7. Support Services—This item represents a definite pillar of assistance to the school district's instructional program. There are a variety of services administered by the logistical management segment of the superintendent's administrative team. Such services are vital not only

to the school district's instructional goal, but to its very existence. These services are:

a. Purchasing and Warehousing Management
b. Pupil and Nonpupil Transportation
c. Food Preparation and Service
d. Operations and Maintenance
e. Clerical Support (central office and building level)
f. Internal Postal Service, U.S. Postal and private postal services coordination

THE LOGISTICAL MANAGER'S POSITION
ON THE SUPERINTENDENT'S ADMINISTRATIVE TEAM

Today's Superintendent

Since the 1960s the superintendent has been faced with a number of challenges. The decade of the 1960s brought out a militancy in teachers, students and the lay public. The drift from the status quo had a direct influence upon elected officials in the congress, statehouses, city councils, county commissions and local boards of education. There was a clamor for new course offerings to more meet the variety of needs of school children. Parents demanded greater input into the problem solving and decision making tasks of school administrators. Teacher organizations through a collective force demanded greater remuneration, benefits and alterations in working conditions for its members.

The zenith for education's age of unrest was during the early 1970s—a point from which the nation began to drift more to the conservative right in an attempt to once again grasp the "peaches and cream" era of conservatism witnessed during the 1950s. Conservative shifts in society sent Richard Nixon and Ronald Reagan to the White House and fostered national fiscal austerity upon public education. With the White House's pacesetting mechanism tuned for America, elected officials at state and local levels followed suit. Another series of problems for education began to spring forth during the middle and late 1970s. They were:

1. Decreasing enrollments
2. Double digit inflation
3. Taxpayer rebellion
4. Increasing unemployment
5. The shrinking education dollar which brought about:
   a. Hiring freezes

    b. Staff reductions

    c. School closings

    d. Program reductions

    e. Program terminations

    f. Service reductions

    g. Research reductions

6. Public clamor for a more basic approach to education

Today's superintendent must work within a sphere of austerity, anxiety and increasing encroachment by private schools. However, the process of public education must continue with the superintendent maintaining overall responsibility and authority of the local district's educational program.

The Superintendent's Administrative Team

Occupying the office of superintendent of a local school district does not guarantee that one has a detailed knowledge of each administrative zone of activity. Many superintendent's can be termed as a "Jack of all trades, but master of none." The vacuum created in this situation necessitates the need for delegation of authority by the superintendent (see Figure 3). A superintendent or any administrative figure can delegate authority to a subordinate to act as his/her representative, but the sphere of responsibility remains with the individual of superior status.

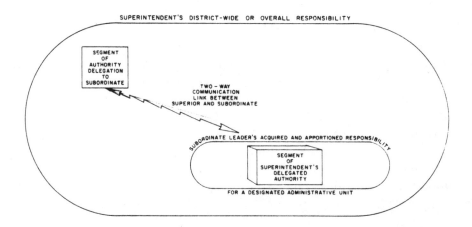

Figure 3. The Superintendent's Delegation of Authority to the Subordinate Administrator.

Delegation of specific duties to lesser central office administrators opens the door to the team concept. Organization of the team and its size will depend upon such factors as:

1. District size
2. District needs
3. District goals

The increasing size and obligations of the school district along with its increasing workload will generate the need for various team specialists. A smaller district does not require the need for numerous specialists, because of the attaching of additional duties to the smaller central office team. A small school district team member may be responsible for two or more major tasks.

In larger school districts one may find that team members have an opportunity to delegate authority to subordinate administrators within their sphere of overall responsibility. This will later be brought out in greater detail in discussion of the organization of the Logistical Manager's zone of operation.

Figure 4 presents a hypothetical illustration of the superintendent's administrative staff of a medium to large size school district. The deputy superintendent acts as a chief of staff who coordinates the numerous tasks of the various team members, also, the deputy superintendent disseminates information, assigns tasks and assists the team in actions and project undertakings. The deputy superintendent is the sole administrative link between the superintendent and the team. However, it must be mentioned that some central office team organizations do not provide for the position of deputy superintendent. Whenever a situation of this nature exists, the sole superior to the team will be the superintendent. A situation of this nature does not provide for delegation of authority to an intermediary administrator.

Whether led by the superintendent or his/her deputy, team action through regularly scheduled meetings should be jointly focused for participation in:

1. Decision Making
2. Planning Process
3. Promoting of Internal and External Communication
4. Goal Establishment
5. Training
6. Program Construction
7. Program Evaluation
8. Problem Solving
9. Zones of Responsibility
10. Zones of Authority
11. Public Relations Activities

The Logistical Manager's Team

It is the duty of the Logistical Manager to provide for all essentials and services needed by other members of the superintendent's team. Coordi-

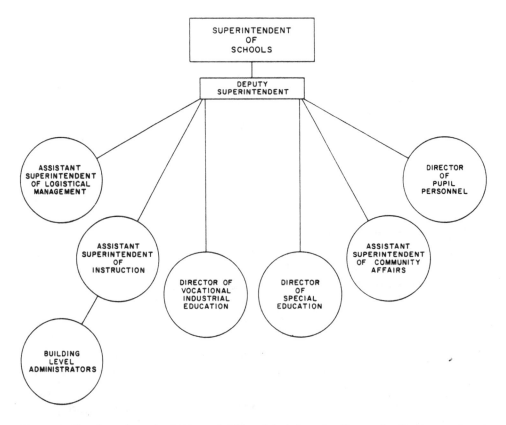

Figure 4. The Superintendent's Central Office Administrative Team of a Medium-to-Large Sized School District.

nated logistical support by the Logistical Manager will enable other team members to carry out their segments of the total education effort in the school district. These essentials and services cover a broad spectrum ranging from dollars to people to gasoline and chalk. A prime point to consider is that the Logistical Manager first needs policy from the local board of education which will enable him/her to function effectively. Logistical policy will offer the Logistical Manager: (1) a foundation from which to set the wheels of logistical support into motion, (2) a prescribed guideline to follow in carrying out a particular task, (3) the perimeter which provides a zone of authority into which the Logistical Manager and his/her staff must conduct their daily operations, (4) methods of procedure which contains the steps to be used in carrying out logistical policy and (5) an established reference point from which unauthorized and unorthodox elasticity are prohibited. It must not be forgotten that logistical policy, like any other type of policy should be periodically reviewed, evaluated and at times be altered or terminated to facilitate the achievement of logistical objectives.

A closer view of the essentials and services provided by the Logistical Manager's staff to the superintendent's central office team indicates coordination. This coordination will involve interaction with peers (assistant superintendents and/or at the directorship level of lesser staff administrators (see Figure 4).

Administrative areas covered by the Logistical Manager's staff are (see Figure 5):

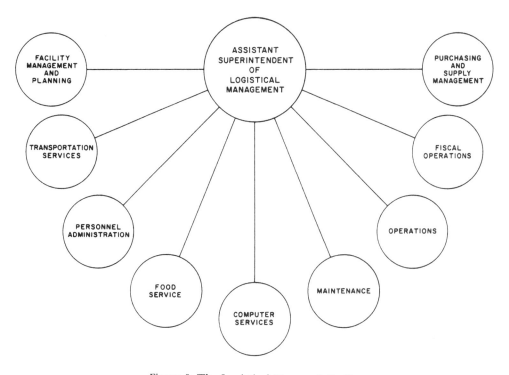

Figure 5. The Logistical Manager's Staff.

1. Facility Management and Planning
   a. Plant Projection
   b. Plant Construction
   c. Internal Usage of School Buildings
   d. External Usage of School Buildings
   e. Coordination with School Plant Planning Personnel
   f. Coordination with School Architects
2. Transportation
   a. Operation of the Pupil Transportation System
      (1) Driver Level Maintenance of Board Owned School Buses

(2) Board Transportation Departmental Maintenance of Board Owned School Buses

(3) External (or Contracted) Maintenance of Board Owned School Buses

(4) Routing and Scheduling Procedures

(5) Student Conduct on School Transportation

(6) Driver Personnel

(7) Nonacademic Use of Pupil Transportation Units

(8) Pupil Transportation Units Coordination with Building Level Administrators

(9) Operation of the Nonpupil Transportation System — Board Owned Automobiles and Trucks

    (a) Driver Level Maintenance

    (b) Board Transportation Department Maintenance of Public Owned Automobiles and Trucks

    (c) External (or Contracted) Maintenance of Board Owned Automobiles and Trucks

    (d) Controlled Usage of Board Owned Automobiles and Trucks

    (e) Purchasing, Control and Usage of Petroleum Products

    (f) Purchasing, Control and Allocation of Spare Parts

3. Personnel Administration

    a. Providing of Noncertificated Work Force (Clerical, Custodial, Maintenance, and Food Service Personnel)

    b. Recruiting, Screening, Hiring and Training

    c. Inservice Programming

    d. Labor-Management Relations

    e. Wage Scales and Fringe Benefits

4. Food Service

    a. Administration of Food Preparation and Mass Feeding Operations

    b. Purchasing and Procuring of Foodstuffs, Kitchen Equipment and Cafeteria Furniture

    c. Master Menu Planning

    d. The Lunch Program

    e. The Breakfast Program

    f. Food Services for Special Occasions

5. Computer Services

    a. Administration of the School District's Computer Program in the areas of:

        (1) Operations, Maintenance and Security

        (2) Personnel

        (3) Office Administration and Procedures

        (4) Student Personnel

      (5) Fiscal Affairs
      (6) Planning Projections
      (7) Instructional Assistance
      (8) Guidance and Counseling
      (9) Library Administration
      (10) Food Service Administration
      (11) Purchasing and Supply Management
      (12) Transportation Administration
      (13) Research
      (14) Communications
      (15) Information Storage

6. Plant Maintenance
    a. Inspection
    b. Replacement
    c. General and Detailed Repairing
    d. Periodic Servicing
    e. Personnel
7. Plant Operations
    a. Housekeeping
    b. Sanitizing
    c. Waste Removal
    d. Heating
    e. Cooling
    f. Grounds Care
    g. Security
    h. Preventative Maintenance
    i. Security of the Plant
    j. Energy Conservation of Utilities
    k. Safety
8. Fiscal Operations
    a. Budget Formulation—Approval and Administration
    b. Accounting Procedures
    c. Auditing Procedures
    d. Financial Reporting
    e. Payroll Preparation
    f. Risk Management
    g. Management of Capital Funds
9. Purchasing and Supply Management
    a. The Purchasing Agent
    b. The Upward Flow of the Requisition—Purchasing Process
    c. Bidding and Specifications
    d. Quality Control

    e. Warehousing Management
    f. Inventory Control
    g. Distribution Procedures

Through the Logistical Manager's responsibility for the previously mentioned tasks, it is imperative that he/she must have direct interaction with the superintendent and the other members of the central office administrative team. The Logistical Manager is the superintendent's primary envoy concerning fiscal matters and logistical services involving interaction with the (1) Local board of education, (2) State officials, and (3) Federal officials. He/she (the Logistical Manager) being in authority over all fiscal and logistical matters should have direct knowledge and access to the school district's financial and inventory picture at all times. Such knowledge is imperative if the Logistical Manager and the school district are to operate in an efficient and synchronized manner.

Through maintaining a direct knowledge over fiscal and inventory situations, the Logistical Manager can inform the central office logistical team members of their individual unit conditions concerning:

    1. Current Programs
    2. Projected Programs
    3. Past Programs

In working with current programs, status can be given central office administrators concerning fiscal and budgetary matters, personnel, supply conditions, equipment conditions and the flow of the various services involved.

The Logistical Manager (with the authorization of the superintendent can also provide public relations data to the community regarding fiscal-budgetary matters, personnel situations, service offerings, equipment plus supply conditions. By having proper communication with the lay public along with the dissemination of bona fide information, the school system can reap great dividends in the form of goodwill for present and future situations.

The Foundation of the Logistical Manager's Team

There must be an in-depth supporting system for the educational organization provided by the Logistical Manager's staff. Without a support for the structure of logistical management, there would be no springboard from which to operate the service and supply machine for the school district. Therefore, there is a need to explore the dark inner depths of the surface operations of public school logistics.

1. The first point of operation (as previously mentioned) is for the Logistical Manager to operate by policy presented by the logistical management policy book. This book will provide not only a basis for all logistical operations,

but that of the spheres of limitations in which the various facets of logistical movement will operate. Policy will also be a reference point from which logistical operations will take place. The logistical management's policy book should be evaluated on a periodic basis to determine if there is a need for alteration or termination. All policy formulation, alteration and termination should be approved by the superintendent along with final and binding approval by the local board of education.

2. The Logistical Manager, in order to have a successful team and a successful operation, needs to have a staff of subordinate administrators that are knowledgeable and dependable. A similar approach must be taken concerning nonadministrative staff operating within the logistical movement. Both situations point to the need for an excellent recruiting selection and evaluation procedures.

3. There is a need for the Logistical Manager to construct the organizational framework from which the logistical movement will operate. The organizational structure should stand periodic review for possible alterations or terminations. Organizational structure must not be entirely rigid and permanent, but allow some form of elasticity. This enables change to take place if needed.

Construction of an overall plan of service is required along with the commencing and operating of the logistical program for the:

a. Fiscal year (local, state and federal)
b. Academic year
c. Calendar year
d. Any prescribed time period required in the operational phase

4. To develop and keep open internal two-way lines of communication with all members of the logistical team.

5. Personnel that are part of or attached to the various segments of the logistical staff must have direct involvement in various forms of training and inservice. These actions directly concern the performance and expected improved performance of logistical staff members. There is also a requirement for personnel management leaders to execute the evaluative phase of work performances by the logistical staff.

6. The Logistical Manager must keep all personnel operating within the sphere of logistics well informed of all current and projected and logistical operations.

7. There is a definite need for liaison and coordination between the various central office team units and within the various logistical staff units.

8. Constant and close supervision of all work performance by staff members of the various units.

9. Top level administrators are required to impress and enforce upon

subordinate administrators (of the logistical staff) proper methods of decision making within their zones of operation.

To ensure that the logistical staff is operating from a true platform
which will assist the Logistical Manager in reaching the logistical unit's
overall goal (of providing adequate logistical services to the school district's
instructional program).

LOGISTICAL SUPPORT AT THE BUILDING LEVEL

The smallest administrative unit encompassing both instruction and logistics within the local public school district is that of the school building
(elementary, middle, or secondary). At building level the principal and
his/her administrative staff [the assistant principal(s)] become the overseers
of a microcosmic logistical system and effort which supports the building
level instructional machine. Services and functions such as:

1. School Plant Services
2. Fiscal Services
3. Purchasing and Storage Management
4. Transportation
5. Food Services
6. Clerical Operations
7. Personnel Administration

are present at the building level and are reinforced by being a part of the
total district-wide central office logistical operation. Building level logistical
operations are subordinate to the larger logistical movement at central
office.

The Principal's Dual Thrust

The principal has a dual responsibility to his/her building. They are:

1. Instruction
2. Logistical Support

Instructional leadership is the primary role of the principal in his/her effort
to reach the overall goal of educating the children of the school's community
(see Figure 6). To be the building's instructional leader, the principal must
from an administrative viewpoint, plan for the overall instructional process
of the building. This includes being involved in specific planning for the
academic year as it concerns the academic segments (such as primary and
intermediate courses of study and objectives along with departmentalized or
self-contained classroom management organization. The principal must also

be able to grasp or have a general understanding of the general instructional process in his/her building. It is also necessary that the principal be a troubleshooter concerning curriculum action in progress at the schoolhouse, and probable problems that may develop at community level.

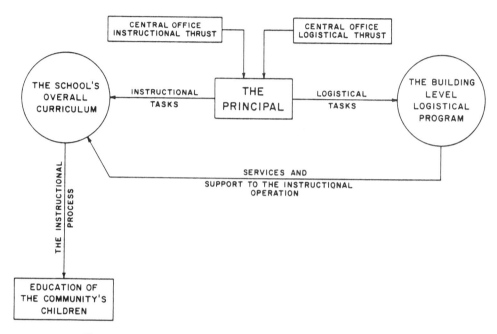

Figure 6. The Dual Responsibility of the Building Administrator.

Leadership of the curriculum process will also involve a series of administrative undertakings which include:

1. Setting the example to the faculty.
2. Fostering the faculty to a positive approach regarding the instructional process.
3. Assisting the faculty with specific (subject and/or grade level) projections regarding:
   a. Course unit content
   b. Time line (accomplishments, grading periods—quarters—semesters—academic year)
   c. Evaluations of students
   d. Evaluation of teaching faculty
   e. Expected outcomes or goals
4. Organization of course unit of instruction
5. Overall appraisal of course unit(s) of instruction and objective accomplishments

6. Preparation for possible alterations and/or termination of instructional course units.

The building level curriculum program does not maintain an innate power to bear a situation of definite supportability. Therefore, there is a need for logistical support in the areas of:

1. Supply
2. Equipment (initial installation and replacement)
3. Textbooks
4. Teaching aids
5. Computers
6. Audiovisual aids
7. Library and reference support
8. Laboratory support
9. Field support
10. Space needs and building management
11. Fiscal support (instructional portion of the building budget)
12. Personnel support (both certificated and noncertificated)
13. Time allocations
    a. Planning
    b. Fiscal year
    c. Academic year
    d. Calendar year
    e. Elapsed time periods
    f. Past periods
14. Clerical support
15. Auxiliary services
    a. Food services
        (1) Breakfast program
        (2) Lunch program
        (3) Special dining situations
    b. Transportation services
16. Facility upkeep and service

If the principal is to be successful as the instructional leader, he/she must be just as successful in being the building level Logistical Manager. The academic program must be supported through an adequate, accurate and synchronized logistical system.

Building level logistics must occupy a portion of the principal's workday, yet like the curricular thrust it (logistics) cannot become overbearing to the general administrative function. Other tasks such as student control, public relations and central office coordination will also consume the typical workday.

There are three prescriptions that offer the principal relief and assistance in carrying out administrative functions. They are:

1. Delegation of authority to trusted subordinates
2. Coordination of the logistical and instructional duties
3. The principal's exertion of his/her zone of overall responsibility.

In managing the logistical thrust of the building, the principal will be working or coordinating with noncertificated personnel such as clerks, custodians, food service workers, maintenance workers, librarians, field personnel, bus drivers, warehousemen, etc. The golden key to success in working in these areas are supervision (personal and/or delegated to assistant principals) and troubleshooting—personal and/or delegated). It is up to the building administrator to establish, work with, plus conserve the delicate balance between logistical management and curricular administration.

Central Office—A Buttress to the Building Level Logistical Program

In order for the building level logistical program to succeed, there must be adequate support and cooperation from the central office logistical management machine. All support services to the building level are administered from central office by the Logistical Manager and his/her staff. Policy concerning the logistical operation has its center of control at local district headquarters. Principals will find that conformity with central office zones of operations, limitations and policies are necessary to properly carry out the logistical program in the school plant. Principals must also be aware not only of board of education policies, but state and federal laws associated with the logistical function. It will also facilitate the logistical operation if there was a uniform building level logistical policy for the school district.

Communications flow between the logistical operation at central office and that of school building level must be adequate plus two-way in both the processes of transmission and reception. There is also the need for these above mentioned actions to take place concerning the logistical flow between the principal and his/her subordinate leaders of the building's various academic and nonacademic units (previously mentioned concerning the principal's dual thrust). Without the appropriate communications flow (both transmission and reception) between building and central office, plus the necessary flow of traffic between intrabuilding units, serious problems can develop. Pressure points of inadequate service offerings will reveal themselves and slowly cause deterioration in not only the logistical program, but also that of the building's instructional timetable (see Figure 7).

School buildings do have the opportunity to provide a highly accelerated link between the building-central office communication zone. Also included

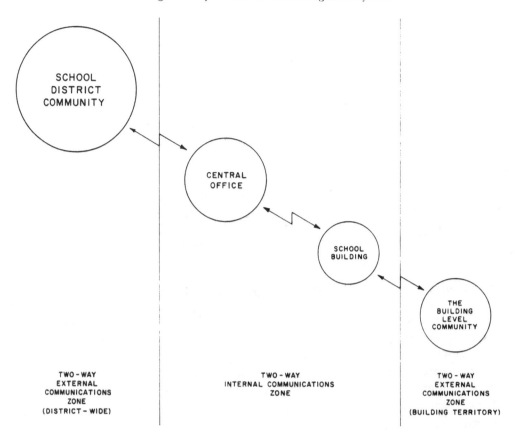

Figure 7. Internal and External Communications Zones of the School System.

along this line is the intrabuilding zone of communication. The medium for creating assistance in this area is that of the central office computer with the remote terminal(s) located at building level. Enormous storage capabilities are also provided by the computer's data bank. The building level remote terminal also will allow the principal's office to:

1. Input data
2. Receive data
3. Process data
4. Make alterations
5. Receive desired output of data

Computer capabilities allow for information resources needed by the Logistical Manager's staff at central office. Access is also open for information resources desired by the building administrator and his/her staff. It must be remembered that the computer is not the sole source of logistical communication flow. There still will be need for communication devices such as:

1. The printed word
2. Electronic mediums
3. The spoken word

Delegation of Authority at Building Level

Discussion has been made indicating the dissemination of authority between the Logistical Manager and his/her staff. Smaller school systems with a decreased number of specialized staff members will reduce delegation and increase the task-load of the Logistical Manager and other central office administrators. The same situation is true for the small school building. There may be an absence of the assistant principal(s), instructional departmental heads, head custodians, and other leader types found at building level in both the instructional and noninstructional levels.

Delegation is in order whenever qualified and trustworthy subordinates are available. By other individuals assuming the principal's authority in certain directed building operations, he/she (the principal) is free to participate in other areas that may be more demanding in regard to direct and personal attention. The shifting of authority from the principal to a subordinate staff member gives that member the principal's power in a particular designated area. The principal, however, maintains overall responsibility as it concerns the particular operation in question. This particular responsibility is included in the overall responsibility for the building. Staff members that take one delegation area are directly responsible to the principal for that particular assigned zone of authority. Yet they (the subordinates) operate the particular zone with considerable autonomy as long as it does not clash with building level and/or board policy.

Delegation becomes necessary for the building administrator in carrying out logistical tasks (due to the time consuming nature for these tasks). For example, many principals will delegate the actual recording of accounts in the building's accounting system to a member of the clerical staff. However, the principal should periodically supervise and check this operation, because of his/her overall responsibility for school's accounting system. The accounting system is a segment of the building's overall financial picture. Delegation for supply and equipment inventory procedures many times is moved in the direction of the teaching staff. Here again the principal needs to provide overall supervision to insure his/her position of responsibility. However, the principal is again committed to overall responsibility of the building's entire inventory task.

Summary

The local public school district performs dual functions in providing an instructional program to the populace along with a logistical program which supports the instruction phase with a number of services.

With the superintendent maintaining overall responsibility and control of district's business, there is a central office administrative team that contains central office administrative control over a variety of educational segments, such as instruction, special education, vocational education, logistics, etc.

Focusing on logistics which is administered by the Logistical Manager, one notices a very direct relationship with the superintendent concerning logistical matters. The Logistical Manager provides logistical information directly to the superintendent and other members of the central office team.

With the central office Logistical Manager and his/her team offering needed services to the building administrator, one can find almost a duplicated logistical effort at the building level, but on a much greatly reduced scale (which covers only the building's area of operations).

CHAPTER II

MANAGEMENT CONCEPTS AND PROCEDURES

The local public school district is a formal organization that has the overall goal of educating the populace of the community. Many modern day school districts go beyond the standard K-12 organization by offering programs in adult and community education. Also one may find (through other offerings) programs for preschool children. Fiscal support for preschool education could be through special funding and/or the community education program. A "cradle-to-the-grave" concept of education can be found in many public school systems throughout America.

A formal organization, such as the public school district, will require an overall leader and subordinate leaders to provide for a system of control. Control of this nature allows for organizational goals to be successfully accomplished. In the process of operation within the organization, these leaders or managers must provide a balance and coordination of tasks and a variety of personnel.

A more penetrating view of leadership by the manager, as it is carried out with his/her subordinates, will touch upon certain factors. They are:

INTERNAL INFLUENCES

1. Character of the manager
2. Character of the individual subordinate
3. Character of the subordinates as a group
4. Character of the manager's immediate superior
5. Character of the manager's superiors as a group
6. Goal(s) to be accomplished
7. Time allowed for goal accomplishment
8. Organizational structure
9. Chain of command flow
10. Overall organizational attitude
11. Overall morale within the organization.

EXTERNAL INFLUENCES

1. Local, state and federal educational dictates.
2. Local, state and national employee organizational and labor union input.
3. Informal community input.
4. Formal community input (organized pressure groups).
5. Alterations brought about by society in general.
6. Alterations brought about by the judicial system.
7. Universal fiscal austerity brought about by inflation and a negative national economy.

Both internal and external forces will have a bearing on the style of leadership that will be desired of the manager if he/she is to achieve his/her assigned goals on schedule with minimum conflict. The manager needs to allow for elasticity in his/her leadership style in order to accomplish the goal(s) that he/she has been assigned. To compensate for the assortment of internal and external pressures upon the manager's leadership, he/she needs to identify these pressures in an assessment of the situation. The next task to complete would be to determine a desired general character type of the immediate subordinate leaders who will be carrying out the logistical program. Also a study is needed of the managerial authority to lesser subordinates. The supreme manager needs also to determine a prototype character representing the next lower level of lesser subordinates. This can be achieved through reviewing previous goal accomplishments of the unit, past communications feedback, and past appraisals.

The extreme polar regions of leadership style are:

1. Liberal Leadership—Which allows for limited managerial input dominated by subordinates with an "anything goes" type of overall atmosphere.

2. Conservative Leadership—This particular leadership style carries a dominance of influence by the manager over the subordinate force. There is usually one way communication—from superior to subordinate. Input by subordinates is little or none.

Between these extreme polar regions one finds a equatorial zone which allows for an elastical movement from the liberal to conservative area, or the conservative to liberal area. Movement to and fro concerning zone to zone action can be influenced by both internal and external pressure upon the organization.

3. MOR or "Middle of the Road" Leadership (the base point)—Depending upon internal or external forces of influence and consideration of alternatives (whether abrupt or gradual change), elasticity is allowed in order to

meet new conditions and still accomplish the assigned goal(s) of the organization (see Figure 8).

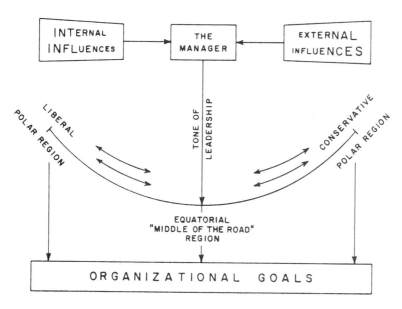

Figure 8. Internal and External Influence Upon the Tone of Managerial Leadership.

MANAGERIAL AUTHORITY, RESPONSIBILITY AND DELEGATION

Managerial Authority

Merriam-Webster [1] gives a precise definition concerning the term, authority: "Power to influence or command thought, opinion or behavior" (by permission from *Webster's Ninth New Collegiate Dictionary* © 1984 by Merriam-Webster, Inc., publisher of the Merriam-Webster ® Dictionaries). The key segment within the definition of authority is that of the concept of power. Invested power is used to determine the avenues of approach on which subordinates will perform their tasks in order to reach the goals assigned to them within their sphere of operation. Inside the zones of subordinate leaders one will find that authority is again exercised with lesser subordinate personnel on a more microcosmic scale.

How is authority invested within top, middle and lower managerial personnel? The focal point of managerial authority will usually rest with some type of legal foundation such as a:

1. Constitutions (federal and state)
2. Statutes

3. Charters
4. Rules
5. Regulations
6. Policies
7. Bylaws
8. Organizational Minutes
9. Robert's Rules of Order

From this legal foundation key managerial positions and the perimeters in which they can operate are usually identified. At times the legal source will provide a certain amount of elasticity to allow the primary managerial level to establish the organizational structure for secondary managerial positions (to assist the organization in meeting goals).

A detailed examination is in order to interpret key, primary and top managerial personnel in contrast to middle, secondary and lesser managerial staff members. Separation between these established tiers of organizational hierarchy is constructed by formally established positions of rank. Interwoven within the system of rank will be found authority. The old military saying of "Rank has its privileges" is also true of the civilian world. Rank's purpose with authority is to guide the organization's daily operation in the areas of:

1. Control
2. Synchronization
3. Efficiency
4. Workload Distribution
5. Supervision
6. Goal Accomplishments
7. Communication Flow
8. Appraisal

(See Figure 9.)

Accountability and Managerial Authority

The legal basis (or bases) provides one with superior rank the right to authority which includes the force of power over subordinates operating within certain perimeters. Caution should be taken in that such a force as derived from authority is not without control. This control factor presents itself within the organization and is known as accountability. Accountability places a retrograding flow from the manager to his/her superiors and/or the legal basis (or bases) which was the creator of the manager's authority. Accountability with its backward surge places the manager in a position where he/she must be answerable to a superior, or to

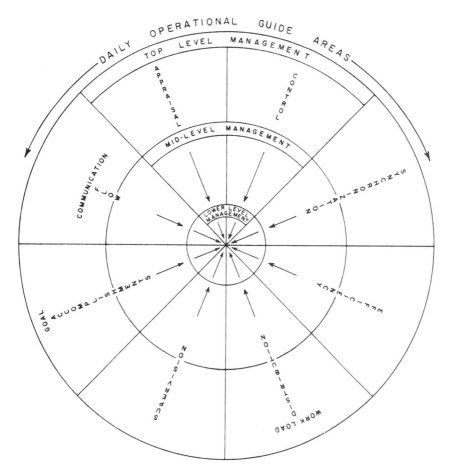

Figure 9. Managerial Rank and Organizational Daily Operational Guide Areas.

legal paper. Public school managerial personnel should view this retrograde action as:

1. Superiors within the administrative corps (assistant principals — principals — directors — to assistant superintendents — deputy superintendent — the superintendent).

2. Superior individuals or groups superior to the school district administrative corps (individual school board members — local board of education — state department of education — state board of education — chief state school officer).

3. Legal papers regulating the educational process (are local board policies — state board rules and regulations — state statutes — state constitution — federal department of education directives — federal statutes — federal constitution).

Accountability is present within and without of the organization. External and internal regulatory procedures are present within organizations of both the public and private sectors. Accountability also places a system of control within the organization which is a check and balance system to all managers whether they are top level, midmanagement or of a lesser position. Another control feature, as was previously mentioned, is the zone of operation which is associated with the position and rank of the manager. The check and balance action of accountability attaches itself to a particular manager and his/her zone, therefore, the responsibility within this zone cannot be delegated to lesser managers. The lesser manager will only be responsible for his/her position and a particular zone of operation. However, delegation of authority is another matter and is brought forth in the next segment.

Delegation in the Organization's Managerial System

The process of delegation provides for an individual to act for, or represent a superior for the performance of a selected task or series of tasks. The party to whom delegation is assigned is invested with the authority, or a division of authority which is inherent to the position of the delegating higher level manager. A delegatee represents his/her superior in an assigned zone of operations, and all subordinate parties must respect and comply with all dictates.

A properly established system of managerial organization will provide a less complex establishment for authority delegation from superior to subordinate. This action will also lay the lines for a convenient communication system. allowing for an adequate system of two-way flow (superior to subordinate and subordinate to superior).

Delegation of authority does not relieve the superior manager of his/her accountability. The overall responsibility for the organization, or a prescribed segment of the organization has priority over the segment that has been delegated (to a lesser manager). Mention is needed here to present the fact that delegation of authority to the subordinate creates a new, but smaller area of responsibility that cannot be delegated to still lower level subordinates. However, delegation of authority can take place among lower level subordinate managers. Attention should also be directed to the fact that delegation of authority can also take place at the lowest subordinate level of the organization.

Delegation should not be exercised haphazardly. Careful selection of reliable and responsible subordinate staff members should be made only after detailed organizational evaluation is conducted of possible candidates. Individuals that are elected to receive delegated authority must represent their superior(s), and the philosophy of the organization.

Policy—The Organizational Keystone

In order that the organization (school district, government, business, military, etc.) operate in an efficient manner, there is need for a legal or paralegal basis from which to function. This basis imposes a series of controls upon the organization's daily operations. One segment of this control device is called—policy. Policy is a principle formulated within the organization after careful planning, great thought, considerable deliberation and has received passage by a governing body (such as directors, trustees, etc.). Policy must be vivid to the point of crystal transparency with a direct to-the-point sharpness. Within policy one will find a control mechanism or a series of control mechanisms which:

1. Observe
2. Record
3. Provide Direction
4. Set Lateral Limitations
5. Provide Points of Termination in Expansion and Depth
6. Provide Standardized Units for Compliance
7. Establish Points of Elasticity Within Limits
8. Provide for Organizational Appraisal
9. Determine Funding and Personnel Needs

Policy or a series of policies are mandatory for the efficient operation of the organization in its daily seeking and accomplishment of objectives. Policy assists the various levels of management (from the highest to the lowest) in defining points of dependence, coordination and liaison between internal units. The enforcement of organizational policy provides for management and the units under their control, a definition of assigned authority and zoned responsibility. Policy can also foster better and more effective relationships, coordination and liaison with units that are external, but vital to the organization. Managerial personnel along with the workers of the organization can look toward organizational policy as both a focal and reference point concerning daily operations.

Policy Formulation Within the Organization

Previous statements were made concerning the careful procedures that must take place within the organization when formulating policy. Factors that must be taken into account concerning the policy formulation cycle are:

1. *Verbal and/or nonverbal alarms*—Within the organizational structure, managerial and subordinate personnel will many times inform their immediate superiors of problems which have a direct bearing upon organizational

goals (which are either secondary or primary). Such problems may be impeding or even terminating the avenue to secondary and primary goal accomplishment. Some warnings or trouble spots may appear through indication by presenting themselves as the culprit which may cause time loss, production loss, and negative objective accomplishment. Many times these warnings indicate problems which are effecting internal synchronization. Such cases may be remedied by new or altered policy.

2. *Detailed description of the problem and its cause(s)*—Once the problem(s) can be identified a detailed and accurate description of the problem along with the cause(s) must be constructed. This description should not be the sole contribution of the ranking manager in charge. Subordinate managers and lesser personnel should also be involved. *Input by subordinate personnel is of major importance.* Another possibility is that of the formulation of an ad hoc committee of directly effected subordinate managers and personnel. They would present and construct the problem and its cause(s) in report form to the ranking manager in charge (for evaluation and possible action).

3. *Obtain clearance for policy formulation from the organization's top manager and/or governing body*—The identification of the problem and the need for new or altered policy may not be sufficient to gain approval from top management and/or the governing board. To be realistic, operating in the human arena may require a style of leadership that is necessary to gain political support from both top management and the governing board. Once this support is gained the construction of policy can be undertaken and approved.

Committee (ad hoc) and/or group action by managerial personnel may be used in the policy construction process. There should also be input by subordinate personnel which are effected by the problem in question and the potential policy influence. Final acceptance and presentation to the chief management figure and/or the governing board should be made by the ranking manager involved in the policy construction process.

4. *Administration and enforcement*—Once the governing board of the organization accepts the proposed policy it becomes valid, and it is a bona fide principle within that particular organization. It will be the duty of various levels of management to administer the newly approved policy (through the carrying out of daily administrative tasks). Partial or total noncompliance by subordinates of the new policy must be rectified by managerial enforcement.

5. *Policy review, appraisal, alteration and termination*—All policy of the organization, whether recent or firmly established over the years, should receive periodic review (at least on an annual basis). Such a review would allow examination of the policy's usefulness and its contribution to the organization's goals and philosophy. Further detailed information should be

gathered from the organization's appraisal process which would determine a formal positive or negative effect of the policy upon the organization. The appraisal would also provide information as to whether the original intent of the policy was being carried out in full effect upon daily operations. Data gathered in the appraisal will allow for three alternatives to take place. The reviewed and appraised policy will either be:

a. Altered to meet present needs.

b. Terminated due to obsolescence.

c. Or the maintenance of current policy standing.

(See Figure 10.)

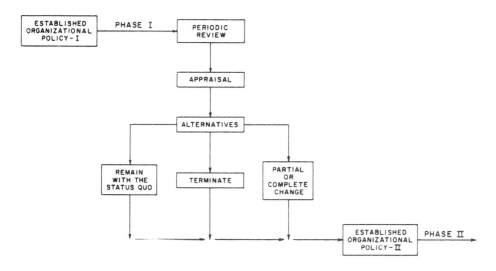

Figure 10. Periodic Policy Review.

Managerial Decision-Making

Standard daily operations will create problems, or a series of problems in the synchronized movement of the organization. These problems may be brought about by:

1. Human interaction or human influence.

2. Technological interaction or influence.

3. A combination of human and technological influence.

The human, technological or combined causes of organizational problems may be either external or internal.

The existence of a problem does not always present itself (directly) to those involved in daily operations. There may be an indirect negative response which may hamper the operational functions of the organization. Sometimes a direct negative response will result from and identify the problem. Identification of the problem itself does not solve or curtail the issue at hand. There is need for further action on the part of the manager(s). Further action will involve an analyzation of the problem in panorama and depth to determine:

1. Cause of the issue (direct or indirect).
2. Is there a constant or intermittent presence?
3. The effect of the issue upon other units of the organization.
4. Is the issue human or technical or a combination thereof?
5. How long has the issue been in existence?
6. Is the origin of the issue internal?
7. Is the origin if the issue external?
8. What are the identified units and/or personnel effected by the issue?

Upon completion of the analyzation procedure, the manager must go into action if an attempt is to be made concerning a solution. First a selection should be made as to the plan of action to be employed in attempting to solve the problem. The term, *attempt,* is used throughout this section to inform the reader that some problems are never solved. For example:

1. The decline of the ice house and ice delivery industry for commercial and residential purposes.
2. The decline of the blacksmith industry.
3. The decline of the privately owned corner grocery.
4. The decline of railroad passenger service in the United States.
5. The almost total disappearance of the hitching post along with its manufacturers.
6. The disappearance of the Packard Motor Company and the General Motors LaSalle Division from the rank and file of the American luxury automobile industry.

Strategy should be planned concerning the types of approach that will be made in attempting to solve the problem. Analyzation in panorama and depth is required to determine the method to be used in combating the problem. Alternatives that can be selected (after input representing the analyzed data of the problem has been introduced) are:

1. Delegation to subordinate managers and/or units.
2. Direct the problem to a standing committee for problem solving action.
3. Direct the problem to an ad hoc committee for problem solving action.
4. Seek external assistance (consulting firms, universities, specialists, etc.)
5. Confer with primary managerial personnel (top management and its staff of specialists).

6. Confer with primary members of management and concerned subordinates.

After a selection of personnel groups and approaches to be used in solving the problem, there is a need to select a particular plan of attack. This should be the nucleus of the decision making process. Before making the ultimate decision, the following steps should be taken:

1. A review of alternative plans of attack.
2. A review of probable outcomes concerning the plans of attack mentioned in item 1.
3. Selection of the primary plan of attack.
4. Selection of a secondary plan of attack.
5. Carrying out the decision.
6. Appraisal of the results of the decision.

If the problem still exists after the decision is made to terminate, management must review appraisal data and repeat the cycle again.

MANAGERIAL CONSTRUCTION OF OBJECTIVES AND PROJECTIONS

Organizational objectives are determined by management in order to direct and coordinate efforts. These thrusts may be direct and/or indirect, with the intent to accomplish a particular task. Objectives may be singular, multiple or grouped in series form.

Organizations establish objectives for a variety of reasons. They are:

1. It (the organization) must comply with the policy what has bore its existence, established the guidelines, and determined limits in which it must operate. Objectives and the accomplishment thereof gives the organization proof in accountability for its creation.
2. Objectives provide the vehicle to assist the projectional thrust.
3. To provide a guide to the decision-making process.
4. To provide a guide for policy alteration and construction.
5. To assist in establishing and coordinating systems of communication within the organization.
6. To provide a means for appraising the organization.
7. To clearly define the perimeters in which the organization is to operate.
8. To firmly establish a service offering.

Objectives should only be established after very deliberate consideration has taken place. Objectives are usually established by governing boards after consideration of input by management. The movement of input data from management to governing board may vary from the "rubber stamping" approach by the board to that of political games and tactical maneuvering, or extreme conflict and chaos. Irregardless of the method of acceptance, by the governing board, there are a series of steps that allow for a synchronized approach to the implementation phase (of a concentrated effort of objectives achievement. They are:

1. Alert involved personnel (managerial and staff or designated committee(s)) that objective formulation is to take place within a specified time frame.

2. Make a thorough review of the organization's exigency data to allow the construction of a priority status.

3. Develop a panacean-optimum type of objective.

4. Reduce the optimum to a more realistic approach. (Consideration must also be made concerning available resources and the positiveness concerning the probability of accomplishment.)

5. Obtain top management approval.

6. Presentation of the plan for objective accomplishment to the governing body.

7. Obtain approval of governing body.

8. Commence implementation phase by:
 a. Orientation of midmanagement.
 b. Orientation of lower management.
 c. Orientation of the staff.
 d. Distribution of policies, tasks (individual and unit) and directions to be taken in accomplishing objectives.
 e. Presentation of objectives (for individuals and units) in prioritized form.

9. Follow-through of the implementation phase.

10. Constant observation and supervision of the objective reaching process.

11. Periodic appraisal of the objective reaching process.

12. Processing of appraisal data.

13. Critique of appraisal data.

14. Possible alterations and/or termination of objective approaches.

15. Continuation of the objective reaching process after review and or modification.

The previously mentioned cycle of the construction of objectives and projections is ongoing until a particular objective, or a series of objectives receives the order of termination. With the introduction of new or altered objectives the cycle will repeat itself until the appraisal process requires:

1. Continuation of the status quo.

2. Alteration or

3. Termination.

FUNCTIONAL STRUCTURE OF THE MANAGERIAL EFFORT

The position of Logistical Manager was designed administer the support and service element of the local school district's instructional program. Within the scheme from which the position of Logistical Manager was established are built-in activities which are called functions.

Some of the functions required of the Logistical Manager have been discussed, but will be reviewed to show their position in the managerial effort. These functions are:

1. *Projection Construction.* This involves the study of chronographic dimensions from the standpoint of future operations. Before the construction of a particular projection, data should be collected from the current and elapsed dimensions to determine if there are clues or trends to future operations. A study should also be made of prioritized needs and possible alternatives before the die is cast (for establishing objectives).

2. *Perimetrical Authoritative Control.* Once the logistical objectives of the school are established, the Logistical Manager and his/her subordinate managers will commence to guide the entire logistical operation and its staff. Such guidance will be within limits established by management's authoritative control through the processes of:
   a. Observation
   b. Supervision
   c. Problem Solving
   d. Decision-making
   e. Evaluation

3. *Establishment of the Functional Structure Scheme.* In order to accomplish an objective, there must be an effort to procure resources such as finances, supplies, equipment, services, personnel and the specific attachment of the chronographic dimension (past and present fiscal years, 5 year projection, 10 year projection, etc.). Once all of the resources are collected, the Logistical Manager must construct these items into a particular arrangement to meet the logistical objectives of the school district.

4. *Establishment and the Maintenance of the Communications Network.* There should be five primary terminals in the school district's logistical system. These primary terminals of communication need to be located within the following units:
   a. The Logistical Manager's Personal Unit
   b. The Superintendent's Personal Unit
   c. The Central Office Administrative Team Unit
   d. The Logistical Manager's Subordinate Managerial Team and Staff Units

    e. External Sources Involved with Logistical Matters (such as jobbers, insurance companies, dealers, brokers, etc.)

Paths between all five primary terminals must be two-way to allow for adequate input concerning:

    a. Problem Identification
    b. Problem Solving
    c. Decisions
    d. Need Identification
    e. Meeting the Need
    f. Priorities
    g. Evaluations
    h. Alterations
    i. Terminations
    j. Dissemination of Information
    k. Feedback
    l. Acceptance
    m. Rejection
    n. Morale Indicator
    o. Official Requests
    p. Authorizations
    q. Union and organizational climate

The Logistical Manager's communication system needs to be reviewed periodically by means of troubleshooting and periodic observation. Assurance that communications lines are operational is of prime importance to the Logistical Manager. This action will allow for balance in the synchronized logistical movement.

The blending of (1) establishing the functional scheme, (2) constructing projections, (3) defining perimetrical authoritative control, (4) and establishing and maintaining an organizational communication's system form the keystone of the functional structure of logistics. Planning for program support service becomes a definite action when objectives are established, accomplished and evaluated. Upon entry of a new program the process will repeat itself (see Figure 11).

LOGISTICAL AND PROGRAM COORDINATION

Coordinating logistics and the school district's instructional program involves a meshing of support services with operations required to meet established organizational goals. Logistical management must provide all the services required to keep the instructional program in working order.

The process of meshing logistics with instruction will require that there

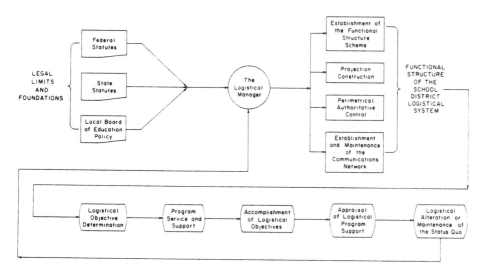

Figure 11. Functional Structure of School Logistics Management.

be prior planning to insure that the proper services are performed at the appropriate time. Such planning should consist of:

1. *Projections* from the standpoint of a future fiscal period(s) to determine whether an academic program is to be continuous over a great or short period of time. Most logistical planning in the public school district involves the projection of a forthcoming fiscal year.

2. *Instruction* as it concerns the type, method, duration, established goals, desired outcomes and actual outcomes of past experiences. Records of past logistical services used in similar instructional programs along with formulated needs for the program in the planning process. Formulation of a time line with points representing primary secondary goals. These items should be indicated along with the logistical needs at specific locations within the district.

3. *Logistical buildup* must take place in order to coordinate service support with the school district's instructional program. There must be a study of the resources readily available, or those resources to which there is unrestricted access. Logistical services must be in a position to supply the need(s) at a particular point in time as presented by the instructional time line. The Logistical Manager and his/her staff must be able to call on their resources to meet the instructional needs at designated points in time. The overall logistical effort of the school district must be in cadence with the instructional program to provide instructional personnel and the pupils with required services. This action is necessary to keep the educational program in progress. Instructional and logistical projections should be coordinated in the planning as well as the process stages (see Figure 12).

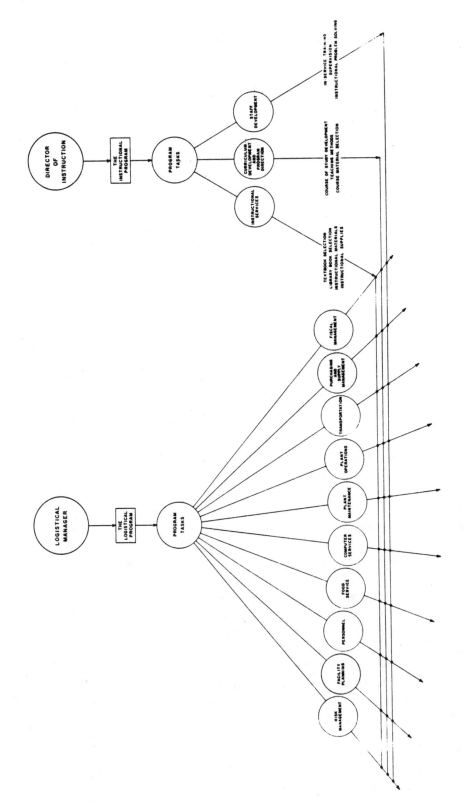

Figure 12. Logistical and Program Coordination.

STAFFING REQUIREMENTS

The previous chapter listed personnel as one of the primary management resources involved in the logistical support of the school district's instructional program. There is a definite need to classify into two main categories those staff members needed to perform the various duties required. They are:

1. Certificated staff members—Those staff members that are directly involved in the instructional process. That is from the direct role of teaching, supervising or administering. Certification may also be required (according to various state laws) of those administering supporting services such as food services, pupil personnel, transportation, teacher personnel, etc. In order that these individuals perform their assigned duties legally, they must possess certification or licensing from the state.

2. Noncertificated staff members—Those staff members that are not required to hold a state certificate or license to perform their assigned duties. This class of employees usually are not concerned with a direct role in the instructional process. Exceptions to this concerns the paraprofessional teaching aide. Other exceptions of this particular class of worker would be:

    a. The school bus driver or truck driver who may be required to hold a chauffeur's license to operate a board vehicle, or

    b. A heating engineer who may be required to possess a state license, or

    c. A food service workers that may be required to be the holder of a food handler's health card.

Though the above mentioned workers are not certified in the instructional process (direct or indirect) they are required to have a state or local license to perform their support service tasks.

Both certificated and noncertificated staff members will be concerned with objectives that are established for personal and unit achievement. Proper construction of objectives by management (with staff input) is imperative in order that achievement of the desired outcome is realistic. Once an objective is formulated, a spot evaluation should be taken to determine whether or not it has the intended potential, and authenticity required before implementation. Questions that need to be answered in determining whether or not objective implementation should take place are:

1. Are the objectives worded in a clear and concise manner to allow freedom from multiple interpretation?

2. What type of relationship is required with other units (internal or external) in order to achieve the objective?

3. Has consideration been given to the area of chronographic dimensions?

4. Is it an assumption or actual fact that all resources are readily available

within the specified time frame required (for the objective to be accomplished)?

5. Has consideration been given the staff and the district's needs in the objective construction phase?

6. What type of appraisal system will take place upon accomplishing the objective?

The Logistical Staff

The majority of membership of the logistical staff will fall in the area of noncertificated personnel. However (as was previously mentioned), there are certain slots that may require certification or licensing. Logistical staff members provide those services that are needed to keep the instructional program operational (in a direct or indirect manner). Logistical staff members will include:

1. Clerical Personnel
2. Food Service Personnel
3. School Maintenance Staff
4. School Operations Staff
5. Transportation Personnel
6. Data Processing Staff
7. Warehouse Personnel
8. Logistical Managerial Personnel
9. Fiscal Management Personnel (Accountants)
10. Property Custodian
11. Risk Management Custodian
12. Security Personnel

The foundation of the logistical staff personnel program is that of board of education policy. Policy will serve as a reference which provides guidelines and zones of limitation for the logistical staff's operation within the school district. This policy should be formulated by the Logistical Manager and his/her staff and after careful review forwarded to the superintendent. If satisfactory, the superintendent will grant administrative approval. Upon the superintendent's approval the policy should be advanced to the board of education for legislative approval in which the policy then becomes a valid part of the school district machine.

After the recruitment and selection of a logistical staff member (greater detail will be brought forth in Chapter IX), the legislative power of the board is brought forth in its acceptance of the individual for a position of employment.

To prevent the overlapping of duties in the logistical program there is a need for the logistical managerial staff to formulate job descriptions for each position within the various service units.

Job descriptions will also assist the logistical managerial staff in determining the number of needed personnel. Whenever pressure points or bottlenecks present themselves within the logistical system, job descriptions may also indicate the need for additional or reduced personnel. The restricting elements included within the job description itself will present points of limitation regarding courses of action and those obligations that are included with a particular job.

Another key factor concerning staffing requirements of the logistical program is that of the provision of in-service to both new and established logistical workers. The catalyst that disrupts the status quo of the logistical operation, or a segment thereof is termed modification. Such modification may be the result of undetermined and gradual growth within the system; or it may be induced by personnel and/or innovation. In-service is a medium by which training (short or long ranged) is used by management to bring the segment of modification to an alternate level representing the newly established status quo. The new status quo is gained as the job performance of the worker(s) reaches a level of managerial acceptance.

What should be the targets of a well planned inservice training program? They are:

1. Determining suspected deficiencies in the organization's previous training programs and correction thereof.

2. Presentation to the staff of the modification (planned or unplanned) that has taken place within the organization and its effect upon the assigned operation.

3. Review and explanation of possible alterations within the job descriptions of personnel concerned with the in-service presentation.

4. A presentation of managerial involvement as it concerns the particular inservice features.

5. A clear and concise presentation concerning alterations in the logistical operation to combat or terminate the previously mentioned modification.

6. Encouraging in-service participants to incorporate newly learned skills in their segment of the logistical operation.

7. Encourage in-service participants to use the organization's communications links between units, managers and central office.

In summary the in-service program should be appraised along with the on-the-job performance of the in-service participants. These results will inform management whether or not the in-service program has merit and has met the needs of the logistical organization. If there have been negative results, there are three alternatives. They are:

1. Change the method of in-service presentation.

2. Investigate and remove personnel responsible for undesired modification.

3. Change the structure of the troubled unit to better meet the needs of the logistical effort.

APPRAISAL OF THE SCHOOL DISTRICT'S LOGISTICAL SYSTEM

Appraisal of the school district's logistical system is a must, particularly if the optimum of program service is to be gained. This action demands that a yardstick of some type be developed to measure the:

1. Quality of service(s)
2. Punctuality of the service offering
3. Amount of time consumed by presentation and engagement of the service offering into the instructional program.
4. Performance of the service personnel
5. Adequate resources
6. Obstacle free supply lines
7. Free flowing lines of communication
8. Adequate coordination and liaison with the instructional units and their objectives.
9. The number and severity of logistical bottlenecks.
10. The attaining of logistical objectives.

The foundation from which the logistical appraisal will get underway and maneuver through the process of operation, is that of board of education policy. Policy should be formulated which will:

1. Construct the polar extremes concerning limitations and the operating zone therein.
2. Define the period of elapsed time which will be covered by the appraisal.
3. Name the particular method of appraisal and the type of instruments involved.
4. Spell out the logistical leadership involved in the appraisal process.
5. Prescribe the method of collection of appraisal data.
6. Prescribe the method of appraisal of data analysis.
7. Prescribe the methods in which appraisal results will be studied for possible alterations and terminations in the logistical program.
8. Establishment of logistical criterion desired, and
9. Establish appraisal costs as part of annual logistical budget for the fiscal period.

Once the policy for appraisal is established, the appraisal cycle is in order. The Logistical Manager and his/her staff should:

1. Review all primary and secondary objectives of the school district's logistical component.

2. Review board of education criterion desired and which coincides with each objective (both primary and secondary).

3. Use of a rating system to determine the logistical unit's level of achievement of the objective(s) along with the established criterion.

4. Implementation of an appraisal data collection system.

5. Analysis of appraisal data.

6. Listing of all action ratings of the logistical objectives.

7. Determination of countermeasure(s) for low and/or mediocre logistical action ratings.

8. Periodic appraisal of countermeasures installed in the logistical process to determine effectiveness in improving low and or mediocre ratings.

9. Analysis of countermeasure appraisal.

10. Decision as to the action of terminating current countermeasures and the establishment of new countermeasures to increase effectiveness of original low and/or mediocre ratings.

Areas of the logistical service effort that are open to appraisal encompass the entire logistical support system. A complete evaluation of each internal unit of the logistical arm along with its goals provides a 360° knowledge coverage of the level of service offered. The service offerings and their position on the rating scale are also a reflection of the logistical managerial staff.

Primary logistical areas that should be appraised are:

1. Fiscal Management and Reporting
2. Purchasing System
3. Supply and Warehouse Management
4. Risk Management
5. Property Custodianship
6. Capital Fund Management
7. Office Management and Support Services
8. Transportation Services
9. Food Preparation and Service
10. Plant Maintenance
11. Plant Operations
12. Data Processing
13. Security
14. Personnel Management
15. Facility Construction Management
16. Central Office Team Coordination

Appraisal results along with remedies for improvement of services will enable the school district to offer a high level of logistical assistance to the instructional program.

PUBLIC INPUT

Individuals and groups outside the local educational organization have the power to place pressure upon the school system and those associated with it. These are the people who pay the taxes to support public education. They are also the individuals whose children attend and receive educational offerings by the school district's instructional mechanism. Members of the community often demand accountability when the question arises concerning the tasks of an administrator or a teacher.

Community members many times will exercise their power by the combined force of pressure groups (which may represent for right wing and/or for left wing political organizations, religious organizations, para-military organizations, civic groups, economic groups, and parent associated groups). These organizations will many times have the influence and the power to remove administrators, teachers and non-certificated personnel.

The Logistical Manager must be aware of the strength of external forces within the school community. As the chief administrator in charge of:

1. Budget Preparation and Fiscal Management
2. Pupil Transportation
3. Plant Maintenance
4. Plant Operations
5. Plant Planning and Construction
6. Labor Relations and Collective Negotiations
7. Food Services
8. Security

He/she (the Logistical Manager) is bound to meet the ire of a community segment in some way. Administrators have long known the fact that it is almost impossible to gain total favor of the populace. By being the custodian of the school district's purse alone is enough to raise the eyelids of suspicion in various sectors of the lay community.

It is almost impossible to clear all suspicion and doubt among the members of the community, but the Logistical Manager's use of (1) tact, (2) decorum, (3) community liaison, (4) community coordination, (5) community input, (6) community awareness, and (7) the maintaining of a two-way system of communication with the populace will be of great assistance.

Public awareness and input into the school district's logistical machine should be in accordance with:

1. The school district's philosophy.
2. According to school district policy.
3. The relationship of the school district with the school community.

4. The presentation of the logistical function at the average level of the lay community.

5. Strive for positive relations between the logistical program and the community.

6. The requiring of a 100% effort on the part of logistical personnel to make school-community relations contacts successful.

7. To illustrate to the public that the logistical effort is a segment of the total school operation.

The Logistical Manager must set the example to his/her staff in maintaining positive relations with the public. Positive community support is needed to insure a successful education program. School board policy should be established as to allow public input to the point that it is beneficial to the logistical program. Also the Logistical Manager must be aware that he/she maintains responsibility for the school district's logistics, regardless of the impact and intent of public input.

INTRA-DISTRICT COMMUNICATION FLOW

Communication flow between the logistical unit and other elements within the local school district is essential and must not suffer any form of interruption. The flow must be two way in nature, therefore, allowing traffic that is outgoing and incoming to subordinate units within the logistical system. This action will also apply to building level logistical units of the school district (see Figure 7).

The communications thrust by the Logistical Manager and his/her staff can be classified according to:

1. The *Service/Product Requester*
2. The *Service/Product Recipient*
3. *Service/Product Data* in accordance with:
   a. Compliance
   b. Fund Disbursement (Fiscal Administration)
   c. Obtaining the product or service
   d. Inspecting product or service guidelines
   e. Delivery of product or service performance to recipient
   f. Passage of appraisal information regarding product or service
4. *Managerial Mandate(s)* that set the operation in motion after the initial action by the service requester.
5. *Managerial Surveillance* (that is overt, covert and/or electronic in nature) to appraise outgoing and incoming data to determine whether the logistical effort is satisfactory.

In the communications process of the logistical program there are a series of primary conductors transmitting both the incoming and outgoing flow patterns. These conductors are:

1. Personnel (logistical staff, other school district staff members, and possibly the school community) that are directly effected (such as through transportation, food service, data processing reports, etc.)
2. The requested product or service itself.
3. The logistical system itself.
4. Logistical policies
5. Logistical controls
6. Logistical evaluations
7. Budgetary and fiscal controls
8. Inventory and warehousing procedures and controls
9. Product or service acquisition
10. Product or service recipient's appraisal concerning both the requested item(s) or service(s) along with the time consumed between request and reception.

Items of communication received by the logistical managerial staff can be classified into two main groups. Those that are formal and those that are informal in nature. Formal communications may be in the form of letters, memorandums, requests, shipping forms, and other formal communications documents. Informal communications may be through evident bottlenecks, trouble spots, or various problems within the logistical works. Informal communication reports need to be evaluated on their authenticity before managerial action takes place. Foregoing a thorough evaluation of the information received can bring forth negative returns and lost time in the logistical operation.

Managerial evaluation of all communications should involve the following checklist:

1. Identification of the sender.
2. History and reliability of the sender.
3. Is there correlation and synchronization between the communique and the particular situation at hand?
4. Does the communique present a situation or situations similar to those in the past?
5. If the communique brings forth an unprecedented situation, further study will be required before the engagement of managerial action.
6. Take the appropriate managerial action.
7. Evaluation of the action taken.

Communication fosters action within the logistical bailiwick which in turn allows the unit to provide a better service. The Logistical Manager must construct a communications system that ties his/her unit with all sections of the school district and the community served by the district. The logistical leader needs to inform his/her subordinate leaders to act properly, quickly and appropriately to all communiques received whether they be formal, informal, human, or technical.

Summary

The organizational philosophy is created and kept intact by the ideas of managerial personnel along with their various methods of engaging in operational tasks. Perpetuation of the organization is highly dependent upon the actions of the managerial corps in their exercise of authority over subordinate personnel. This would also involve the setting of the work effort in motion to accomplish assigned goals. In viewing the panoramic scope of managerial authority (at higher and mid-level positions), it is virtually impossible to be in direct authoritative contact with various subunits. Therefore, it becomes necessary for management to delegate to lower level managerial personnel, a segment of the total authority picture. However, if delegation takes place, the action of overall responsibility for the delegated action remains with higher management.

The accomplishment of the organization's primary and secondary goals does not become fact upon happenstance. There is need for interaction and synchronization of tasks by the organization's managerial corps. These tasks are entwined with: (1) Authority—which legally gives the managerial corps the power to function and attempt goal satisfaction; (2) Responsibility— the legal obligation of management in its particular zones of coverage; (3) Delegation—the investing of authority upon subordinates in order to increase direct managerial observation of performance and goal accomplishment.

Another beacon for the organization is the formulation of objectives and projectional thrusts by management. Objectives must be constructed with great care and be within reason. The same input must also be used in the projectional or planning phase by management. An objective or planning project does not initially reside in reality until: (1) A performance of tasks; (2) The infusing of personnel, services and support; (3) A coordinated predetermined tracking system has provided guidance; and (4) The chronographic dimension of elapse time has been consumed. Venturing into projected dimensions requires caution and a well developed scheme to forecast the unknown.

There are certain general functions that will be required of the school district's Logistical Manager in his/her operation of the support services program. These functions cover: (1) Projection construction, (2) Perimetrical Authoritative Control, (3) Establishment of the functional structure, and

(4) Establishment and the maintenance of a communications network.

Coordination between the school district's logistical unit and its multitude of instructional programs requires not only adequate communications, but clear concise planning and liaison (between logistics and instructional programs). Coordination is also the key within the logistical organization and its staff members. An adequate number of qualified and responsible logistical workers are needed to provide adequate services to the instructional programs.

Effort by the school district Logistical Manager also involves creating and maintaining communications within and external to the logistical program. An adequate communications network is required if satisfactory or impressive goal achievement is to be a reality.

Logistics within the school district must be coordinated with the instructional program if there is to be proper supplying and servicing. Instructional projections and objectives cannot become reality unless there is adequate logistical support. There is need for logistical buildups in advance of instructional program operation to insure that adequate and quality service can be offered.

Next to fiscal management, staffing is the second most important item in exercising both the instructional and logistical programs of the local school district. Both certificated and non-certificated personnel must be orientated to organizational objectives and the proposed area of achievement. In order to obtain staff members who have the potential to comprehend and work toward achieving objectives, there must be managerial channel markers. They are: (1) Active Recruitment; (2) A Proper Section Process; (3) An Adequate Job Description; (4) Continuing In-Service Training; and (5) Adequate Supervision and Measured Work Performance.

Evaluation of the school district's logistical system is a major requirement. Data of this nature is important in informing the Logistical Manager of the status of his/her unit. Appraisal results also provide a springboard from which to reconstruct any negative or mediocre facts of the logistical program. Reconstruction can be brought about by: (1) Program termination; (2) Program alteration; and (3) Complete new program construction.

Periodic evaluation of the logistical program is necessary in order to collect data which will indicate variance (both positive and negative) as a form of preestablished benchmark.

Direct public contribution into the educational program had been open since the inception of American education, however, a mass thrust on this avenue of approach did not come about. Since the explosive 1960's, direct parental involvement in educational matters has become stylish among the lay citizens. Positive relations with laypersons should be maintained by the Logistical Manager in his/her daily tasks which influence the lay community.

Lay input should be allowed to assist the logistical program in order to facilitate its operation to be of high caliber. Also, lay action can provide the school district with goodwill (which can bring later dividends).

Communications between the Logistical Manager, the logistical units, and other segments of the school district must be established, maintained, and allow for two way flow (between superior and subordinate personnel and various units). Data received through the communication's channel must be evaluated before taking decisive action. Communication is the key to successful operation of the logistical program.

PART TWO
LOGISTICAL LIMITS
AND OBJECTIVE DIRECTION

CHAPTER III

THE LEGAL PERIMETERS OF
SCHOOL LOGISTICAL MANAGEMENT

The American public school system is a creation of the American legal system. The legal system provides the foundation supporting the structure from which the educational process takes root. The supreme tables of law forming the legal foundation are the federal constitution and each individual state constitution (covering the fifty grand divisions of the nation). Federal and state constitutions provide a body of law from which government (both federal and state) can function in carrying out its obligations to the populace. Also, constitutions will point out the rights of individual members of the populace. Being that the federal constitution does not provide for a national system of public education in the United States the function is, therefore, delegated to the individual states. Each state's constitution provides for (directly or indirectly) a public system of education to educate its citizens.

Federal constitutional delegation of duties to the states concerning matters not directly of federal concern has automatically placed public education upon the states. The involvement of the federal government in education has been the result of the constitution's general welfare clause (which will be brought forth later in this chapter). With the general welfare clause as a release mechanism, the United States Congress has seen fit to enact legislation concerning education. However, a balancing effect is due in respect to federal statutes and presidential executive orders in that they must be in accord with the federal constitution.

State Constitutions provide for the establishment of legislative bodies which construct legal statutes representing the state's laws. Statutes concerning public education are processed into law creating state departments of education, chief state school officers, and state and local boards of education. State laws will provide guidelines for the previously mentioned bodies and positions to operate in carrying out their respective duties. Statutes will provide for not only state administration of the public school system, but the administrational operation at the local level. These laws will cover a multitude of items such as:

1. Local School District Operation
2. Fiscal Management

3. School Property
4. Personnel Management
   (Certificated and Non-Certificated Employees)
5. Teacher Certification
6. Collective Negotiations, Employee Unions, and Organizations
7. School Calendar
8. Curriculum
9. Student Discipline
10. Accreditation
11. Selection of Textbooks
12. Logistical Services (Transportation. Food Service, Purchasing and Supply, etc.)
13. School Safety and Security
14. Special Education
15. Vocational Education
16. Career Education
17. Community Education
18. Computer Education
19. Private Schools
20. Special Programs
21. Agricultural Education
22. Pupil Personnel
23. Delegation of Authority to:
    a. Chief State School Officer
    b. State Department of Education
    c. State Board of Education
    d. Local Boards of Education
    e. Local Superintendents

Mention needs to be made of the previously mentioned term, balancing. Balancing concerns the keeping in constitutional line all policies, rules, regulations, state statutes and federal statutes. All of the above mentioned principles must be within those perimeters identified by both the state and federal constitutions. Balancing will also need to take place concerning the legal interpretation of policies, rules, regulations, state statutes and federal statutes. Interpretation can be the key to the survival of the principle's original intent.

The next question that may be asked is the identification of the individual or body determining balancing according to constitutionality and interpretation. The correct answer would be the American judicial system. This system is divided into: (1) the federal courts and (2) the state courts. These two groups can be represented as dormant and massive watchdogs with golden collars and chains. The gold chains are attached to a jeweled mace which is the standard of the American judicial system. The watchdogs do not awaken unless litigation tugs upon their chains. Courts do not act as enforcers of the law, they render decisions concerning the constitutionality and the interpretation of the law. Issues which come forth in litigation may be settled in federal or state courts. Or it is possible for litigation to travel from the state to the federal court system. The courts provide the balance which is needed to keep governmental operation and individual rights in proper order.

FEDERAL IMPACT UPON PUBLIC SCHOOL SYSTEMS

As discussed previously, the federal constitution makes no mention of public education. However, Article I, Section 8 states:

"The Congress shall have power to lay and collect Taxes, Duties, Inposts and Excises, to pay the Debts and provide for the common Defence and General Welfare of the United States. . . . " This particular feature of the constitution has been used by Congress to pass federal legislation for the benefit of public schools. The general welfare clause has not been without its problems and conflicts which date back to the 18th century. During the formulation of the constitution where was considerable discussion and controversy between James Madison and Alexander Hamilton. Madison looked upon the general welfare clause as referring to other powers listed in later clauses. In addition, Madison looked upon the federal government with both limited and enumerated powers and the power to tax and spend for the general welfare according to those listed legislation fields given in trust to the congress of the United States (reprinted from "Public School Law: Cases & Materials," with permission of the West Publishing Company) [1].

Alexander Hamilton occupied the opposite and extreme view concerning interpretation of the general welfare clause. He (Hamilton) supported the fact that the general welfare clause placed upon the United States Congress a real power to tax and expend for those purposes that would provide for the nation's general welfare [2].

In later years the Supreme Court has sided with the Hamiltonian view of the general welfare clause rather than the Madisonian belief. The legal cases of United States v. Butler [3] and Helvering v. Davis [4] were decided by the high court and gave Congress the right to spend under the less restrictive interpretation of Alexander Hamilton.

Federal Guidelines and The Logistical Manager

Through the years the federal government has provided monies to the states in support of specific educational programs. The main emphasis for obtaining federal funds will be brought forth at the local school district level. Construction for the grant proposal should originate with the concerned member of the superintendent's administrative team (that is the administrator in charge of curriculum, or special education, or vocational education, etc.). The specific area of the grant will dictate action to the specific team member(s) involved. There is a need for coordination between the concerned administrative team member, the superintendent and the Logistical Manager prior to and during the proposal writing stage. The Logistical Manager will base his/her input according to the specifications required by the U.S. Department of Education. Logistical input will involve:

1. The time period to be covered by the proposed grant. This time period must be further broken down according to:
    a. The federal fiscal period(s) October 1 to September 30
    b. The state fiscal period(s)
    c. The academic year(s)
    d. The calendar year(s)
    e. Possible future periods (identical to the above if grant can be renewed)
2. Financial Management
    a. Preparation of the proposal budget according to the federal fiscal period(s) required by grant guidelines.
    b. Budget breakdown according to:
        (1) Personnel
        (2) Travel Expenses
        (3) Supplies
        (4) Equipment
        (5) Services
            (a) Accounting
            (b) Auditing
            (c) Communications
        (6) Evaluation
        (7) Consultants
        (8) Contractual Arrangements
        (9) Indirect Charges
            (a) A percentage of the total budget charged for existing overall administration, services and expenses not directly involved in the area of the proposed grant
3. Personnel Management

     a. Qualification, Determinations
     b. Recruiting
     c. Selecting
     d. Housing and Space
     e. Pre-Service and In-Service Training
     f. Salaries
     g. Fringe Benefits
     h. Coordination With Employee Organizations and/or Labor Unions
     i. Termination Procedures
     j. Total Personnel Requirements

4. Travel
     a. Staff Travel
     b. Non-Staff Travel
     c. Room and Board
     d. Gratuities
     e. Taxicab, Limousine, Automobile Rental

5. Supplies
     a. Clerical Supplies
     b. Instructional Supplies
     c. Other Non-instructional Supplies

6. Equipment
     a. Rental Equipment
     b. Purchased Equipment
     c. Instructional Equipment
     d. Non-instructional Equipment
     e. Equipment Maintenance
     f. Equipment Disposal

7. Procuring, Providing and Coordination Support Services Needed for Federal Programs

8. Establishing Evaluation Procedures for Logistical Support of the Program

Once the coordination between the concerned administrative team member, the superintendent and the Logistical Manager is made, the proposal constructed and approved by the local board of education and the U.S. Department of Education, the logistical program should commence operation. Even before federal approval a minimal amount of preplanning should have been made concerning:

1. Availability of qualified personnel.
2. Vendor availability concerning possible supplies needed.
3. Vendor availability concerning possible equipment needed, and maintenance services projections on proposed equipment.

4. Availability of proposed needed services.

5. Possible merging of accounting and auditing procedures with established system.

6. Availability of proposed services.

Upon receiving the "green light" from the federal agency, the Logistical Manager must place his/her program into action, and closely adhere to the stipulated federal guidelines. There needs to be a synchronized meshing of logistical support with the federal program. Evaluations of the logistical support plan needs to be made in order to eliminate any problems that may arise. Alterations and or termination procedures concerning logistical services may have to be made in order to meet the program's demands.

Once the federal program has run its course, the Logistical Manager once again must follow federal dictates including procedures, disposal of supplies and equipment, termination of employees, and procedures concerning surplus monies.

STATE OPERATION OF THE PUBLIC SCHOOL SYSTEM

In addition to the constitution's general welfare clause (which has been used to provide federal funds to education), the Tenth Amendment delegates powers to the state level.

"The powers not delegated to the United States by the constitution, nor prohibited by it to the states, are reserved to the states respectively, or to the people." The word education is not mentioned here, but legally it is presumptive that it has been reserved to the states or to the people.

In order that the individual state establish a system of public education, there must be a supreme legal paper to provide a foundation. This supreme legal document is the state constitution. The state constitution gives the state power to tax for, construct and provide maintenance for a public system of education. A state constitution also creates a power body within the state which can create legal statutes, offices, and official positions to operate a system of education. That power body is the state legislature. Each state has a variety of statutes concerning the establishment and maintenance of a public school system. The legislature can also create (by statute) a department of education, a board of education and a chief state school officer. State legislatures (by way of statute) delegate powers concerning education to state boards of education and state departments of educations. Also there are powers delegated by the legislature to local boards of education. The breadth and depth of local board delegation will vary from state to state. The only exception to this is the state of Hawaii which has no local school districts.

Mention needs to be made that state legislatures do not constitutionally delegate their legislative power to lesser bodies such as state school boards, state departments of education or local boards of education. It is the conferring upon these lesser bodies authority by discretion to construct policy, rules and regulations. However, such policy, rules, and regulations by these lesser bodies must be in line with state statutes and the state constitution.

The Logistical Manager must constantly be aware of changed or new directives coming from the legislature, the state board of education, the state department of education, or the local board of education. It is also the duty of the Logistical Manager to orientate his/her staff on any legal changes which have a bearing on school logistics.

State statutes, rules or regulations which would most likely be of concern to the Logistical Manager would probably be in the area of:

1. Accounting, auditing, budgeting, and financial management procedures
2. School property
   a. School sites
   b. School buildings
   c. School equipment
3. School emergency preparedness
4. School safety
5. School security
6. School transportation
7. Food service
   a. Breakfast programs
   b. Lunch programs
8. State level administration
9. Local level administration
10. State school funds and funding procedures
11. School bonds for capital outlay programs
    a. Limit of bonded indebtedness
12. School surety bonds
13. Performance bonding
14. Personnel laws
    a. Teacher certification
    b. Prescribed teacher duties
    c. Collective negotiations
    d. State labor law
    e. Retirement procedures
15. School census, attendance, and pupil assignment procedures
16. Textbook selection and purchasing procedures
17. Contract laws
    a. Teacher contracts
    b. Contracts with external units

18. Computer usage and procedures
19. State fire laws
20. State health laws
21. Bidding and purchasing procedures
22. State insurance laws
    a. School property
    b. Liability
    c. School personnel
    d. Bidding procedures
23. School organization
24. State tax laws
25. Election laws concerning public approval of school taxes and bond issues

The Logistical Manager should have ready access to the various state codes and their annual pocket supplements (addendum). There is also a need for state and federal periodicals which will list a review of any changes or additions to the existing codes. There are times when judicial decisions on matters of litigation may call for alterations in statutes and logistical procedures.

THE LOCAL SCHOOL DISTRICT'S RESPONSIBILITY FOR PUBLIC EDUCATION

Public education in the United States is generally accepted as a state function (except for the District of Columbia). School property and school monies legally belong to the state. However, the main emphasis for administration comes from the local school district level. State statues have created the local school board and have delegated a series of powers to them to control public education at the local level. These powers are:

1. Permissive powers—Where the state gives the local school district the right to offer programs or services, but the state does not demand that the local district offer a particular program or service.

2. Prohibitions—Where the state forbids the local school district to be involved in certain acts and procedures.

3. Mandated powers—Where the state requires that all local school districts undertake certain practices and procedures.

4. Fiscal dependence—Where the state requires all local school districts to obtain local governmental approval (city, county or metropolitan government) on all fiscal matters, for example, budgeting, purchasing, bidding, etc.

5. Fiscal independence—Where the state allows the local school district to grant its own approval on all fiscal matters.

The above mentioned powers are invested in a group of officials called the local board of education. Their sovereignty is gained through state statute and the individual board members are usually elected by the populace of the local school district. Acting as a body, the local board of education is mainly involved in decision-making and policy formulation. Board minutes are kept to record board proceedings and are a matter of public record. With decision-making and policy formulation as the main directive thrusts of the local board of education, the superintendent and his/her administrative team carry out the directives of the local board. Board policy is the legal foundation for the local school district. It (policy) provides direction, gives principle, and provides concept to the overall school operation.

Emphasis must be made toward the fact that local board policy must be in line with state law, state rules and regulations, the state constitution and the federal constitution. Administrators, teachers and staff employees of the local school district in carrying out their duties must adhere to local, state, and federal legal directives.

The Logistical Manager and Local Board of Education Policy

As previously mentioned local boards of education must keep their policies within state laws and constitutional guidelines. However, local boards of education may improve or become more specific concerning broad statements in existing laws. Board policy relating to the Logistical Manager should first be aimed at:

1. Basic Logistical Structure and Responsibilities—The Logistical Manager, his/her administrative staff and the departments which make up the logistical arm, for example:
   a. The Assistant Logistical Manager
   b. Food Services Manager
   c. Transportation Director
   d. Maintenance Supervisor
   e. Operations Supervisor
   f. Payroll Clerk
   g. Chief Secretary
   h. Director of Safety and Security
   i. Warehouse Manager
   j. Chief Accountant
   k. Insurance Custodian
   l. Records and Property Custodian
   m. Personnel Director

Qualifications, duties, and responsibilities of the Logistical Manager and his/her staff should be indicated in local board policy. When personnel are replaced these qualifications, duties, and responsibilities should be reinforced by the Logistical Manager. Top quality personnel are a must if the logistical operation is to function satisfactorily.

Certain fiscal management policies that the Logistical Manager and his/her staff need to adhere to are:

1. Accounting Procedures
2. Audits
3. Bonding
4. Budget Procedures

Local board policies concerning personnel that concern the logistical staff are:

1. Personnel Contracts
   a. Issuance date of the contract
   b. Contract terms
2. Fringe Benefits
3. Credit Union Privileges
4. Employee Insurance Programs and Tax Sheltered Annuities
5. Payroll Deduction Procedures
6. School Property Insurance
   a. Crime Insurance
   b. Liability
   c. Athletic Insurance
   d. Surety Bonds or Blanket Bonding
7. Payroll
   a. Salary Schedules
   b. Separation Pay
   c. Deductions and Deduction Laws
      (1) Taxes
      (2) Retirement
      (3) Insurances
      (4) Credit Union
   d. Payroll Records
   e. Check Preparation and Issuance
8. Employee Leaves
9. Recruiting and Hiring Procedures
10. Terminations

The Logistical Manager must adhere to local policy concerning purchasing procedures. Policy should cover the following areas:

1. Purchasing Agent Designation
2. Requisition Procedures
3. Specification Guidelines
4. Accounting Coordination
5. Bidding Procedures

Other areas of policy that concern the Logistical Manager are:

1. School Plants
2. School Plant Planning
3. Remodeling and Renovation Procedures
4. School Plant Maintenance and Operation Procedures
5. School Property Trespassing
6. Custody of School Property
7. The Right of Eminent Domain
8. Acquisition of School Property
9. Inventory of School Property
10. Inspection of School Property
11. Safety on the School's Property
12. Disposal of School Property
13. Use of School Property
14. Issue of School Bonds
15. Purchase of Property
16. Safety and Security
    a. Locker Searches
    b. Search of Persons on School Property
    c. Container Search
    d. Vehicle Search
    e. Use of Metal Detectors
    f. Use of Search Animals
    g. Search by Law Enforcement Agencies
    h. Procedures Concerning Drugs and Contraband
    i. School Use as a Weather Shelter, Disaster Shelter, etc.
    j. Conformity to State Fire Marshall's Codes
    k. School Vandalism
    l. First Aid Treatment
    m. Emergency Movements and Crowd Control
    n. Playground Equipment Inspection
    o. Athletic Facility Inspection
17. Food Service
    a. Personnel Qualifications
    b. Food Service Managers — Duties and Responsibilities
    c. Food Service Personnel — Duties and Responsibilities

    d. Health and Safety Procedures

    e. Vending Machines

    f. Free and Reduced Breakfasts and Lunches

    g. Food Service Equipment and Supplies

18. Clerical Services (Central Office and Building Level)

    a. Personnel Qualifications

    b. Duties and Responsibilities

    c. Computers and Office machine procedures

19. Custodial Personnel

    a. Personnel Qualifications

    b. Duties and Responsibilities

20. Paraprofessionals

    a. Personnel Qualifications

    b. Duties and Responsibilities

21. Facilities for the Handicapped

22. Travel Regulations for School Personnel

23. Risk Management Program

24. Reporting

25. Warehouse and Storage Procedures

26. Warehouse Inventory

27. Accounting for Building Level Funds

28. In-service Training Programs (Certificated and Non-certificates)

29. Employee Organizations and Labor Unions

30. Collective Negotiations

31. Pupil Control

32. Health Department Coordination

33. Food Storage

    a. Freezer

    b. Refrigeration

    c. Dry Storage

34. Garbage Collection and Removal

35. Workmen's Compensation

36. Pest Control

37. School Transportation Services

    a. Student Conduct

    b. Extra Curricular Affairs

    c. Driver Selection and Training

    d. Transportation Safety Procedures

    e. Transportation of the Handicapped

    f. School Bus Servicing and Maintenance

    g. School Bus Contracted Services

38. Weather Reporting

39. Bidding and Vendor Selection
40. Logistical Evaluations

Some local level policies may be broader or more specific in detail concerning items related to the Logistical Manager and his/her operation. Breadth and depth of the policy is of concern, but adherence is the major key. Adherence involves both the Logistical manager and the logistical staff. Coupled with adherence are the requirements of logistical management and its staff to have a thorough knowledge of the local board's logistical policy.

Checking and Balancing by the Judicial System

There are foundations in both the federal and state constitutions (or state statutes) which allows for both a federal and state court system. The court systems provides an outlet where litigation can be heard challenging legislation or actions taken by governments (federal, state and local). Judicial action provides for a checking and balancing to the governmental function. State courts are involved with state matters while federal courts deal with federal legal questions. There also can be concurrent jurisdiction which allows for litigation in either a state or federal court. The prospective litigant may select the court system (federal or state) which may be more beneficial to his/her cause. Cases having their beginnings in the state court system can be appealed to the federal system if it can be determined that a federal question does exist.

Organization of the state court system varies from state to state. Two primary facets of state court systems are:

1. A court of entry of original jurisdiction
2. An appellate system to allow movement to higher state courts.

In some states there is a trilevel system which allows for the entry court of original jurisdiction along with an intermediate appellate court, and the court represented or the state's highest court. Within each state's court system the terminology of each level of court will also vary.

The federal court system is an independent part of the triumvirate power structure established by the federal constitution — the judicial, the legislative, and the executive branches. Each provides a check and balance system to the other. For example, the legislative branch's ability to override a veto of the executive branch. The judicial branch's option to declare any statute passed by the legislative branch illegal or unconstitutional. During the 1970's Watergate investigation, the judicial branch ordered the executive branch to release a series of presidential conversation tapes. Past federal legislation has provided for a trilevel organization of the federal court system which is represented by:

1. Federal district courts which are the courts of entry of original jurisdiction. Of the fifty states one will find from one to four district courts. A federal judicial district may also be subdivided into divisions with cases being heard at different geographic points within the division.

2. Federal courts of appeals which reviews appeals from lower district courts within its region. A decision at this level can be made, or there can be a move to the next higher court (the U.S. Supreme Court), or the federal court of appeals can remand the case to a lower court. There are eleven circuits representing eleven courts of appeals in the United States.

3. The United States Supreme Court—the highest court in the land from which there is no appeal. All decisions made by this court are final and its decisions apply to all states of the union.

Legal issues concerning public education travel through both the state and federal court system. Many educational cases are solved at the entry of original jurisdiction level at either the federal or state system. Some cases move through appellate procedures (both state and federal) to higher courts for decisions. The Logistical Manager must keep himself/herself informed of the constantly changing legal situation effecting the management of the public school system. Areas of law in which judicial decisions may influence operation of the public school logistical system are:

1. Torts and Liability—Concerns here could involve school personnel, pupils, community persons through direct or indirect functioning of the school district logistical system.

2. School Property—Besides being an avenue of possible tort situations, the acquisition (eminent domain or standard purchasing procedures) selling and acquiring of property can lead to a variety of legal entanglements.

3. Equal Opportunity Compliance and Affirmative Action—Discriminatory conflicts with racial, religious, females, homosexuals and the handicapped in recruiting and hiring practices, promotions, job assignments, seniority issues, layoffs, terminations, salary schedules and working conditions can open more than "Pandora's box" and lead to serious alterations as the result of court decisions.

4. Employee Organizations and Labor Unions—Legal decisions concerning labor laws, collective negotiations, labor agreements and grievances can result in litigation which could have far reaching effects upon the Logistical Manager's operation.

5. Contracts—Items of concern in this area are:
   a. The school district's authority to enter into contracts.
   b. Intra-district contracts
   c. Contracts with external agencies
   d. Bids and contracts

Litigation commonly results from contracting parties in which one party alleges that the other party did not fulfill agreed upon obligations. School districts are no exception to the rule.

6. Computer Reporting and Records—The use of computers to compile reports and maintain records through its storage capability can open the doors of litigation because of unauthorized entry into the computer system or electronic tampering by authorized and unauthorized personnel. As computer usage increases, there will be a need for legislation to control computer operation and computer crime.

A Logistical Manager that is well informed can better provide a smooth operating logistical service to his/her system. Court decisions can have a binding effect upon logistical movements. Also, it must be remembered that the legal picture associated with public education is almost constantly changing.

Summary

Logistical Management is not given a free reign from which to undertake its daily operations within the public school district. Legal boundaries have been established at both the federal, state and local levels. Some of the legal perimeters are expressed directly. Such is the case with the federal general welfare clause, due process, state prohibitions and mandates to local school districts. Others are more indirect in nature such as the federal delegation of unidentified duties to the states, state permissive powers to local school districts, and unidentified duties delegated to local school districts by the state (such as some areas of local board policies and administrative policy at both the central office and building level). All policy at the local district level must coincide with state statutes, the state constitution, federal statutes (if federal programs are involved), and the federal constitution.

The Logistical Manager must have knowledge of all federal and state statutes, plus local board policies that have a bearing on the logistical operation. He/she (the Logistical Manager) must also keep abreast of legal alterations due to decisions of legal cases by the American judicial system. The national judicial mechanism operates on a dual system representing both the federal and state governments. Knowledge of the state framework concerning logistical operation is imperative, and there must be a steady watch regarding judicial decisions in this area. Observance of the federal court system is also a necessity concerning not only interpretation of federal statutes, but issues on constitutionality, affirmative action, equal opportunity compliance, and labor issues.

Local logistical policy should be reviewed on an annual basis to evaluate whether or not policy is in step with attaining logistical goals. If goals are not being met, there should be a call for policy modification or termination. With the main state emphasis for public education placed upon the local district, there is need for the entire local machine, to be informed and coordinated concerning legal perimeters.

CHAPTER IV

PLANNING PROJECTIONS
OF THE LOGISTICAL MANAGER

The process of planning should take place at all levels (administrative and staff) of the public school district. Planning's primary emphasis should be at the central office with the superintendent and his/her administrative team providing leadership down to the individual building planning situations of the principal.

Central office group planning of the superintendent's team will encompass the school district's primary goal of educating the populace. The Logistical Manager will find planning as the heartbeat of his/her operation. Logistical planning touches the planning operations of all segments of the superintendent's administrative team. Services and support must be received by all other operations within the school district. To the Logistical Manager, planning is a tool which provides a blending of chronographic dimensions (past, present, and future); acquired knowledge; accordable action; and a project affirmation of controlling future operations to a particular course of action. The Logistical Manager will be faced with the tasks of coordinating other team members and being able to: (1) obtain needed supplies and services from internal and external sources; (2) being able to obtain and budget financial resources; (3) having the ability to tap the labor pool for the type(s) of personnel needed; (4) and being able to provide those service's needed at the desired projected time.

Reviewing past planning programs will provide excellent data to consider when planning for future programs. Any negative aspects presented by past planning should create alterations for corrective measures (in order to attempt to obtain improved results).

In preparing for planning action, the Logistical Manager needs to use a construction guide. There may be a need for the Logistical Manager to coordinate with member(s) of the superintendent's administrative team (in order to provide logistical support to a particular area of the team member's zone of operation). In formulating a plan, the following steps should be utilized:

1. Identification of the plan.

2. Signed and date stamped permission of the board and/or superintendent to commence the planning process.

3. A listing and signatures of the individuals that were involved in the construction of the plan.

4. The direction(s) and intention of the planning operation.

5. Presentation and breakdown of the master issue of concern.

6. Evaluation of resources needed to get the planning process underway.

7. A detailed study of all directions offered.

8. Selection of primary course of action.

9. Selection of secondary course of action.

10. Projected outcomes.

11. Signatures of those individuals that have approved the completion of the plan along with the stamped date of completion.

12. Evaluation of the planning operation.

13. Signatures of the evaluators.

14. Stamped date and time of completion of the evaluation.

15. Formulation of summary and recommendations of the planning venture.

EVALUATION OF RESOURCES

Before launching a planning project there is a need to observe the surrounding resources that have a direct effect upon the operation. From a legal point of view there may be local board policies, state laws, rules, and regulations, and/or federal laws that may be of concern to the planning operation. Another point of concern is the probability of both problems and/or restrictions within the school district and external to the school district. For example conflicts with other educational programs or problems with external vendors. The moves and philosophy of the community may have an effect upon planning. It is normally in the best interest of the schools and the community, if the local school district abides by such unwritten laws. Economic and political situations within the school community and/or outside the school community can have a definite influence upon the district's planning operations. For instance, high unemployment creates a dampening effect upon tax revenues (federal, state, and local) which may reduce or even eliminate the impact of the planning process.

Consideration concerning resources can be input from a variety of areas such as:

1. Upper, middle and lower management
2. Staff members
3. External resources, such as consultants, industrial representatives, lay community members, etc.
4. Employee units

5. Other school districts
6. Retired employees
7. Past planning evaluations
8. Board of education members
9. Teacher organizations
10. Labor unions

Once there has been input by both external and internal groups regarding the proposed planning venture, there should be coordination. Coordination in this area should involve the needs which have created the issue which initially necessitated planning. Alarm signals within the community may be individual in nature, but once individual problems are discussed collectively through formal or informal organizations, they are grouped into major issues or problems. Many times these problems are presented to the board of education which acts as an ombudsman device for the community. Boards of education in turn will present these problems to the superintendent for study or action. The superintendent's administrative team could use the following course of action in working with the presented problem:

1. Transforming the problem into a definite need.
2. The gathering of concepts to satisfy the need.
3. Selection of a method to accomplish need satisfaction.
4. Team input in determining the plan and its objective desired upon completion.
5. Presentation of the plan for approval by the superintendent and the board of education.
6. Commencing of the planning process.

An item of importance at this point is the Logistical Manager's input concerning an instructional plan of the school district. He/she (the Logistical Manager) must have the logistical staff ready to provide all services and support needed by the proposed operation. The Logistical Manager needs to take an in depth observation of the plan, and the concepts that created its existence. Knowledge of this nature can have a bearing on magnitude and the quality of logistical effort.

First, the Logistical Manager needs to review the initial problem and its nucleus. For example — Is there need for remedial science instruction? Why is there a need for remedial instruction in science? What is the socio-economic status of the target group involved? Does it cut across all socio-economic lines? Is the problem at the elementary level, the secondary level, or both? Information of this type can have a bearing upon the type of logistical support needed in planning for a remedial science program. Items such as finances and financial sources, equipment, personnel, supplies and various support services can be influences by the specific school population targeted. Also another factor which can influence planning of the logistical element, is the direction and/or method to be used in the overall planning process.

Second, the Logistical Manager needs to review the essential characteristics of the overall plan in determining the logistical portion required to provide satisfactory servicing. There must be coordination within the logistical planning process while maintaining liaison with the direction of the overall plan.

Third, a pre-evaluation of the proposed plan is necessary to determine the probable outcome. Comparisons with past plans or similar plans would be in order. Both the negative and positive aspects of past plans are necessary in developing a yardstick for the pre-evaluation process. Computer assistance could aid greatly in this area. The results of such an evaluation could greatly assist the Logistical Manager in preparing for logistical support in the planning process. A wealth of information could be gained through past planning programs that failed and the reasons for their failures.

Fourth, the Logistical Manager in preparing his/her portion of the master plan needs to review the chronographic dimensions aspect as follows:

a. How much time has been allocated for the overall planning process?
b. How much time has been allotted for the Logistical Manager's logistics plan?
c. What was the time factor in previous planning ventures?
d. Has there been an input for elasticity in the time factor?

In summary, there is need to know the total cost of the overall plan and the cost of the logistical segment of the plan. Data gathered here should be reviewed for possible austerity moves in any areas or potential areas of waste.

The Logistical Manager is the central figure and should embark upon all compass points. This action is needed to gain information concerning the cause of problem origin; the problem itself; board and administrative staff alertness to the problem; and administrative team planning. By studying and using previously mentioned resources, the Logistical Manager can be in a better position to construct the logistical plan of supporting the administrative team's master plan.

CONSIDERATION OF VARIOUS ALTERNATIVES

Once the die has been cast for a particular plan, it has been the result of selection from a number of alternate courses of action. The more complexity involved in a particular plan, the greater will be the alternatives from which to select the main thrust. With two or more alternatives, there is a need for detailed study and appraisal before the primary plan is selected. The selection process should be the effort of the central office administrative team with the superintendent making the final decision. In regard to the logistical segment of the overall plan, the logistical staff needs to come up with the primary alternative. Here again the superior administrator (the Logistical Manager) should give final approval.

The selection process of an alternative route for a planning operation must coincide with school district policies. This keeps the entire venture within the legal limitation points of the school district's zone.

Before selecting a course of action for a planning operation, there are three major items that should be reviewed in establishing anticipated outcomes. They are:

1. *The major and minor goals of the school district*—The local district is charged with providing education to the students of the school district according to:
    a. Communication skills
    b. Ciphering skills
    c. Problem solving through appraisal research fundamentals and investigation skills.
    d. Understanding of psychological principles
    e. Understanding of its fine arts
    f. Being a good citizen
    g. Maintaining good mental and physical health
    h. Knowledge of the work ethic
    i. Relationships with others
    j. Understanding of the people of other nations and their governments.

2. *The major and minor goals of the planning operation*—This portion of desired outcomes are wholly attached to the planning action, and involves a segment of the school district's major goals structure. The plan may provide for a new course for high school vocational students in computer assistance for food preparation and services. The major goal for students who successfully complete this course would be the attaining of computer knowledge as it relates to food preparation and services. Secondary goals could be programming and the problem solving phase. Adequate instructions, practical and field work in this area would prepare the successful student in being able to be qualified for employment with this particular skill. This secondary skill ties in with the school district's major goal(s) for providing education to the populace.

3. *Major and minor goals of the logistical support system*—Once the planning operation is launched by the central office administrative team, the

Logistical Manager will be charged in planning for logistical support. Let's stay with our hypothetical computer assistance program in food preparation and services. The Logistical Manager must construct a logistical plan that will allow for the:

a. Obtaining of personnel needed for computer instruction.
b. Obtaining computers and other appropriate equipment.
c. Providing for needed supplies.
d. Providing for other needed appropriate services.
e. Obtaining funds needed to operate the new program.
f. Projecting the time line for:
   (1) Instructional planning
   (2) Commencement of instruction
   (3) The period involved
   (4) Evaluation of instructional program
   (5) Repeat processes if necessary

AVENUES OF APPROACH

The existence of varying alternatives probable to use as the prime planning process opens the door to evaluation. All alternatives must be taken into the evaluation process in order to select the plan that best meets the needs of the organization. Consideration needs to be given to certain points which may influence the selection of an alternative. These conditions may be:

1. *The purpose of the plan*—What are the reasons for which the plan has been formulated. These reasons need to be broken down into both major and minor categories.
2. *The goal(s) intended to be achieved*—A thorough check of the goal(s) that are desired through usage of a particular plan. If more than one goal is envisioned, classification into major and minor categories is necessary. Such classification will provide better insight to those involved.
3. *Consideration of legal limitations*—Laws, policies, regulations will have a definite influence upon selecting the proper alternative to meet a proposed goal.
4. *Accessible logistics*—Does the school district maintain a complete logistical support capability for a particular project? Is there district access to a direct line concerning external logistical sources? Are funds available to invest in logistical supplies and services as called for by a particular plan? Can the need for person-power be satisfied? All logistical questions must be answered and coordinated toward achieving the goal(s) of the master plan.

5. *Operations within the planning time block* — The total amount of time that will be consumed in the planning process is critical to the planner. Study will also be required of particular points of accomplishment within subunit time blocks as part of the overall time frame. Are these particular segments of time reasonable or unreasonable? Do they coincide with the goal(s) of the master planning process?

6. *A critical review of the planner(s) involved* — What is the experience and qualifications of the plan's constructors? Have they been successful or unsuccessful in previous operations? How was the plan created? What particular tools did they use in constructing the plan?

PRIMARY AND SECONDARY PLANS OF ACTION

Primary Plan of Action — Appraisal

The primary drive towards the final selection of a particular plan will be the appraisal of the various alternatives offered by different plans. A uniform yardstick should be established beforehand to appraise each particular plan. Specific points along the evaluative device need to indicate measurement in:

1. Reviewing of the original problem and the quality of the plan (and its goal(s)) to solve the problem.
2. The possibility of unforeseen events taking place during the planning process.
3. What is the school district record concerning outcomes of similar plans?
4. Recognition of the time factor in planning construction, and in carrying out plan operations.
5. Characteristics of the planner(s) and the quality of their produced work.
6. The desired outcome.
7. Local board of education planning policies.
8. Fund consumption.
9. Time consumption.
10. Other logistical consumption.

Data gathered from the above mentioned areas will supply the evaluator(s) with enough information to place a mark of evaluation upon each plan. These resulting marks could then be categorized into three rating groups. For example:

1. High
2. Medium
3. Low

Plans in the low rating category could be listed for terminating procedures. Plans listed with medium ratings could be either terminated or kept for later modification. Those plans in high classification should be reviewed and taken into the secondary plan of action.

Secondary Plan of Action — Goal Probability

Scholars of the ages have stated that the only certainty in the lives of men and women is that of death. No matter how extensive and how well constructed a plan may be, the achievement of the stated goal is not certain. This thought brings about a secondary evaluation of placing a weight of probability of goal achievement by each plan within the previously mentioned high category. Planners must place this secondary mark of probability upon each high ranking plan to assure that the best plan will be selected as the final choice. However, certain factors should be adhered to in classifying the likelihood of the intended occurrence(s) becoming fact. These factors should not be taken lightly and are in need of detailed study.

1. *A peripheral review of all know possible outcomes of the plan.* This action will require a study of similar plans of the past. Computer assistance and brainstorming could also prove to be of valuable assistance in this particular phase.

2. *What guidelines were used by the school district in past planning projects?* Are there board policies, state or federal laws that must be adhered to in this particular planning project? All planning work must be kept within legal standards. By avoiding these restrictions the plan is subject to possible disaster once the goal(s) are met.

3. *Carry out an internal review of past school district planning projects.* Determine why they were successful or unsuccessful.

4. *Carry out an external review of past planning projects in other school districts and other organizations (such as business, industry, government, etc.).* Study the reasons for success or failure.

5. *What is the projected amount of time consumption involved with the plan from commencement to termination?* This is a critical phase in determining the final selection of a proposed plan, and its ability to achieve the proposed goal.

6. *A detailed cost analysis study should be made of each plan to determine per hour, per day, per month, per individual, etc. and the grand total cost of the planning venture.* Austerity minded boards of education and administrators are in need of cost information. This factor alone may have the greatest bearing on goal probability.

THE FINAL SELECTION—
COURSE OF ACTION—FOLLOW THROUGH

Once the goal probability factors are studied in detail, a decision must be made on the plan to be used. The decision will set the planning process upon a specific course of action. It is important that the selected course of action be correct in adequately meeting the established goal(s) within the time period allotted. It is usually detrimental to make major alternating adjustments once the plan is in progress.

In exploring the term, decision, Merriam-Webster [1] defines it as, "a determination arrived at after consideration." Decisions involve judgement calls made after deliberation has taken place. After the previously mentioned action is undertaken with a group of individuals, or through a process of committee action, two types of results may be evident. There may be a vote with the decision riding with the majority. Or there may be reports given by the supporters of the varying decisional outcomes. In this situation the major administrator usually makes the final choice after weighing various presented alternatives.

After the planning programs have gone through the primary and second-ary plans of action (in which appraisal and probability values have been established) action should be taken to determine the final selection of the plan to be used in solving the initial problem. Once the selection is made the planning operation should go immediately into operation on the appointed day of commencement. The entire course of action should receive a final check before actual operation takes place. Administrative personnel and their staffs should be orientated to the plan and all its segments before commencement. Emphasis also needs to take place to the overall particular sequences of events that are to take place within certain time frames. Special importance should be given by each involved member of the central office team to his/her staff and their scheduled contributions to the selected plan. This action will include the Logistical Manager's unit and their contributions. Logistical support must be merged within the prescribed time periods to allow for proper synchronization with the other contributors of the selected planning process.

Evaluation of the selected plan is a must in order to:

1. Determine if the plan's prescribed goal(s) were met. If not, why?
2. Was there time gain in the overall planning venture?
3. Were there time loss in the overall planning venture?
4. What were the time gains in individual unit segments of the plan?
5. What were the time losses in individual unit segments of the plan?
6. Where did bottlenecks occur and why?

7. What were the areas where synchronization did not take place?
8. Place all areas of the evaluation data on record for future reference.

Evaluation data can be useful to future planning operations. Both negative and positive aspects of an evaluated planning operation will provide planners with a wealth of information during current planning preparations.

COMMUNICATION AND THE PLANNING PROCESS

Merriam-Webster [2] defines communication as, "a process by which information is exchanged between individuals through a common system of symbols, signs, or behavior. . . . " (By permission. From Webster's Ninth New Collegiate Dictionary © 1984 by Merriam-Webster, Inc., publisher of the Merriam-Webster ® Dictionaries.) Ask the question — How does the process of communication conform with the process of planning? Planning merges itself with other processes. For example:

1. Research
2. Brainstorming
3. Classification of tasks
4. Classification of personnel
5. Operations
6. Administration
7. Evaluating

The previously mentioned processes are definite and can be looked upon as fact. However, in merging with the planning process there is uncertainty. Planning operations have been constructed through human input that is the result of carefully thought out projections. There is not a sure 100% guarantee that a particular planning process will work according to projection and particular goal achievement.

Communication is more fluid than the seven above mentioned processes in that it covers all processes and provides for a vehicle for which to transmit the flow of two-way traffic needed to complete the planning operation. Not only does communication provide transmission from the planner(s) to the operators (of the plan), but between the operators. A properly established communications network will also provide a reverse flow from operator to planners (or to those administering the planning operation).

The plan in its entirety must be sent along communication lines to those individuals that will be the doers or operators. These individuals will be involved in the overall plan by carrying out their tasks in a variety of major and minor segments (which make up the overall plan). If communication is hampered or not allowed to flow freely, complications can occur.

In regard to planning one will find a communication cycle. This cycle begins with the sender who selects a carrier to transmit to the receiver. The receiver will decipher and act out the instructions. Receivers may communicate in return to the original sender, or disseminate information to his/her subordinates. In other words, through conversion and the need to communicate, the original receiver can become the new sender. If transmission is made directly back to the original sender, he/she (through conversion) becomes the new receiver. Communications should cut freely among and between lines of rank in the following manner:

1. Superior to peer
2. Superior to subordinate
3. Subordinate to peer
4. Subordinate to superior

Transmission

Next there is need to analyze the reason for using a particular line of communication as brought forth by the above mentioned communications channels between the four classifications of personnel within the organization.

At either the superior or subordinate levels, the initial phase will be the *presentation of a situation.* The situation may be grouped into one of three categories, which are:

1. Positive
2. Neutral
3. Negative

Once the situation is presented to the prospective transmitter, he/she immediately go into the second phase which is to *resolve the need* brought about by the situation. When the prospective transmitter has become aware of the need(s) he/she will *outline a plan for satisfying the need* in question. The next phase of the communications cycle will be that of *selecting the method of transmission.* This can involve the use of:

1. The written symbols
2. Actual or electronic voice transmission
3. Visual symbols
4. Audible signals
5. Electronic signals
6. Sensory signals and symbols

Upon selection of the means of transmission *the act of transmission* itself will become the final phase of the transmission segment.

Reception

The second segment will involve the phases of reception by the receiving party. Once the transmission is released and directed toward the receiver, responsibility will change hands to the receiving zone of operations. The initial phase of reception should be *the collection of transmission language.* In this particular phase the transmission language may go through first a recording process within the receiving unit for storage purposes and then through dissemination to concerned individuals within the unit. Once past the initial phase of reception, the second phase of *transmission breakdown* which involves the deciphering of the received message which allows for further dissemination to the directly affected unit or individual. The reception process is further advanced by taking the results of the transmission breakdown and formulating it into the next phase which is *the formulation and interaction of operating procedures.* At this point direction is taken to coincide with the original transmission's logic. Upon completion of the next preceding phase, reception is presented which is *the culmination of operating procedures.* The final phase of communication reception is that of *evaluation of operating procedures.*

In order to complete the act of communication and to place it into cyclical form, the receiver will become the new transmitter to convey the last two phases of the reception segment (culmination of operating procedures and the results of evaluating those procedures). The direction of communication's flow may be to the original sender of the first transmission or to concerned personnel that may be in the previously described category of superior, subordinate, or peer (see Figure 13).

Mention also needs to be made that transmission and reception of communication may be undertaken by nonhuman objects. Such objects may also complete all phases of the communications cycle without human assistance. For example, computers, robots and other computer assisted devices. It must be remembered that these electronic devices must be programmed and taken through troubleshooting action by trained and skilled personnel.

Planners must be able to use fusion in the blending process of planning along with communications input. Planning without communication or proper communication techniques can lead to disaster resulting in the nonreaching of projected goals. There are certain factors that need to be kept in mind when launching out on a planning project, and keeping aware of proposed communications needs. These factors are:

1. The planning team must be aware of forthcoming communications needs.
2. There must be an awareness of the type of communications mediums available.

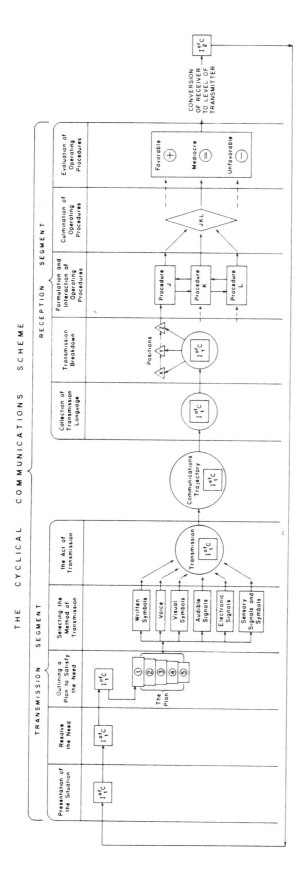

Figure 13. The Cyclical Communication Scheme

Legend

I of C = Item of Communication – 1
  1

I of C = Item of Communication – 2
  2

3. There must be an awareness of the type of communications mediums needed.
4. Communications history of the intended group.
5. Elimination of known communications bottlenecks and preparation to meet potential trouble areas.
6. Providing for elasticity of communication to coordinate with planning goal(s).

Summary

In order to commence the planning process there must first be an evaluation of the resources that the planner or planning team must draw upon. Input from resources that are a part of the organization as well as those that are external.

Steps that follow the evaluation of resources are:

1. Review of the initial problems.
2. Review of the characteristics of the overall plan.
3. A pre-evaluation of the proposed plan.
4. A review of chronographic dimensions as they are associated with the plan.
5. The segmented and overall cost of the plan.

No plan should be established without the consideration of various alternatives. Multiple alternatives should be considered prior to the final selection of a particular planning project. This would include the:

1. Major and minor goals of the school district.
2. Major and minor goals of the planning operation.
3. Major and minor goals of the logistical support system.

Along with the final selection of the intended course of action will be those administrative decisions (with serious forethought) for which there can be no turning back. Movement is then carried forward to the outcome phase.

The outcome (whether negative or positive) needs to be appraised for immediate and future needs. Both success and failure should be measured. This can greatly assist future planning efforts.

PART THREE
THE CONTROL OF ELECTRONIC SERVICES

CHAPTER V

MANAGING THE COMPUTER SERVICE SYSTEM

EXIGENCY AND THE
SCHOOL DISTRICT'S DATA PROCESSING SYSTEM

Within the last decade there has been an increase in the use of computer services. One can observe the numerous capabilities that these electronic machines offer along with the decrease of unit size. Other features include the factor of some models having portability. Computers are also being used to program robots in assisting to relieve mankind of menial and nonmenial chores. Along with business, industry, government and the military, education has found use for the computer within its daily operations. The chief administrator for managing the school district computer program is the Logistical Manager. Before the establishment of any kind of computer program, or additional computer programs within the school district, there should be a study of school district computer needs.

When a school district decides to introduce a program of computerization to its operations, or extend an already established activity, a careful and detailed study is in order. Such a study will assist the Logistical Manager and the superintendent in determining approval or disapproval for computerization or an extension of computerized services. If approved, such a study would assist the central office administration in determining the extent of services needed and the district's affordability for such a venture. While participating in a study of computer needs, the Logistical Manager and his/her staff (or an ad hoc committee established at central office) should from a general point of view, establish and list the *desires* of the various units within the school district. Once the desires are listed, there should then be a listing prepared of the district unit's actual computer *needs*. Desires that are not placed in the needs category, or are not practical, unorthodox or not affordable should be discarded. Further sifting will be involved as other considerations are taken into account.

After the general needs are subtracted from the district's general desires, a more specific study is in order. First there should be a *review of the school district's organization and goals.* Those overall goals and the goals of computerization services. Another point to consider is that of *the direction of the school district and the proposed computer program.* Next in line would be *a study of alternatives to the previously two mentioned points.* Consideration for alternatives are necessary, because primary thrusts may be thwarted by direct or indirect actions, or by seen or unforeseen circumstances.

Observation should be taken to determine if *alteration should be made of the established predetermined needs.* If so, then such alterations should be evaluated and then made to present a more current and precise listing of the district's computer needs. Once the previous actions are taken the Logistical Manager and his/her team, or the ad hoc study committee should come up with a majority or consensus thought on district goals, direction, actual computer needs, and why the existence of such particular thought is maintained. Upon completion of establishing this particular standard and being able to give support for its creation will complete the first phase.

The second phase will further develop the established needs by *reviewing those manuals and established computerized services that are in existence.* The Logistical Manager's study group's direction should answer the following questions:

1. What are the requirements listed in manuals and are present in functional computer systems?
2. What are the results of past evaluations of the existing systems?
3. What are the specifications of the existing systems?

In obtaining responses to the above three questions, the Logistical Manager's study group (or committee) should be able to *develop a set of specifications for the proposed computer equipment; project a master planning operation for district computerization; project planning tasks for specific units of the school district; and establish new computer goals for the school district.*

The third phase of the Logistical Manager's study group would be to develop *a plan of action* from which the district computer program would embark. There would be need for:

1. Reviewing the existing manuals or functioning computerized systems
2. A study of existing limitations (internal and external)
3. Establishing the specific functions to be performed
4. Feasibility tests
5. Functional test
6. Time consumption
7. Training requirements
8. Overall costs
9. Implementation
10. Evaluation
11. Quality control

(see Figure 14).

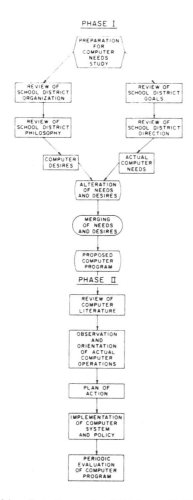

Figure 14. Establishing Data Processing Within the Public School District.

Upon completion of the Logistical Manager's study team's (or committee's) assessment of computer needs, there will be need for approval by the Logistical Manager, the superintendent, and the board. More specific direction will involve the choice of having all computer operations originate from a central point within the district, or from independent terminals (located at building level or other units tying in with a central computer). Study is also needed here (possibly with the help of a consultant) as to which plan best fits the individual district. There are both negative and positive points to both central computer location and terminal usage tying in with a central computer location. Positive features of maintaining centrally located computer use are:

1. Centralization of all computer activities.
2. Easier enforcement of computer policies.

3. Easier management control.
4. Economy of use.
5. Noncomplex accounting for unit time usage.

Negative points concerning centralized computer usage and location are:

1. Computer policy centralized and does not make allowances for individual subunit participation.
2. Loss of computer control by individual user.
3. Precedence procedures for subunit use.
4. High cost due to almost constant or constant business hours of operation.

The positive points that individual terminal usage offers are:

1. Tailor made usage for the individual user.
2. Direct user control.
3. Direct cost application to the user.
4. Direct user knowledge of input, process and output.
5. Minimum time usage.

Negative features of individual terminal usage are:

1. Greater installation and maintenance costs.
2. Complexity in establishing uniform computer policy for the entire school district.
3. Allowing for variance in subunit approaches to computer application.
4. Overall computer goals of the school district are greatly dispersed.

Completing a study of needs and the establishing of computer program specifications and implementation opens yet another avenue of approach to operation. That particular avenue concerns computer selection. Specifications will tie in directly with the type of equipment needed along with its capabilities. This will influence the decisions to be made in purchasing or leasing equipment. State law and local board of education policy will dictate the bidding procedures to be used concerning purchasing or leasing costs. There are several computer companies vying for marketing leadership. Careful study of the computer's capabilities along with specifications and cost is essential.

Another point of importance about organizational usage of the computer concerns sharing. Some school districts may find themselves sharing their computer with local government, or other school districts. Sharing computer time with other organizations may present problems with (1) priority usage; (2) determining cost; (3) time consumption; (4) computer overload; (5) personnel conflicts; (6) and computer espionage. Sole usage of the computer system by the individual district will eliminate the above mentioned problems, but the school district may well find the factor of cost higher than if the services were shared. Careful consideration should be made before making a decision in this area.

PLANNING FOR COMPUTER STORAGE AND INFORMATION RETRIEVAL

Security—A First

Before the establishment of the computer's storage capability and retrieval operations, the organization needs to develop a program of computer security. Stored data should not be at the beck and call of unauthorized personnel who may gain entry into the system and its stored data. Some types of information maintained by the school district's computer mechanism may be considered classified and protected by legal statute. For example, transcripts, bidding information, personnel records, etc. A properly established computer security program will help to decrease the probability of unauthorized access to data storage.

Security of the computer and its storage capability will involve a number of factors such as:

1. Manual or electronic personnel checks at entry and exit areas of the computer area.
2. Identity cards for all computer personnel.
3. Security and security procedures concerning all hardware and software items.
4. TV monitoring of the computer area and its exit and entrance points.
5. Security and security procedures of the storage area, storage equipment and the data files.
6. Surveillance and control over internal personnel (administrators, staff members, etc.) and external personnel (dealer representatives, service personnel, consultants, etc.) having business in the computer area.
7. Periodic checks and surveillance of assigned computer personnel.
8. Emergency procedures for computer area in case of disaster.
9. Computer security policy constructed, evaluated, and modified by the Logistical Manager and computer management on a periodic basis.

The responsibility for security will rest with the Logistical Manager and the management of the computer team. Overall responsibility for the computer program's security will be that of the Logistical Manager. The supreme paper of computer security will be that of policy constructed by the Logistical Manager and lesser computer managers. Any newly prepared security policy is then forwarded to the superintendent and the school board for approval. Areas to be covered in the policy should include:

1. A table of organization for security positions of computer management and staff (these positions would be in addition to the primary position already assigned).
2. Security job description of the computer managers and staff.
3. Specifications for prime computer facility location (including fire-proofing, waterproofing, heating, ventilating and cooling features).
4. Security of terminals.
5. Security of lines between terminal and computer.
6. Security of hardware and software.
7. Availability of proper electrical voltage and emergency generating capability.
8. Control of computer input and processing through codes.
9. Establishment of periodic code books.
10. Control of computer output materials.
11. Control of personnel.
12. Security of the information storage area.
    a. Provisions for a fireproof and waterproof storage facility and equipment.
    b. Control of personnel entry into storage area and materials.
    c. Ensure compliance by computer personnel with policies, rules and regulations and statutes concerning entry into storage materials.
    d. Establish procedures for terminating storage materials.
    e. Codify entry in order to control retrieval of stored data.
    f. Electronically secured storage area.
13. Electronically monitored computer and storage areas.
14. Control of all computer supplies through signout and inventory procedures.
15. Establishment of an alternate secured storage facility for alternative reasons such as possible disasters.
16. Provision for managerial spot-checks of the entire computer system.
17. Control of the computer communications system.

One cannot establish the fact that an organization's computer and storage operations are 100% secure. There is need for managerial establishment of security procedures and policies in protecting not only the computer itself, but also the storage and retrieval operations. Denial of entry by unauthorized persons is a must if the near optimum of security is to be reached. An important fact that should be remembered is—Security is only as effective as its enforcement.

Storage and Retrieval

Computers have the capability to store or retain information within its system. Just as easily as is stored, data can be accessible to unauthorized retrieval and processing. Storage capabilities will vary according to manufacturer's offerings in the computer marketing arena. Organizational computer storage capabilities should be designed by a consultant. The consultant should use his/her expertise in:

1. Reviewing organizational requests.
2. Determining organizational storage needs.
3. Average daily storage input needs.
4. Average daily storage input time consumption.
5. Average daily retrieval needs.
6. Average daily retrieval time consumption.
7. Frequency of storage.
8. Frequency of retrieval.
9. Storage limitations.
10. Cost of storage.
11. Cost of retrieval.

The Logistical Manager and/or the computer manager must be ready to orientate the computer staff to be able to coordinate the mass of data coming in for storage and processing. Records must be kept for identification purposes, consumption of time, and storage space. Computer control in the storage and retrieval processes should be kept at central control with terminal capability (if the school system has installed terminals throughout the district).

Responsibility for data storage and retrieval should be with the Logistical Manager and the head manager of the computer operation. The authority of a managerial position can be delegated to lesser managers, but the factor of responsibility cannot. Managers involved in storage authority and responsibility must ensure that board policies in this area are adhered to by users and the computer staff.

Responsibilities that computer managers should cover in the managing of storage and retrieval operations are:

1. Storage needs of the organization.
2. Retrieval needs of the organization.
3. Coordinate with user personnel regarding storage and retrieval operations.
4. Construction of criterion to be used in storage and retrieval operations.
5. Consultation of storage of retrieval matters to other central office and building level administrative personnel.
6. Administer inservice training to computer staff personnel and other

noncomputer personnel on a *need-to-know basis.*
7. Overall supervision.
8. Provide security.
9. Assist users in storage and retrieval matters.

The mechanism that has been developed to allow the processes of storing and retrieving information is known as the data bank, or sometimes the centralized data base. This electronic reservoir allows for the input of various types of information to the computer system or storage tapes or discs and remains stored until called upon for retrieval and processing purposes. The result of the processing action is called the output. Information placed into the input situation is verified and then placed in specified areas of the data bank (see Figure 15).

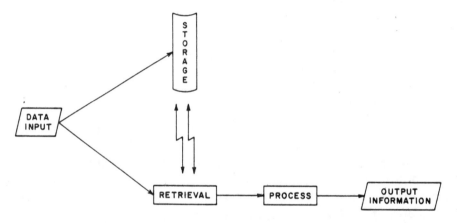

Figure 15. The Data Storage, Retrieval, and Processing Operation.

Typical storage areas and retrieval implementations that could be applied to the average school district could be:

STORAGE CAPABILITY AREA	RETRIEVAL AND IMPLEMENTATION AREAS
1. *Fiscal Management*	a. Accounting
	b. Auditing
	c. Reporting
	d. Payroll
	e. Revenue and spending estimations
	f. Capital fund
	g. Student activity funds
2. *Personnel Administration*	a. Evaluations
	b. Workload distribution and need

    c. Personnel records
    d. Construction of wage and salary schedules
    e. Reduction—in force procedures
    f. Training

3. *Office Management*
    a. Word processing
    b. Record keeping
    c. Communications
    d. Office form and report design
    e. Computer operation training

4. *Instruction*
    a. Instructional presentation
    b. Testing
    c. Grading
    d. Computer training
    e. Problem solving exercises
    f. Semipractical applications

5. *Research*
    a. Linear and outline form
    b. In depth

6. *Student Personnel Administration*
    a. Student record (standard and academic)
    b. Class scheduling
    c. Student activities
    d. Registration
    e. Guidance and counseling
    f. Attendance
    g. Job placement
    h. Medical information

7. *Facility Maintenance*
    a. Maintenance scheduling
    b. Service projections
    c. Replacement projections
    d. Staff needs
    e. Workload distribution
    f. Staff assignment
    g. Work activity coordination
    h. Maintenance program needs

8. *Facility Operations*
    a. Daily, weekly, monthly, semiannual, and annual operations scheduling
    b. Staff needs
    c. Workload distribution
    d. Staff assignment

e. Operation's program needs
f. Daily work activity
   coordination
g. Facility priorities
h. Heating control
i. Air conditioning control
j. Ventilation control

9. *Food Service Operations*

a. Recipe file
b. Daily menu planning
c. Master menu planning
d. Inventories
e. Automatic reorder
f. Freezer control
g. Refrigerator control
h. Automated baking, frying,
   broiling, and warming
i. Humidity control in dry
   storage areas
j. Workload
k. Staff needs
l. Staff assignment
m. Food service accounting
n. Portion control
o. Meal preparation
   cost analysis
p. Meal preparation
   time consumption
   (individual dish and/or
   course offerings)
g. Meal selection popularity

10. *Transportation*

a. Driver information
b. Passenger information
c. Vehicle information
d. Vehicle maintenance
   scheduling and record keeping
e. Route and bus stop
   information
f. Scheduling data
g. Transfer point data
h. School site mounting and
   dismounting points
i. Passenger accounting

	j. Petroleum oil and lubricant products inventory controls
	k. Spare parts inventory control
	l. Tool assignment and control
	m. Driver training
	n. Pupil discipline recording
	o. Automatic reorder of transportation item needs
11. *Library System Administration*	a. Book classification and placement
	b. Collection development
	c. Circulation
	d. Research
	e. Library user information and records
12. *Extracurricular Activities*	a. Event planning and scheduling
	b. Transportation requirements
	c. Chaperone assignments
	d. Compliance checks
13. *Audiovisual Management*	a. Equipment classification and placement
	b. Circulation
	c. Maintenance and service schedules
14. *Purchasing*	a. Requisitioning
	b. Automatic reorder
	c. Financial coordination
	d. Purchasing order preparation
	e. Vendor listing
	f. Catalog preparation
	g. Specification construction and listing
	h. Recording
	i. Reporting
	j. Communicating
	k. Payment authorization
	l. Construction and listing of the purchasing calendar
	m. Need determination
	n. Quality control
	o. Product appraisal
15. *Warehouse Management*	a. Inventory systems

	b. Stock locator system
	c. Space management
	d. Receiving organization and monitoring
	e. Distribution organization and monitoring
	f. Catalog preparation
	g. Handling and storage safety
	h. Requisition compliance
16. *Cost Analysis Data*	a. Determining:
	(1) Per pupil cost
	(2) Per employee cost
	(3) Per school cost
	(4) Per unit cost
	(5) Per period (daily, weekly, monthly, semiannually, annually, etc.) cost
17. *Planning Projections*	a. Network analysis
	(1) Critical-Path Method (CPM)
	(2) Program Evaluation And Review Technique (PERT)
	(3) Resource Allocation And Multi-Project Scheduling (RAMPS)
	(4) Other programs
18. *Security*	a. Controlled entry
	b. Controlled exits
	c. Smoke and fire sensing/communications link with fire department
	d. Forced entry alarms/communications link with law enforcement agencies
	e. Television surveillance
19. *Communications*	a. Printout
	b. Computer-telephone connections
	c. Data entry and display station
	d. Audio response units
	e. Visual signaling

20. *Evaluation*

   f. Televised communications
   a. Compiling of evaluation data
   b. Calculating evaluation results
   c. Producing evaluation comparisons

The school district's computer programmer should have the flexibility to design programs that would allow stored data to be obtained and placed through a variety of processes. This flexibility would conform with school district needs. Storage capability areas that would be general in their appeal to the district-wide education program and interwoven with other storage capability areas are:

1. Fiscal Management
2. Personnel Administration
3. Office Management
4. Research
5. Audiovisual Management
6. Purchasing
7. Warehouse Management
8. Cost Analysis Data
9. Planning Projections
10. Security
11. Communications
12. Evaluation

ADMINISTRATION OF COMPUTER PERSONNEL

School district size and needs will determine the type and capacity of the computer system to be selected. The computer specifications will in turn determine the computer unit's personnel needs. People that are involved in computer work, whether management or staff, need to be highly trained and skilled in data processing (if a level of success is to be reached). Sources that provide the above mentioned qualified employees are:

1. The employing of university, community college and business college trained individuals from outside of the organization.

2. Training people already within the organization's employ to operate and maintain the computer system.

3. Or a combination of item 1 and 2.

4. Computer contractors.

The training of internal personnel for computer operations can be through university, community college or business school sources. Also, many computer manufacturers will offer training courses through their own schools, or they will bring classes to the organization. A third method would be for the organization to provide for its own training program with qualified instructors hired for the purpose of training a computer staff to be operational.

Employees that are to be considered for computer training should be tested, screened and interviewed (through some bona fide accepted medium) before final selection. There should also be background checks concerning possible past criminal activities. Only individuals with unblemished backgrounds should be selected for computer work. Any computer system offers an opportunity to the dishonest to become a perpetrator of "high tech" crime.

Computer services can be contracted through firms offering their services for a fee. The advantages of this type of an arrangement would be that of no personnel costs such as wage, fringe benefits, or union inspired costs such as monies lost, to grievance investigations, wage increase demands, etc. Disadvantages would be that of: (1) Loss of direct action to assigned tasks; (2) User priority due to other organizations contracting with the computer firm; (3) convenience; (4) Personal attention to projects and problems; and (5) The contractor's familiarity with public school operations.

The Computer—Personnel Dilemma

The age of the computer has produced several new jobs and careers for managers, operators, clerical and service-maintenance employees. Within the last two decades many colleges and universities have added computer science to their curriculum offerings. Trained computer personnel will be in demand until a universal point of saturation is reached.

Computers have the ability to assist organizations in an electronic manner that is way beyond the ingenuity of mortal beings. Processes such as:

1. Originating
2. Data collection
3. Recording
4. Classifying
5. Sorting
6. Processing Analyzing and Calculating
7. Summarization of Processing Results
8. Electronic Information Breakdown
9. Electronic Communication Process
10. Data Storing
11. Retrieval Action
12. Written and Visual-Graphic Reproductions

13. Projections, and
14. Audible communications

can be accomplished on an immense scale which offers a lightning quick electronic means of operation. This action can, therefore, eliminate lengthy periods of manual interaction. In addition, all of the above mentioned processes can assist management in policy making, problem solving and decision-making tasks. With the organization preparing or extending itself in these electronic computer age processes, there will be a need for computer trained staff, or the addition of external personnel to the organization's computer operation. There also may be a need to terminate outmoded manual and/or machine processes. If this step is taken, there will probably be a cancellation of personnel services in those areas. An action of this type will give the organization four alternatives. They are:

1. Terminate displaced employees
2. Train displaced workers in the various areas of computer operations
3. Transfer displaced workers into other units within the organization
4. The reduction of manual and machine workers through natural attrition.

In some situations fears and uncooperative actions may result from an organization's plan to install a computer system within its domain. Employees and their unions or organizations may establish formal or informal defenses to computer operations. In order to successfully operate an organizational computer system and obtain satisfactory results and proper goal accomplishments, *there must be staff cooperation.* The fears of computers replacing humans must be neutralized by management. Employees need to be shown that computers will assist in organizational tasks and will not provide an instant and direct takeover of duties within the organization.

Employee uncooperativeness with computer systems may be serious and damaging to the organization. Some prime examples are:

1. Not providing data for input purposes.
2. Not providing correct data for input purposes.
3. Improperly filling out various computer forms, etc.
4. Establishing negativism with computer output.
5. Poor effort.
6. Overt and covert hostility.
7. General negative cooperations with the overall computer operations.
8. Organized efforts to hinder or halt computer operations.
9. The inducement of low morale standards.

Employee sabotage has presented itself to the world in a variety of ways. Patton brings forth the point in history of the resistance of French workers to the Industrial Revolution. In order to halt machine production, the French workers would hurl their wooden shoes or sabots into the machines in order to stop production. Thus the word, "sabotage" was coined (from the *World Book Encyclopeadia* © 1984 World Book, Inc., by permission of World Book, Inc.) [1]. Other negative employee defenses against management that have been used in similar situations. Sometimes with the assistance of labor unions and/or other employee organizations are:

1. Featherbedding
2. Labor-management contractual stipulations
3. Employer penalties
4. Favorable legislation (passes by legislators supporting union causes)

One may ask the question, why do people combat change within organizations? An organization may seek change from the status quo in order to become more efficient, increase profit, save time, or a number of various reasons. Employees at times will be dissatisfied with the managerial challenge to the status quo. This new challenge (as far as the employee is concerned) transforms itself into a threat. The threat itself can be further be reduced to:

1. Job loss
2. Replacement by younger high technically trained workers.
3. The destruction of the labor force hierarchy.
4. Psychological losses
5. Domestic losses
6. Financial losses

In order to have a successful computer operation, management will have to deliver to the work force a plan which will disperse employee computer fear. Such a plan needs to include the following measures:

1. Develop a sound and fair personnel transfer plan which will not include employee termination (due to direct introduction of a computer system).
2. Orientate the employees concerning computer system introduction.
3. Provide training for employee operation and cooperation with proposed computer operations.
4. Allow for active employee participation in various phases of the computer process.
5. Managerial appraisal of the overall conversion scheme.

Staffing The Computer Unit

Once settlement has been made concerning the hiring and/or training of various computer personnel, along with the total number of individuals needed, a table of organization should be constructed. In order to move into this construction phase there is need to:

1. Construct the mission of the computer unit.
2. Establish the philosophy of the computer unit.
3. Develop job descriptions.
4. Develop employee job specification tables.
5. Establish managerial needs and focal points within the computer unit.

Upon establishing and meeting the above mentioned needs, managerial and staff personnel should be established into the following divisions of the computer unit:

1. Office Management Team
2. Computer Operators Team
3. Computer Programmers Team
4. Systems Analysis Team
5. Research Team
6. Troubleshooting Team
7. Electronic Communications Team
8. Data Storage Team
9. Clerical Team

A manager should be in charge of each of the eight teams along with a primary director and an assistant director (of the computer unit). Staff needed to operate in each of the eight teams will be dictated by school district size and type and size of the computer system. An organizational format as presented would appeal to medium to large size school districts. Small districts would place more than one team duty to possibly one or two managers. Also, a typical staff member would wear a number of task hats in the area of performance in small school districts (see Figure 16).

EVALUATION OF THE DISTRICT'S COMPUTERIZATION EFFORT

There should be two types of evaluation concerning the school district's computer unit. They are:

1. Project evaluations—Which are an appraisal of the processing and outcome of a particular project. Did the project meet the needs of its originators and those concerned? Was the waiting time (if any) and processing time held to a minimum and within reason? Did the programmer execute his/her duties in a proper manner? Was the assistance of the computer unit's teams adequate? Answers to these and possibly other evaluative inquiries will determine the ranking of a satisfactory computer service to those involved with a particular project.

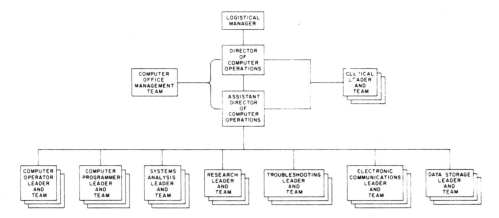

Figure 16. Table of Organization for a Computer Unit of a Typical Medium-to-Large Sized School District.

2. Periodic evaluations — Evaluations of this nature will encompass the entire computer operation and each member of the operation (both management and staff). Information gathered here will determine the level of quality of the computer unit's performances. Critical views should be taken of whether or not the unit is offering a financially sound operation at the lowest possible cost. Another area of appraisal would be the quality control aspect of production. Evaluation of computer unit personnel would present a yardstick of individuals carrying out their duties and a marking of individual and team participation along with cooperation within the computer process.

Evaluation results would indicate to the chief computer manager and the Logistical Manager where alterations or terminations would be needed in order to offer a more satisfactory service.

Summary

Today's school system will find a definite need for installation of a computer system within its organization. The need to reduce costs and accelerate the execution and accomplishment of various tasks will increase the demand for computer modification of the school district. Actual establishment of the computer system within the district will call for a study of the type of system needed, and whether to train present employees or to hire computer trained personnel external to the organization. Another point of consideration is that of purchasing a computer system for sole use by the school district, or sharing the cost and the services with local governments or other school districts.

The installation of a computer system within the school organization will call for the expansion of the security program to involve the data processing unit. Computer crime or white collar crime is making its presence felt in society. The school board must enact policy that will counter the opportunity for criminal acts in the computer arena. The superintendent, the Logistical Manager, and the director of computer services must see to it that such policy is enforced and abided with by the computer and district staffs.

The computer's capability and capacity to provide for data storage and retrieval operations must match the needs of the school district. These two tasks along with the third function of processing, represent the foundations of the school district's computer system.

Some people have a fear of being replace by computer to become a member of the ranks of the unemployed. The use of tact, proper reassignment and the computer training of present employees by management may well reduce fears of this nature. Managerial personnel must be able to guide a painless transition of the computer system over the manual and/or less sophisticated machine operations of the school district. Resistance to computer change should not be allowed to formulate by staff members. Managers must lead the way by illustrating to staff members that they are a part of the change, and that they are included within the change features.

In order that the computer operation is properly synchronized and successful there is a need for the correct organization of the computer unit. The creation of positions within the computer unit and the personnel assigned to these positions will fall into the classifications of: (1) management, (2) operators, (3) programmers, (4) systems analysts, (5) researchers, (6) troubleshooters, (7) electronic communication experts, (8) data storage team, and (9) clerical team members. Medium to large sized school systems may well have personnel in each of the above nine categories. Smaller systems may require their computer personnel to double or triple the previously mentioned tasks to each individual staff member.

Evaluation of the school district's computer program should be ongoing. Appraisal is needed not only of computer personnel and their duties, but also of the computer processing and how it is meeting organizational goals.

PART FOUR
MANAGING THE SCHOOL DISTRICT'S
FINANCIAL NERVE CENTER

CHAPTER VI

THE BUDGETING PROCESS

The budgeting process (as it concerns public education), denotes a segment of the chronographic dimensions in the projected sense which is related to financial management. Progress concerning this venture is covered within a time period called the fiscal year. Two chief factors relating to the budgeting process are the projections of forthcoming revenue and the projection of forthcoming school district expenditures. Those that are involved in budget preparation and administration must be concerned with a variety of time frames concerned with the budgeting process. Such time frames are:

1. The local school district fiscal year.
2. The state fiscal year.
3. The federal fiscal year.
4. The academic year.
5. The calendar year.

Budgeting at the local school district level will require that the school district's fiscal period will be interwoven with the four other above mentioned time periods.

A local school district budget involves the total financial picture and a series of individual financial representations of individual school buildings plus other administrative units. The budgeting process offers the district and its various branches a provision for administrative control and economy of financial resources.

The chief administrators that are involved in budget preparation are the superintendent and the Logistical Manager (or the budget team). While the superintendent has overall responsibility, prime delegation for the actual overall budget preparation will be placed in the hands of the Logistical Manager. However, administrative input will be made by other members of the central office administrative team, building principals, and unit administrators (such as transportation, food service, operations, maintenance directors and others). Budget approval must be made by the local board of education and that unit only if the school district is operating under the system of fiscal independence. Fiscal independence offers the local school district complete authority over all financial matters including the budget. If a school district is operating under fiscal dependence, budgeting must not only be approved by the board, but by a local governmental body city council or county commission). Fiscal dependence requires that financial matters must have local governmental approval.

Administration of the budget will involve the superintendent, the Logistical Manager, the central office administrative team, building level administrators, and the various unit leaders throughout the district. Budget adherence is necessary in order to have proper control. Also, overall adherence is the key to the district's financial economy.

THE PREPARATORY TASK OF THE BUDGETING PROCESS

The Logistical Manager needs to look toward the chronographic dimension of elapsed time (to previous fiscal periods) before attempting to construct the budget for a forthcoming fiscal period.

Vital information regarding past fiscal periods could be through district-wide postbudget evaluation data. This action could give the budget team (the superintendent and the Logistical Manager) important budgetary information from all segments of the school operation. Input could be gained from:

1. Each member of the central office administrative team and his/her sphere of operation.
2. Building level administrators.
3. Secondary and middle school department heads.
4. Elementary school primary and intermediate level leaders.
5. Teachers.
6. Logistical services directors and subordinate leaders.
7. Logistical staff.
8. Unit administrators and their staffs.
9. Public relations administrators.
10. The lay community.

Processed budget evaluation information can offer the budget team an illustration of the highs and lows of previous fiscal periods, and how the various unit objectives were reached plus their individual levels of success.

Other areas that the budget team could take into consideration that could assist in preparation are a review of all state and federal codes concerning school financial management to see if there have been any alterations. There should also be a study of all pupil census projections for the forthcoming fiscal period. This should be observed from a central office point of view, individual administrative units, and each individual elementary, middle and senior high school. Data from individual schools can provide an important segment of the financial picture due to socioeconomics, ethnic groupings, special programs, curricular offerings, population shifts, logistical needs, and miscellaneous instructional needs.

Another area of concern in which evaluative data could assist is that of budgetary communications (between the central office, school buildings and other various units of the school district). As in other areas, there must be a two-way communications flow involving budgeting. Also, the communications action must be adequate in order to have compliance and control.

A review procedure concerning the obtaining of budgetary data representing the needs of school district employees should be established. This information needs to represent the present and past fiscal periods. Information of this nature could be obtained through an evaluation process, or through a needs assessment study by central office, building level and unit level administrators. Employees at all levels should have input into the study of needs. Needs should be listed in priority by the budget team in order to fund those items that are the most critical.

Another item that should be considered before the actual budget preparation commences is that of quality control (as it relates to the school district's educational program). In these days of economic uncertainty coupled with rising costs, there is great temptation to cut the educational program to a minimum. In fact one may even find lay support in this direction. The budget team needs to keep in mind that a quality educational program must be offered to the local community's children in order that goal of educating the populace is accomplished. However, with the availability and dependence upon public monies the program must operate within certain fiscal limitations. The budget team must be able to allow the funding of a premium program within the projected range of funds available.

In order for a planned and approved budget to reach the stage in which it is to be managed by the school administrative corps, it is possible for four years of managerial input to have taken place. A breakdown of the time that could be consumed in this action is in order. For example:

1. During the 1989–1990 fiscal period, review, planning, formal presentation and formal selection (by the local board of education) will take place for the 1990–1991 fiscal year. While reviewing and planning for the 1990–1991 fiscal period, administrators will also take a preliminary projection of 1991–1992 financial picture. Projected tasks and specific projects that are to be funded for the 1990–1991 period may well run into the 1991–1992 fiscal year. Projected dollars and cents needed beyond the 1990–1991 budget period should be considered along with the projected revenue to cover the intended expense of 1991–1992. This first year (1989–1990) of the budget cycle can be termed the *Preview Year.*

2. The second year of the cycle (1990–1991) will involve the actual adminis-

trative working period (performing the tasks of reviewing, planning, the formal presentation to the board and the budget acceptance by the board) will take place for the next fiscal period, 1991–1992. This second year is termed the *Administrative Working Period.*

3. Actual administration of the budget will take place during the third year by central office administrators, building level administrators, unit administrators, and lesser leaders throughout the school district during the 1991–1992 fiscal period. The third year is known as the *Administrative Implementation Period.*

4. The fourth year period, 1992–1993 or the *Appraisal Period,* will find the evaluation phase of the budgeting cycle taking place for the 1991–1992 fiscal year. Appraisal will be made by the local board, the school district administration, and local government.

Budgeting for a specific fiscal period covers a total four fiscal year segments of working time consumed in the educational process. The third year involves the actual expenditure of the school district's funds with the fourth year as pure appraisal.

Attention needs to be given that the above mentioned four year scheme involved a prototype school system that had fiscal independence. This allowed the local board of education to accept and approve the administration's budget without forwarding the financial package to the local governmental level for further approval. Fiscal independence allows for the local board to have final jurisdiction over all fiscal matters.

School districts operating under the principle of fiscal dependence must not only have their budgets approved by the local board of education, but also a local governmental body such as that of the city, county, or metropolitan legislative body. School districts operating under the fiscal dependence method may well find the budgeting cycle of a more complex nature due to additional legislative input.

Preparation is the key in constructing the four year budget cycle. The main emphasis will come during the first two years of the cycle's formation. Once the *Preview Year's* (First Year) information has been collected, formulated and processed, review and preparation should commence with the beginning of the second year (the Working Period). A time line or calendar which coincides with the fiscal year should be constructed to be used as a guide during the entire budget cycle. Let's assume that the standard local school district fiscal period is being used (July 1 to June 30).

| Phase I Preview Year (1989–1990) | July-June | Observations and projections based on information collected during the period. (Also forecasts for 1991–1992 budgetary period.) |

Phase II Administrative Working Period (1990–1991)	July	Budget team led by superintendent and Logistical Manager undergoes a review of Preview Year's information and other financial needs for the district's education program.
	August	Principals and other unit administrators collect financial data requested by subordinate leaders within their organizations regarding program operation.
	September	Principals and other unit administrators forward (after approval of subordinate input) financial data to the central office budget team.
	October	Meetings with teacher union and/or organization plus other employee unions regarding salaries and fringe benefits.
	November	Obtain financial data concerning educational programs for next fiscal period. Obtain financial data for school plant operation and maintenance.
	December	Obtain financial data regarding all other logistical operations.
	January	Accept employee union and organizational input regarding salaries and fringe benefits.
	February	Collect all recommendations from administrators, teachers, staff employees and lay community members.
	March	Construction of the budget.
	April	Presentation of the budget to local board of education and the lay community.
	May	Board approval and adoption of the budget. (If operating under a system of fiscal dependence, local governmental approval and adoption would also take place during the month of May.)
	June	Administrative and staff orientation of the new budget.
Phase III The Adminis-	July–June	Administration of the new budget.

trative
Implemen-
tation Period
(1991–1992)

Phase IV	June–July	Appraisal of the previous fiscal period's
Appraisal		budget. (Some secondary appraisal may
Period		have been undertaken during the
(1992–1993)		Administrative Implementation Period.)

It is essential that conformity be maintained concerning the budget cycle's time line or calendar. There are times when unforeseen circumstances will disrupt the planned schedule. However, elasticity should be built into the system to allow for spontaneous acceleration in order to recover lost periods of time.

Preparation of the budget is not without criticism, therefore, the central office budget team and administrators at line level (principals) must be able to support their claims for financial requests.

ADAPTING AVAILABLE FUNDS AND PROJECTED REVENUES TO THE MONETARY NEEDS OF THE SCHOOL DISTRICT

The School Program

The key to the use of monies to pay for the school district's educational process is the educational program. To be more specific one will observe that the *quality* of program to be maintained or desired by the local board, the school administration and the community is of prime importance. Boards and administrators may desire a high quality of educational program, but the community may indicate noncompliance through the failure to pass local tax increases (for public schools) during elections. There is also the possibility that local boards or segments of local boards being against spending increased amounts for higher quality educational offerings. The same can also be said of the school administration.

Akin to the quality of school program to be desired or maintained are the goals expected to be accomplished by the school district. In order that program goals are reached there must be adequate funding to assure reasonable accomplishment without a great amount of complexity.

Before the attaching of dollars and cents to the various budgetary segments, a critical review should be taken of the present educational program and the possibilities of program improvement, program termination, or the middle ground called program adequacy. Program adequacy funds would require neither an increase in funds (outside of an inflationary adjustment), nor a shifting of funds to another budgetary area. Program areas that should be taken into consideration are:

1. Policies that result in expenditures
2. Pupil-teacher ratios
3. Union or employee organizational contracts or segments of contracts that require expenditures
4. Enrollment data
   a. Total number of children attending school within the district
   b. Apportionment of children by grade level
   c. Apportionment of children by chronological age
   d. Apportionment of children according to specific geographical areas within the school district
   e. Apportionment of children according to socioeconomic class
5. Curriculum offerings
   a. Preschool program
   b. Kindergarten
   c. Elementary
      (1) Primary
      (2) Intermediate
   d. Middle school
   e. Senior high school
   f. Special education
   g. Gifted education
   h. Vocational education
   i. Career education
   j. Community education
6. Housing conditions and needs
   a. School plant facilities
   b. Nonschool facilities
7. Earnings
   a. Certificated personnel
   b. Noncertificated personnel
   c. Paraprofessionals
   d. Contracted personnel (without fringe benefits)
8. Other logistical services and support such as:
   a. Food service
   b. Transportation
   c. Purchasing supply and warehousing management
   d. Clerical service
   e. Data processing
   f. Risk management
   g. etc.

The superintendent and the central office administrative team (including the Logistical Manager) must make a concerned effort in estimating and establishing program needs to maintain proper operation of the educational process. Once establishment has been made of the type of educational program to be offered (including expenditures) then another critical review must be taken concerning revenue.

Projected Revenue and Available Funds

State and federal monies for local school districts are fixed at certain rates according to formulas established by state and federal laws. State monies are the most concrete and have maximum intended stability. Many soft money programs offered by the federal government could well not be around the next fiscal period due to executive and congressional cutbacks. The superintendent and the Logistical Manager will have to make an accurate or mostly accurate projection of federal and state monies coming into the school district for the budgetary period. The following actions to be taken by the budget team (superintendent and Logistical Manager) will be that of projecting the amount of revenue to be received the local district from local taxes. The primary local tax for the school district's educational program is the property tax. The rate of the local property tax for school support is set by the local board of education under fiscally independent situations. If there is fiscal dependence local boards must have local governmental approval upon property tax rates. If the needs of an established educational program are not being met due to financial restraints, local boards of education must then promote tax increases to be placed before the electorate for approval.

Estimates for local tax revenues can be placed more in the accuracy zone through the budget team's study of past fiscal periods and their graphic presentations. Notice also needs to be given to the tax delinquency rates during elapsed fiscal periods.

A study should be made of any available surplus monies and how these funds could be used in the projected budgetary period. Care should be used here in establishing the priorities concerning the spending of surplus monies in the forthcoming period's educational program.

Once the grand total and various segmented dollar figures are projected for the budgetary period, another review of the proposed educational program is in order. This action would allow the budget team and possibly the central office administrative team to make a *final* match of program segments and grand program total with the projected revenue of local, state and federal funds. Last minute adjustments would be in order at this time before the final draft for presentation to the board (see Figure 17).

CONTROLLING SCHOOL EXPENDITURES

Once the budget is planned, constructed, and approved by the super-intendent, approval is in order by the local board of education and local government (if fiscally dependent). The approved budget is then returned to the school district for administration. The superintendent, the Logistical Manager, the central office administrative team, building principals and other unit administrators will also commence with the process of ad-ministratively controlling the budget operation within the zone of their authority.

One may question the fact as to why must there be a control of the budget when the various accounts have been allocated specific sums of money. In order to bring forth an adequate response, a backward glance is in order. A review indicates that the budget is a planned and projected representation of needed monies for the district's operation. These needed monies are depen-dent upon projected revenues from federal, state, and local governments, plus other revenue sources. Governmental sources are dependent upon tax collections. Delinquent taxes are more sharply felt at the local level and can have more of a direct influence upon the local school district's operation.

In observing the revenue collection — the school expenditure picture pres-ents a formation of the balancing act brought about by administrative control. This administratively induced balancing operation keeps school expenditures directly in line with available resources. If local tax revenues are less than the level projected, those individuals that are involved in budget administration must either petition the local board to obtain needed funds through borrowing, or create a program of austerity to match the available revenue. In either case there is a balance between revenues and expenditures.

Administrative participation in budget control procedures should be involve the entire administrative corps from central office to building level principals to those administrators in charge of external units such as transportation centers, warehouses, food preparation centers, etc. These administrators should be distributed copies of the overall school district budget and a division of the budget which applies to their particular zone of operation. As each administrator matches his/her allotment of funds with the proposed expenditure for their unit's function, the con-trol function becomes more precise and to the point. Procedures of this nature will also allow for more coordination between the lower echelon administrator and the Logistical Manager. In addition, such coordina-tion permits elasticity and better control over budget administrative practices.

In order to enhance the above mentioned points on administrative coordi-

BAYBERRY HARBOR CITY SCHOOLS
BAYBERRY HARBOR, TENNESSEE
GENERAL PURPOSE OPERATION AND MAINTENANCE BUDGET FOR FISCAL YEAR, 1991-1992

PAGE ONE

PROJECTED REVENUE FOR FISCAL YEAR, 1991-1992

Account Number	Current Tax Sources for Revenue	Actual Fiscal Year 1989-1990	Estimated Fiscal Year 1990-1991	Projected Fiscal Year 1991-1992
110.0	Bayberry Harbor City Revenue	$ 5,000,000	$ 5,000,100	$ 5,005,000
120.0	Mountain County Revenue	3,000,000	2,800,000	3,100,000
130.0	State Revenue	6,000,000	6,000,100	6,001,000
140.0	Federal Government Revenue	300,000	300,000	250,000
111.0	Nontax Revenue	250,000	245,000	250,000
115.0	School Food Services Revenue	300,000	250,000	300,000
112.0	Adult Education	60,000	50,000	60,000
4090.0	Summer School	25,000	20,000	25,000
98.0	Balance from Previous Year	269,800	260,000	270,000
GRAND TOTAL FOR REVENUE (ACTUAL, ESTIMATED AND PROJECTED AND INCLUDING INFLATION FACTOR)		$15,204,800	$14,925,200	$15,261,000

BAYBERRY HARBOR CITY SCHOOLS
BAYBERRY HARBOR, TENNESSEE
GENERAL PURPOSE OPERATION AND MAINTENANCE BUDGET FOR FISCAL YEAR, 1991-1992

PAGE TWO

GENERAL ACCOUNT CATEGORY
APPROPRIATIONS FOR FISCAL YEAR, 1991-1992

General Account Number		Actual Fiscal Year 1989-1990	Estimated Fiscal Year 1990-1991	Projected Fiscal Year 1991-1992
2100	General Administration	$ 290,000	$ 312,000	$ 315,000
2200	Instruction	7,000,000	7,500,000	7,800,000
3600	Instruction--Special Education	427,000	434,000	463,000
3700	Instruction--Vocational-Technical	1,000,000	1,107,000	1,200,000
2300	Truancy and Attendance	40,000	43,000	45,000
2400	Medical and Dental Services	2,000	2,100	3,000
2500	Pupil Transportation Services	316,000	334,000	361,000
2600	School Plant Operation	1,000,000	1,100,000	120,000
2700	School Plant Maintenance	425,000	465,000	543,000
2800	Fixed Charges	710,000	756,000	850,000
2900	Cafeteria and Food Services	546,000	663,000	680,000
3100	Community Relations	12,000	11,500	14,000
3200	Capital Outlay	157,000	226,000	425,000
3300	Community Education	8,400	8,200	10,000
3500	Adult Education	84,000	93,000	105,000
4000	Miscellaneous Programs	20,000	20,000	25,000
	Federal Programs	3,167,400	1,350,400	2,302,000
GRAND TOTAL (INCLUDING INFLATION FACTOR)		$15,204,800	$14,925,200	$15,261,000

Figure 17. A Typical General Budget Statement for A Public School District.

nation and control over budgetary matters, there is need to establish bi-weekly or monthly financial reporting from all administrative units to the Logistical Manager's office. This procedure would allow those involved in fiscal administration to have a reading of the district's financial heartbeat on a periodic basis. Information of this nature would allow an extention of control procedures. If the school district is fortunate to have computer services, the financial status of the school district would be available at a moment's notice, therefore, allowing almost instant control.

The chief element of budget control is the school district's accounting system. An accounting system may be manual or it could be operated by a highly sophisticated computer system. A properly operated system of accounting will govern the school district's fiscal system in illustrating the expenditures and cash on hand picture in total and according to each individual account. Greater detail as to the school district's accounting process will be mentioned later in this book.

Another element of controlling the budget is the administrative control design. A fiscally wise administrator will review his/her allotted funds and construct a design which will keep unit subordinates within fiscal limitations. Before actual construction of the control design, the unit's goal(s) should be prioritized according to organizational and fiscal needs.

Achieving budgetary success can only come about through administrative control during the fiscal period of operation. Administrators cannot just look upon the budgetary document and hope for a fiscally osmosis type of influence to guide unit subordinates along proper money lines during the fiscal year. There must be administrative input concerning how and when funds will spent within the unit. Above all there will be administrative enforced fiscal limitations on unit spending in accordance with unit goals and policies.

EVALUATION OF ADMINISTERING THE
SCHOOL DISTRICT'S BUDGET

The optimum that can be reached by the budgetary procedure is to end a fiscal period that has allowed the anticipated revenue and the projected expenditures to be kept in line. Another prime features would be that expenditures were less than anticipated. The windfall results of a balance or surplus would permit funds to be held for possible later emergencies. Administrators should also be careful in creating a year-end balance or surplus to the level that notice is taken by legislative groups (such as local boards and/or local government). It is possible that such groups may view unused monies as a stimulus to cutting funds in future fiscal periods.

Budget appraisal can be performed while the budget is in operation, or after the budgetary period is terminated. In process evaluations may be accomplished by the administrator when he/she prepares the periodic (bi-weekly or monthly) financial report. Obtaining the current financial period and determining whether or not the unit is meeting its established organizational goals. There can be relationships between fiscal strength and a specific unit adequately reaching its objectives. The primary emphasis of budget appraisal comes after the budgetary period has come to an end. Data can be gathered from the periodic in-process evaluations, and from the overall financial operation during the elapsed fiscal periods. Appraisal should be made to determine if the elapsed budget allowed for fiscal and program objectives to be accomplished. If these two areas of objectives were accomplished, to what degree of quality was such accomplishment reached. Administrators at the central office level will collect data from their respective units as well as those administrators operating units in the field (school plants, teacher centers, food preparation centers, etc.). Data should be collected and categorized into central office divisional units of the central office administrative team and processed. Also, results should be obtained from data collected to allow for a quality related observation of the overall budget process. Total and segmented appraisal will allow the administrator corps and the budget team to make possible alterations for forthcoming fiscal periods. Alterations may be made through requests for additional funds, or by reducing varying operational costs.

Appraisal procedures should consider the sources of school revenue (local, state and federal) and the rate of financial support contributed by each governmental level. Another point of consideration in the appraisal process is that of inflation. An established federal inflation figure should find its way into the budgetary process and its appraisal system. Use of the inflation figure would assist in maintaining quality level programs through this annual means of elasticity.

Key areas in budget evaluations that are of major concern are:

1. Budget review
2. Planning procedures
3. Desired educational program
4. Actual educational program
5. Projected revenue
6. Actual revenue
7. Projected expenditures
8. Actual expenditures
9. Budget format
10. Budget administration (all units)

Evaluation results are to be used in assisting the budget team and the administrative corps in budgetary and program quality. In addition to measuring levels of quality, evaluation data will give direction to administrative personnel in making those necessary adjustments to better synchronize future fiscal periods. Appraisal data should not be used as a foundation for professional criticism but as a guide to better future fiscal periods.

Summary

Budgeting is an act which keeps the school district's financial program within designated limitation boundaries. In establishing the use of a budget format, the public school district takes a projected observation of needed expense to operate the school program at a specified level of quality. In addition, the amount of projected revenue from government (federal, state and local) and other sources are taken under study. Once there is a meeting of the minds between expense and revenue, the budget team (the superintendent of the Logistical Manager) along with district administrative and staff inputs, will make preparation for formal presentation to the local board of education. Fiscally independent boards have the right to approve their own budgets and direct authority over all fiscal matters. Fiscally dependent boards of education must obtain budgetary and other fiscal approval from a local governmental body (city council, county commission, etc.).

Budget acceptance and approval by the local board (and local government if fiscally dependent) returns the budget to the school district's administrative corps for compliance and control.

Evaluation of the budget is of prime importance to both the administration and the board of education (plus local government if fiscally dependent). Some evaluation data can be obtained during the budget process, however, the main appraisal effort should come after the budgetary period (the fiscal year) has expired.

CHAPTER VII

ACCOUNTING SERVICES AND AUDITING FUNCTIONS

In association with the term, accounting, some individuals may be brought to mind of a Dickens type of character perched upon a high stool. The Dickens accountant would be well within reach of a pile of various accounting books, an inexhaustible ink well, and the ever present nontiring hand clutching a well used quill. Through the years there has been a transformation in the process of accounting and in the image of the accountant and his/her staff.

First let's take a look at the term *accounting*. The *Random House College Dictionary* [1] defines accounting as:

"The theory or system of organizing, maintaining, and auditing the books of a firm; art of analyzing the financial position and operating results of a business house from a study of its sales, purchases, overhead, etc." (Reprinted by permission from *The Random House College Dictionary*, Copyright © 1984 by Random House, Inc.) Application is given here as to the accounting services of a profit making business organization. However, accounting procedures are also used by nonprofit organizations to achieve the same results concerning the organization's financial picture at a given point in time. The public school district is a nonprofit organization that must keep a record of its financial operations as required by law. Financial management (which includes the accounting process) is the direct responsibility of the Logistical Manager who has the opportunity (in many school systems) to delegate this function to the chief accountant and his/her accounting staff.

SUPERVISION OF THE ACCOUNTING SYSTEM

The accounting process is the heartbeat of the school district's operation. Without finances educational programs and their logistical support would not be able to function. School system accounting is concerned with a public or governmental service to the residents of the school district supported by public funds. Although public school systems are operated at the local level (in all states except Hawaii and the District of Columbia), they are legally considered to be segment of the state's system of public education. This frame of thought places local school districts in a position to be liable for financial decisions to the public. Accounting provides the tool which records:

(1) all financial transactions; (2) the reason for the transaction; (3) justification for the transaction according to local, state and possibly federal guidelines; (4) when the transaction took place; (5) the unit (within the school system) that was responsible for the transaction; and (6) the provision of accuracy as brought forth in the recording process and account balancing procedures.

Within the last two decades, accounting has been moved from the manual realm to that of the computer. Though some school districts may still be involved in manual accounting practices, many are presently operating or converting to computerized accounting systems. Computerized accounting provides for: (1) less time consumption on the part of the accounting staff; (2) greater accuracy; (3) greater availability to financial information; (4) greater ease in preparation of financial reports; and (5) easier access to auditing personnel.

Financial accounting within the local school district is in need of supervision by the Logistical Manager and the chief accountant. The board of education, the superintendent, state and federal auditors, employee unions and organizations, and the lay community will frequently call upon a variety of financial records and reports for review. Management must constantly be aware of the district's financial management operation and the accounting process within.

Many daily managerial tasks within the school system require the use of financial information provided through the district's accounting system. The selection of an accounting system for the local school district may be well be determined at state level. State influenced accounting systems are operated in order to achieve uniformity at the local level within state boundaries. Such a practice for uniformity may push a number of local antiquated manual accounting systems to a computerized operation. State mandates may include procedures for account classification, reporting, reporting procedures, and standards. Another feature provided by state accounting systems for public school districts is the general construction of the individual accounts and their involvement in the total accounting operation. In order to further elaborate in this area concerning the individual account, there are a series of questions that must be responded to by each account:

1. What is the origin for the establishment of the account?
2. What particular unit(s) within the school district are influenced by this particular account?
3. Is this a general type of account that is influenced by the entire school district?
4. Does this account support an instructional activity?
5. Does this account support a logistical activity?

6. What is the source of funds for this particular account?

7. Is this account involved in procuring goods?

8. Is this account involved in procuring services?

9. What is the source of funding for goods and services?

10. What is the numerical identification of the account?

Once the accounting system is established (whether by the state or the local board of education) it must be able to accommodate daily administrative tasks within the school district. For example:

1. Construction of financial reporting systems (for local, state and federal governmental agencies).

2. Abidance with local, state and federal guidelines.

3. Actual receipt of revenue from governmental and other sources.

4. Budget construction, administration, and control.

5. Economy of operation overall and within individual sections of the school district.

6. Availability of data for auditing purposes.

7. Availability of data for the lay public.

8. Assisting both long and short range planning.

9. Assistance in decision making.

10. Assistance in problem solving.

Those school administrators that are involved in the school district's accounting system need to adhere to certain basic rules. These rules are the cornerstone to successful operation of the accounting process. They are:

1. Data produced by the school district's accounting system should provide adequate knowledge that is beneficial to the educational process.

2. That the accounting system can assist in providing budgetary data plus adequate administrative control.

3. The accounting system should indicate proof that responsibility is taking place through the actions of school personnel.

4. Both internal and external audits should take place on an annual basis (along with impromptu audits to assure constant compliance by school personnel).

5. Audit findings should be issued in a report to school personnel and the community.

6. All accounting and financial management procedures must be undertaken in compliance with local, state and federal laws.

7. The local school district's accounting system should be evaluated on an annual basis.

8. That all accounting data *must* maintain a level of pure accuracy.

9. The accounting system is a focal point of reference to administrative

decision making, board of education policy making, administrative and board problem solving, the establishment of instructional plus logistical programs, and assistance in the planning process.

Administrative supervision of the public school accounting system provides for control, compliance, accuracy and general assistance to the overall school operation. The Logistical Manager and the chief accountant must make sure that the above mentioned points are carried out by the accounting staff. An adequate system of accounting is necessary to the operation of a public school district. Money is a definite necessity for program operation and service to the school community.

FISCAL RECONCILIATING AND MONITORING OF ACCOUNTS

Funding

A system of accounting should have uniformity to provide for a reduction in complexity and confusion. As previously mentioned one may find that a state will provide for a uniform system of accounting for its local school districts. First there is need to observe the types of funds a typical school district will be operating with. A fund can be described as an amount of money, or resources that have been allocated by a governmental body, or other types of organizations. These monies or resources are channeled to be used for supporting certain activities within the local school district. There are three primary classifications of school funds. They are:

1. The Restricted Fund—This fund controls those monies that are limited to certain labeled activities, programs, groups, etc., within the school operation (and for their use only). A fiscal restriction is placed into being and provides a measure of fiscal power to a privileged segment of the accounting system (such as organizations, athletic programs, etc.).

2. The General or Nonrestricted Fund—This particular fund is somewhat of a "catchall" type of fund in that its use is limited to those revenues and expenditures that are for the general school population. The general fund is not restricted to any specific segment of the school program.

3. The Food Service Fund—School systems that are recipients of governmental food service funds are placed upon a separate fund which involves only the food service program.

Types of Accounts

Now that we have discussed funding as it applies to the accounting process, our next order is that of defining and classifying the individual account. An account provides the accountant with a title in which financial transactions are categorized in line with:

1. Intention
2. Action
3. Origin

Accounts belong to one of three major categories. These categories are:

1. The Asset Account—Items that are owned by the school district and can be converted into cash. This classification also includes ready cash.

2. The Liability Account—Items which represent a debt to someone or something external to the school district, or something that is owed.

3. The Net Worth or Fund Balance Account—This particular type of account illustrates the difference between items that are owned and those items that are owed.

The previously mentioned information supports the standard accounting equation of:

Assets = Liabilities + Net Worth (or Fund Balance)
A = L + NW (or FB)
or
Assets − Liabilities = Net Worth (or Fund Balance)
A − L = NW (or FB)
or
Liabilities = Assets − Net Worth (or Fund Balance)
L = A − NW (or FB)
or
Net Worth (or Fund Balance) = Assets − Liabilities
NW (or FB) = A − L

Let's further investigate the typical account (whether an asset, liability or net worth account) as it is involved in the accounting process. Entries that are made into the journal (book of original entry) are later posted or transferred to the accounts in the ledger or book of accounts. (This process will be discussed later in the chapter.) Action that has taken place will have a positive or negative influence upon each account. This positive or negative influence is represented by the terms debit and credit.

1. The debit is an entry of the accounting process to the left side of an individual account of the ledger. A debit represents an increase in an asset account, but a decrease to a liability and net worth (fund balance) account.

2. The credit is an entry of the accounting process which is applied to the right side of a ledger account. The credit represents an increase to the

liability and net worth accounts, however, it is a decrease to the asset account (see Figure 18).

Asset Account

Debit (Dr.)	Credit (Cr.)
+	−

Liability Account

Debit (Dr.)	Credit (Cr.)
−	+

Net Worth or Fund Balance Account

Debit (Dr.)	Credit (Cr.)
−	+

Figure 18. Debit and Credits as Associated With Asset, Liability, and Net Worth Accounts.

Account Classifications and Codes

The process of accounting reflects the financial transactions taking place in daily school operations. Whenever such an action is generated, there will be an increase or decrease in the individual account involved. The use of double entry accounting involves the entry of a debit in a specified account, and the entry of a credit in another specified account. Within one particular account the difference between the debit and credit sides will offer the account's balance.

Previously we discussed uniform classification of accounts used in public school systems. The federal government recommended the use of Handbook II through the United States Office of Education during the 1960s. Some states have developed accounting classifications that are to be used by the local school districts. However, in some of the state uniform account classification systems, flexibility is allowed to better fit the individual local school district. Such flexibility may be used through the addition of decimal places to the major category area. (For example Account #0304 may be the general category for resale items with account #0304.1 representing school store materials.)

The state of Tennessee in its *Tennessee Internal School Financial Management Manual* has assigned the following series of accounting codes or numbers for accounting purposes at the local school district level.

1. Account Numbers 1–99. For all balance sheet (a periodic accounting form, usually on a monthly basis, which reflects the balances of all asset, liability and net worth accounts which should balance out according to the accounting equation) accounts. This category applies to those accounts involved with restricted, general and food service funds.

2. Account Numbers 101–199. For revenue accounts associated with food service funds.

3. Account Numbers 201–299. Representing expenditure accounts associated with food service funds.

4. Account Numbers 301–399. Concerns revenue accounts that are involved with the general or nonrestricted fund.

5. Account Numbers 401–499. Represents expenditure accounts that are of the general or nonrestricted fund.

6. Account Numbers 601–999. This extremely large category represents those accounts that are affiliated with the restricted fund. [2]

By classifying and coding accounts, the accounting staff and administrative personnel face less complexity and confusion in interpreting financial actions. Statewide coding systems with built-in flexibility features offer uniformity to the local school district level which makes for greater synchronization in the preparing of state reports. Convenience is also offered to the account workings within the school district.

The Books of Account

Whether a school district is using a manual or computerized accounting system, there are books of account and various recording forms that are involved with daily financial transactions. If a manual system of accounting is being used there are actual books of account in which hand entries have been made. A computerized system of accounting with its storage capability offers the books of account on a video screen and/or as a computer printout whenever electronically called upon.

To prepare for the implementation of an accounting system there is need to construct a *balance sheet* which will show the assets, liabilities and the net worth or fund balance of the school district. This point could also be explained as showing what the school district:

1. Owns
2. Owes and its
3. Wealth or Worth

Once constructed the balance sheet *must* support the accounting equation of Assets = Liabilities plus Net Worth or Fund Balance.

The key action that commences the accounting process is the financial transaction. A financial transaction may be initiated within any unit of the local school district, plus it may be for any type of financial purpose. Whenever the transaction is made it must be recorded into the various books of account. The financial transaction may involve an outflow or an inflow of cash. Use of an accounting book called the *journal* provides space for recording financial transactions. Accountants also call the journal the book of original entry. Some accounting systems will provide what is called a general journal in which all financial entries are recorded. Other accounting systems may use special journals for specific entry purposes such as, the cash receipts journal, accounts receivable journal, etc. Events within the journal are recorded in chronological order and are:

1. The date
2. Identification of account concerned
3. Explanation of the transaction
4. Debit and credit placement of the entry concerned
5. Information concerning posting information

The first event that is to be placed in the journal will be the opening entry from the beginning balance sheet which lists the total assets, liabilities and fund balance or net worth of the school district from the previous fiscal period.

After the opening entry is placed in the journal the various accounts must be posted to the ledger. The term *post* means to transfer entries of the journal to the *ledger.* The ledger is a book into which the various accounts (assets, liabilities, and net worth or fund balance) are grouped. Additional factors that should be remembered are that:

1. Asset accounts usually have debit balances
2. Liability accounts usually have credit balances
3. Net worth or fund balance accounts usually have credit balances.

All other transactions should be processed in the same manner by journalizing (placing the transaction in the journal) and posting the transactions to the ledger. Both journalizing and posting should be carried out on a daily basis.

Another accounting form that should be prepared is that of a *trial balance.*

This item provides the proof that the debits and credits within the ledger are accurate. Before preparing the trial balance all accounts in the ledger must be *footed* or balanced (between the debit and credit sides. The balance of each account is recorded in each account and the trial balance is prepared. The trial balance is constructed with the date and the debit or credit balance of each account. Preparation of the trial balance is made on the last day of each month along with the footing or balancing of each ledger account. The trial balance proves correctness of posting by indicating that the debits equal credits in all of the ledger accounts.

Further analysis of the trial balance needs to be taken and that is done through an accounting analysis form called the *work sheet*. Accountants consider the work sheet a working type of paper and it does not become a permanent part of accounting record books. The work sheet is a distribution point at which the school district's fund balance is calculated. Use of the work sheet also checks the accuracy of all accounting entries. Work sheet functions involve the:

1. Placement of the trial balance and its account balances to the worksheet trial balance format in proper debit and credit balances.

2. Extension of the asset, liabilities, reserves, contributions and net worth (or fund balance) accounts to the balance sheet sections (with the proper debit and credit balances).

3. Extension of the revenue and expense accounts to the statement of revenues and expenditures sections.

4. Total should be made of the revenue and expenditure sections (both debits and credits). Also total should be made of the balance sheet sections (both debits and credits). The difference between both the debits and credits of the revenue and expense sections, plus the debits and credits of the balance sheet sections. These actions will indicate excess or a deficit to the school operation funds. If assets are higher than liabilities, and if revenues are higher than expenses then an excess will occur. However, if liabilities are higher than assets and expenses higher than revenues, a deficit will occur.

The next step of the accounting cycle would be the preparation of probable *local and* state financial reports indicating the excess or deficit status of the school district's fiscal position. Accounting forms representing the above would be taken from the work sheet and are called the:

1. *Revenue and Expense Statement*
2. *Balance Sheet*

The balance sheet items will be used to start the accounting cycle for the next accounting period (or the next month).

A *closing entry* should be made into the journal which transfers current balances of the revenue and expense accounts to the revenue and expense summary account. This is called a closing entry. Information concerning the revenue and expense accounts is obtained from the work sheet.

Next the process of posting the closing entries to the ledger of the revenue, expense, and revenue and expense summary accounts. This action will rule and close the revenue and expenditure accounts.

Asset, liability and net worth (or fund balance) accounts are closed (for the current fiscal period), balanced (to indicate the debit or credit balance for the next accounting period), and ruled to show that the account is closed for the current fiscal period. Single rule lines on accounts indicates that addition calculations have been made. Double ruled lines indicate that the ledger account is closed. Entries made below the ruled double lines indicate that the account has a balance for the next accounting period.

The last item in the accounting cycle is the *post-closing trial balance*. This is a trial balance which is taken after closing entries have been made in the journal and posted to the ledger, plus all accounts of the ledger have been balanced and ruled. Only those accounts that are open or containing balances appear on the post-closing trial balance. The post-closing trial balance is the final checking by the accountant to determine if the ledger balances and it is synchronized to fit into the new accounting period (see Figure 19).

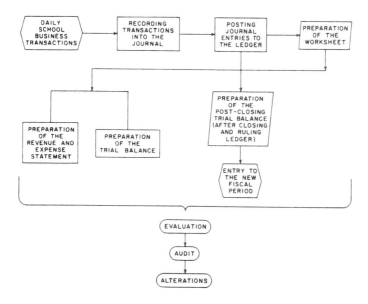

Figure 19. The Accounting Cycle Flowchart With Evaluation, Audit and Alteration Processes.

EVALUATION OF THE ACCOUNTING SYSTEM

In order to evaluate a school district's accounting system, we must first take a panoramic observation of the expected goals. They are:

1. Granting provisions that allow for:
   a. Accuracy in all financial management transactions
   b. Establishment of fiscal limitations and control
   c. Establishing school district projections that are dependent upon finances
   d. Problem solving
   e. Decision making
   f. Policy establishment and alteration
   g. The budgeting process
   h. Granting additional local, state, and federal assistance
   i. Revenue projections
   j. Employee wage and benefit demands through organizations and labor unions

The Logistical Manager, the chief accountant and the superintendent need to ask themselves, does the present system of accounting help or hinder the school district to achieve the previously mentioned goals through its daily interactions. If these goals are being met, is it with or without complexity and extreme effort on the part of organizational personnel. There may be greater ease of accomplishment through the use of other accounting systems. If the above mentioned goals are not being met there is definitely a need for a change in the accounting system.

In order to obtain a feeling of the school district's pulse as it concerns accounting, survey instruments should be formulated by the Logistical Manager and the chief accountant. Distribution should then be made to all district personnel involved in the accounting process. Data should then be formulated to identify the troubled areas. This information should be forwarded to administrative personnel in order to allow for their input for rectifying negative situations. This may be accomplished through:

1. Alterations by the Logistical Manager and the chief accountant.
2. Alterations by the superintendent.
3. Alterations suggested by external consultants such as university personnel, computer firms, etc.

In the process of evaluation, the satisfactory achievement of accounting goals must be remembered. If alterations must be made to allow for satisfactory achievement, there must be careful administrative thought before actual implementation.

INTERNAL AND EXTERNAL AUDITS

Auditing is an official examination of the school district's accounting system by auditors to determine if accuracy was carried out in all financial transactions during a given fiscal period.

Audits may be carried out by governmental units (local—if fiscally dependent, state and federal). Such groups of auditors would be external to this school system. Audits taken by accounting personnel within the school system would be classified as internal.

Audits of the school district's accounting system may be taken on a periodic basis, or it may been taken in an impromptu fashion.

Auditing results cannot only find inconsistency and unethical practices, but also flaws in the accounting system. This information can also assist in the evaluative action.

The auditing process also has certain goals to accomplish. They are as follows:

1. To ensure organizational integrity.
2. To ensure accuracy of all financial transactions within the school district.
3. To check on compliance with local, state and federal regulations.
4. To coordinate with the chief accountant and the Logistical Manager.
5. To check the accuracy of inventory procedures.
6. To ensure the accuracy of auditing procedures.

There are certain items that should be involved in the auditing action. They are:

1. Record of all revenue (taxes and nontaxes)
2. Property deeds
3. Records of debt service for capital outlay
4. Bank accounts (savings, trusts and checking)
5. The school district's computer accounting system program.
6. All books of account
7. Insurance policies
8. Surety bonds
9. Payroll records
10. Inventory of all warehouse storage items.
11. Inventory of all equipment
12. School building internal accounts
13. Food service system accounts
14. Extracurricular activity funds
15. Purchasing data records
16. Vendor payment records

17. Local governmental tax collection records for school support
18. Local governmental tax delinquency records for school support
19. School plant improvement records
20. Budget forms
21. All financial reports for the fiscal period
22. Board minutes for the fiscal period or previous fiscal periods if applicable.

Summary

The Logistical Manager's main thrust into the school district's accounting function is that of supervision. Keeping track of the school system's financial transactions is a full time job which is usually delegated to a chief accountant and an accounting staff (in medium to large school systems), or to an individual that has accounting knowledge in smaller systems. Some smaller systems contract their accounting tasks to private firms.

School district accounting functions are changing from manual to computerized assistance in a number of public school districts across the country. Computerized accounting practices offer greater accuracy, less time consumption, and greater convenience to the administrative operation.

The accounting cycle is the cornerstone to keeping an adequate and accurate set of books. This cycle consists basically of:

1. Recording transactions of school business into the journal.
2. Posting journal entries into the ledger.
3. Preparation of the work sheet to test the accuracy of the ledger's accounts.
4. Preparation of the revenue and expense statement to determine excess or deficit.
5. Preparation of the balance sheet to show the financial condition of the school district.
6. Preparation of the post-closing trial balance to prove the equality of debits and credits after the ledger is closed and ruled.

The school system's accounting system needs to be evaluated by all personnel involved with the accounting function. Data collected through the evaluation should be used to correct any deficiencies within the accounting program.

Auditing is a check upon the accuracy and the operation of the school district's accounting system. The primary tasks of the Logistical Manager, the chief accountant, and the accounting staff is that of assistance to the auditing team.

Negative findings by the auditing team will lay a foundation for alterations in procedure and policies. The auditing action also serves as an evaluative yardstick. Audits may be taken by either internal or external personnel. Also, audits are sponsored by local, state, and federal governmental bodies. Audits may take place on a periodic basis or present themselves in an impromptu fashion.

CHAPTER VIII

PLANT PLANNING, CONSTRUCTION, AND CAPITAL OUTLAY

There is need to house the local school district's educational program. This task is accomplished through the construction of elementary, middle, and secondary school plants. There are a variety of factors that will influence plant construction in a given school district. They are:

1. Age, type of construction and condition of present buildings.
2. Overall enrollment increases or decreases.
3. Enrollment increases or decreases of specified areas within the school district (K–12).
4. Enrollment projections (K–12 for next 10, 20 and 30 years).
5. Educational program needs.
6. Extracurricular program needs.
7. National, state and local economic conditions.
8. National, state and local economic projections.
9. School district financial ability (present and future).
10. Present and future school plant needs.

Often a school district will find itself needing to replace older plants or construct additional ones. In order to fulfill the school district's building needs careful study and thought must be carried out (by the administrative corps, the school board, and the lay community). Additional input should also be allowed by the teaching and school plant support staffs concerning instructional-logistical specifics.

DETERMINATION OF FACILITY NEEDS

The superintendent will usually delegate the task of school plant planning to the Logistical Manager and his/her staff.

To commence action, the Logistical Manager needs to confer with the superintendent and the central office administrative team. The purpose of such a conference would be to obtain input for formulating an ad hoc committee to plan for the proposed school plant(s). This ad hoc group could be entitled, the School Plant Needs Committee. Representation of the following personnel should be included on the committee:

1. Members of the central office administrative team
2. Elementary, middle, and secondary principals
3. Elementary, middle, and secondary teachers
4. Vocational, special and gifted education teachers
5. Instructional supervisory personnel
6. Maintenance and custodial staff members
7. Food service staff members
8. Lay community members
9. Clerical staff members

A chairperson from the central office administrative team should be appointed by the superintendent. This ad hoc committee should be guided to launch a study to identify the school plant needs of the school district and lay community. The committee would also analyze the determined needs. A study would also be made of the existing services offered by present operating school plants. This study could be made by local administrators or consultants. Once the data is collected concerning school plant needs and present plant offerings, final analyzation is in order. A decision would come from the committee concerning school plant needs in the district and a plan of action needed to accomplish the construction of a school plant program. The study would also provide current costs for site and the building. Upon completion the committee would then forward their report to the Logistical Manager who in turn would forward (after approval) the item to the superintendent.

The Logistical Manager should act in an ex officio capacity in relation to the School Plant Needs Committee. However, he/she (the Logistical Manager) needs to keep the committee machinery within certain operational zones. These zones are:

1. Keeping constantly in mind the school program.
2. The breadth and depth of committee input.
3. The scope of external consultant parties.
4. Available and projected funds.
5. Allotted time consumption for committee work and actual building construction.
6. Legal perimeters.

Upon receipt of the building committee's report the superintendent and the Logistical Manager need to take a more penetrating view of the findings. The report has had the input of the central office administrative team, line administrators (principals), logistical staff members, lay community representatives. Contributions by these various groups creates a panoramic offering to the school plant needs of the community. More detailed information must be gained by the superintendent and the Logistical Manager concerning proposed plant construction. Information from consultants, the local Chamber of Commerce, etc., should be gained in the areas of:

1. Actual and projected capacity of existing and future school plants 10, 20, and 30 years into the future.

2. Past community cooperation in funding plant construction.

3. Present and projected birth rates of local, regional and state areas.

4. Projected life span of present school facilities.

5. Present and projected business and industrial development in the local and regional areas.

6. Present and projected residential development in the local and regional areas.

7. Current and projected socioeconomic stratification in local and regional areas.

8. Historical information of local and regional areas.

9. Population movements within the locality, the region and in adjacent areas.

10. Actual and projected business, industrial and residential distributions in local plus regional areas.

11. Population breakdown according to age, marital status, occupation, income, educational level and property ownership or tenantry status.

12. Housing breakdown:
    a. Type of residence
        (1) Single dwellings
        (2) Condominiums
        (3) Rental units
        (4) Trailer courts
        (5) Farms
    b. Rental or ownership
    c. Price range
    d. Location
        (1) City
        (2) Suburb
        (3) Rural

13. Existing roads and projected road construction.

14. Existing commercial and projected commercial unit construction (such as malls and shopping centers).

15. Actual and proposed federal installations in the local and regional areas.

Once the above information has been obtained along with (1) the architect's preliminary plans, (2) input by the state office of education, (3) a projected listing and the cost for equipping and supplying the school, (4) the cost for instructional and logistical staffing, (5) the projected overall cost of the plant construction program (along with the site cost), (6) the projected cost of bonded indebtedness (principal and interest over a specified period of time), (7) and lastly a report should be prepared for presentation to the board of education for approval.

The superintendent and the Logistical Manager must keep the school within the indebtedness limits prescribed by the state and local board of education. Also, they (the superintendent and the Logistical Manager) must be certain that the school system does not go through any financial strain in paying its debts for capital outlay. Local boards of education must approve any school plant construction program formulated school system's administration. Further approval in many states must be made by the citizens of the community in approving a bond issue to finance plant construction. If a school district is financially dependent, additional approval must be granted by the local government (city, county or metropolitan). This will be before the bond issue is placed upon a ballot for public approval. Additional information concerning the financing of school construction will be given later in the chapter.

PLANNING OF THE FACILITY

Site Selection

In planning for the facility consideration should first be given to the building site. A very critical observation should be made of the site before purchasing or selecting. An evaluation instrument of some kind should be used to obtain data on whether the site is favorable or unfavorable. Certain points that should be considered in evaluating the site are:

1. Location
2. Drainage capabilities
3. Access to utilities
4. Size and shape
5. Type of soil
6. Type of terrain
7. Residential and/or commercial surroundings
8. Campus and playground features
9. Parking lot offerings
10. School bus mounting and dismounting offerings
11. Possibilities for external building and athletic facilities
12. Availability for immediate sale
13. Sale price

14. Willingness for sale price negotiations
15. Socioeconomic surroundings
16. Roadways
17. Roadway traffic conditions
18. Availability of public transit
19. Availability of law enforcement
20. Availability of fire protection
21. Neighborhood zoning projections
22. Availability to pedestrian traffic
23. Availability for community use
24. Danger areas
25. Utility hookups

An evaluation in each of the above areas of the potential site will give the Logistical Manager data upon which the superintendent and the board of education can reach a decision. The selection of the site is the foundation upon which the actual school plant will rest. Additional factors involving the site and the proposed school plant are:

1. The educational program.
2. The pupils.
3. School personnel.
4. The community.

Selection of the Architectural Firm

Another key point in planning for the school facility is the selection of the architect. It is imperative that state laws and board policies be adhered to in this aspect. The selection of a certified architectural firm that has good standing is essential to the proper design of the school facility. Architectural firms that have experience in school design should have favor over those that do not.

A study and evaluation of a potential architectural firm should include the following factors:

1. An investigation of the firm's good will.
2. An investigation of school buildings designed by the firm.
3. Is the firm willing to keep their personnel on the site during the period of construction?
4. Is the firm willing to maintain liaison and coordination between engineers, construction and other personnel?
5. Data collection from engineering and construction companies that have worked on school buildings designed by the firm.
6. Does the firm keep the school's education program at the central focal

point while going through the process of building design?

7. Has the firm had a history of project overruns?

8. What has been the firm's experience in school building construction?

9. Is the architectural fee within reason?

10. What is the overall personality of firm members? Of key members within the firm?

11. Are school districts pleased with the firm's design work and the finished products?

12. What has been the reputation of other organizations working with the firm (engineering design personnel)?

13. Obtain and study data from state building inspectors concerning school buildings designed by the firm.

14. Are the firm's projections within the educational goal(s) range?

All of the above information should be obtained before the final selection of an architectural firm. Prior to the signing of a contract between the local board of education and the architectural firm all questions need to be answered and total clarity must be present. State statutes should be checked to insure that all aspects of the contract are legal.

The Education Specifications

Once the preliminary data has been received from (1) the ad hoc School Plant Needs Committee, (2) the central office administrative team, (3) consultants, (4) introductory information from the architect, (5) the Logistical Manager, (6) the superintendent, and (7) the board of education it is time for the table of educational specifications to be compiled by the Logistical Manager and the superintendent for presentation to the architectural firm. The table of educational specifications will be the guide from which the architect will initiate his/her design of the proposed school building.

If the school district wants a class "A" building, time must be taken to construct a class "A" table of educational specifications. The superintendent and the Logistical Manager should first approach the educational specifications needs from the standpoints of additional committee interaction and input. This particular group should be also ad hoc in nature yet differ in mission from the School Plant Needs Committee which was established to ascertain facility requirements. The ad hoc Educational Specifications Committee will study the facility data that has already been formulated. This material will have a great influence upon the forthcoming specifications. The Educational Specifications Committee's work will be more detailed in that its mission will be to obtain information that will contribute directly to the makeup of the proposed structure. The report of this committee (after approval by the Logistical Manager, the superintendent and the board of education) will be submitted to the architectural firm. A specifications report will serve as a keystone of the architect's final plan for the proposed facility.

Members of the Educational Specifications Committee should represent an excellent cross section of the following primary groups.

1. Educational professionals (administrators and teachers)
2. Community lay persons
3. Local board of education representatives
4. Logistical support personnel

Data compiled by this group should be processed by school plant consultants (hired by the board of education) with a final report turned in to the Logistical Manager and the superintendent for approval. After approval at the central office level, the report should be forwarded to the local board of education for final approval. Once the board accepts the specifications report it should be sent to the architect to act as a foundation for actual design.

Educational specifications dispatched from the local school district to the architectural firm should include at least the following items:

1. A detailed account characterizing the school community, its citizens and children, plus its general socioeconomic status.

2. A detailed plan of the educational, extracurricular, and community programs that are to take place in the proposed school building.

3. A retrospective presentation of the school community's involvement in educational programs, activities and past use of educational facilities.

4. Expectations concerning the functions of logistical services within the proposed structure and its grounds.

5. Expectations concerning the use of instructional services and aids within the proposed structure and its grounds.

6. A detailed written presentation of the method of classroom organization(s) (departmentalized, self-contained, open classroom, team teaching, lecture, etc.) to be used in the planned structure.

7. Grade level(s) that are to be operational within the structure (elementary, middle, junion high school, senior high school, adult education, etc.).

8. Enrollment projections for the new structure at opening date and beyond.

9. Local school district philosophy.

10. General goals to be achieved by the local school district and more specifically the goals to be achieved by the new school building and its personnel.

11. A detailed description of the school site and its immediate surroundings including roads, traffic lights, sidewalks, etc.

12. A description of the type of curriculum planned for use in the proposed building.

13. Space management requirements for total and individual programs and services (instruction and logistics).

14. Floor requirements and plans.

15. Types of building materials, stains, and finishes required.

16. Telephone, television cable plus closed circuit capabilities and intercommunication systems required.

17. Thermostatic requirements.

18. Computer system required (for administration, instruction and logistics).

19. Water heating, general heating, ventilating and cooling systems requirements.

20. Fire, security and surveillance systems requirements.

21. Landscaping data.

22. Automatic lawn sprinkling needs.

23. Exterior drainage needs.

24. Acoustical requirements.

25. Illumination needs (internal and external).

26. Utility requirements.

27. Carpeting and other floor coverings.

28. Furniture needs and placement.

29. Cabinet, closet and storage requirements.

30. Wall surfaces.

31. Locker space.

32. Classroom number, shape, and size requirements.

33. Library requirements.

34. Theater—auditorium requirements.

35. Educational media center.

36. Administrative instructional guidance, and logistical office requirements.

37. Male and female faculty lounge areas.

38. Restroom areas.

39. Access points to external areas.

40. Access points to internal areas.

41. Site availability references to possible future expansion.

Educational specifications should not be considered as architectural plans. The architectural firm will use the specification information as part of the input for processing through professional expertise and formulating a detailed plan. This detailed plan which will include blueprints, drawings and scale models, will be the building contractor's guide to construction of the proposed school facility.

THE FISCAL ASPECTS OF CAPITAL OUTLAY

The financing of capital outlay projects by the school district is mostly done through voter approved bonding. Action of this order involves a series of tasks by the local board and central office administration. Through the use of the bonding process, a school district finds itself paying (by way of voter approval of a bond issue which will increase taxes to pay for new or improved facilities) for capital outlay over an extended period of time (for example 10, 20, and 30 years). Extended payments of principal and interest of school bonds that have been purchased places the school district in debt, or bonded indebtedness. Once the educational specifications are formulated and architectural data are introduced a price tag is placed upon the proposed structure. In these times of almost constantly rising prices it also may be necessary to place a quarterly, semiannual or annual price increase index to keep the computed cost of the facility at current levels.

District indebtedness and limitations must coincide with local board of education policy and state law. Use of the school bond results in long term financing which offers the buyer of the bond a return of the principal plus the fixed rate of interest. Local board policy and state laws will govern placing bond issues on the ballot (for voter approval) placement on the bond market and selling procedures by the local school district.

Observing bonded indebtedness limitations placed upon the school district by the policies of the local board and the state statutes, the superintendent and the Logistical Manager are positioned to plan and budget for capital outlay projects. Planning and capital outlay schemes move toward long-range planning. Projections may be made from 10, 20, 30, or more years into the future. The superintendent and the Logistical Manager must take into consideration a number of factors in order to keep the district's indebtedness within the legal zones. These factors are:

1. Enrollment projections
2. Condition and age of present facilities
3. Educational program needs
4. Logistical program needs
5. Community needs
6. Present indebtedness
7. Inflationary conditions
8. Interest rates
9. Community attitudes and history concerning bond issues
10. Building costs
11. Economic stability of the community
12. Projections of residential, commercial and industrial growth in the community.

Information that has been derived from the above factors can assist in the formulation of a capital outlay budget.

Once the need planning, specifications, architect's design, cost, and budget considerations have taken place, there will be need (in some state) to prepare for voter approval of the bonding issue in many states. School administrators must then prepare for an election campaign to persuade community members to approve the bond issue for financing capital improvements. Passage of the bond issue will result in the increasing of taxes. In some areas school officials find themselves at the center of a tax rebellion by a populace that is unwilling to shoulder additional taxes in an inflationary and negative economy. Unemployment and a higher cost of living adds to the possibility of negative voter response. Strategy must be planned by the superintendent, the Logistical Manager, and central office administrators concerned with community and public relations. Outside consulting firms may also be hired to help formulate campaign strategy for bond issue passage. Key endorsements supporting the bond issue by prominent organizations and citizens is a must. The campaign program must have complete 360° coverage to meet every segment, neighborhood, ethnic group, religious group, and socioeconomic groups within the community. Strategy is also needed to combat those organizations and individuals that will be opponents of the bond issue. Opposition can come from:

1. Those citizens and pressure groups against the raising of taxes.
2. Citizens that have their children enrolled in private schools.
3. Citizens that have no children.
4. Citizens whose children have completed school.
5. Senior citizens that have retired.
6. Individuals that are unemployed.
7. Individuals receiving public assistance.
8. Citizens that do not exercise their right to vote (Their nonparticipation is the same as a negative vote).

One may ask—What approach can school administrators take to promote passage of a bond issue? The campaign needs to center about:

1. Providing a two way communication system between the school system and the community.
2. Enlisting the aid of members of the school staff and employee organizations and unions.
3. Enlisting the aid of community supporters and organizations.
4. Making inroads into interdenominational clerical organizations to obtain support.
5. Obtain the support of the local chamber of commerce and like organizations.

6. Obtain support of key members of both the Democratic and Republican parties.
7. Explain the need for school construction and why it is a top priority.
8. Establishment of a desirable date for the election in accordance with state laws.
9. Use of students in promoting passage of the bond issue.
10. Use of newspaper, radio, and TV support in campaigning.
11. Obtain the support of labor unions.
12. Tactfully and systematically obliterate campaign strategy of the opposition.
13. Designing, ordering, and the distribution of campaign paraphernalia.
14. Prepare data to support need for building construction.
15. Prepare computations to show construction costs, and projected inflationary effect if the construction schedule is delayed.
16. Illustrate to the community how proposed building program can promote and improve the quality of education.

If the bond issue fails, an evaluation needs to be taken to determine why it failed. Alterations then should be made in the campaign plans and the same steps repeated again. Another point to be taken under consideration is the selection of an election day (primary, special, or the traditional November election day) for placing the issue again on the ballot. State laws may also influence the selection of a day for placing a school bond issue on the ballot.

When a bond issue passes school officials must then prepare to sell their approved bonds on the bond market. This action will require the assistance of a bond broker. A bond brokerage firm has the professional expertise to oversee the board's marketing venture. A key to marketing bonds is the interest rate. School districts favor a market in which the interests rates to be paid will favor the district, but still be attractive to the potential purchaser. The bond broker will take into account the following points regarding the sale of school district bonds:

1. Past history of the market concerning school bonds.
2. Past history of the school district's payments on bonds.
3. Current conditions of the bond market.
4. Grand total amount of bonds being offered by the district.
5. Durational period of the overall bond issue.
6. Date selection for the bond sale.
7. Current popularity of school bonds.
8. Type of bonds to be offered by the district.

School administrators and the bond broker need to coordinate and work together in market placement and the actual selling. Cooperation is a term, that cannot be overstressed in this venture.

A bond being a note which establishes a promise by the seller to pay on a selected date the principal plus interest. However, the entire principal and interest may not be paid on a prescribed day. It may be paid in installments on selected dates of a certain year or years as brought forth in the agreement during the marketing process.

Bonds are purchased by the buyer in order to make a profit on his/her investment. The school district is obligated to pay to the buyer the prescribed principal and interest on the selected date(s) agreed upon.

There are some prime types of bonds that can be offered for sale by a school district. State laws may determine the kind that can be placed on market. These prime types are:

1. Serial bonds—These bonds mature in small amounts at selected intervals in time.

2. Term bonds—These bonds are issued with the selected due date for payment of principal and interest (at the termination of a given period of time).

3. Callable bonds—Bonds that may be paid by the seller before maturity under certain agreed upon circumstances.

A point to be kept in mind is that the bonding approach used by the school district will depend upon state statutes and local board of education policies. If fiscal dependence is practiced, there could also be additional mandates by local government for school district adherence.

Summary

Housing the school district's education program rests primarily upon the shoulders of the Logistical Manager. Information concerning the district's facility program is presented to the superintendent by the Logistical Manager through needs studies, school plant planning, coordination with consultants and architects, and the final construction of the educational specifications. To assist the Logistical Manager and the superintendent, there are the functions of two ad hoc committees, the School Plant Needs Committee and the Educational Specifications Committee. These two working groups will provide the Logistical Manager and the superintendent with information which is required in establishing the actual construction of a school building. Educational specifications are very detailed factors which are the segments of the overall facility structure.

After the architect's design is completed the school district is ready to present bonds to the bond market in order to finance construction costs. Some states will require that the local populace approve the bonding issue through the voting process. Once approval is established the marketing process will commence through the assistance of a bond broker. The bonds are then sold to buyers who will receive the principal plus interest on specified dates of maturity. Payment of the principal and interest is made through increased local taxes brought about by approval of the bond issue.

PART FIVE
PROVIDING SPECIALISTS, MATERIEL AND PROTECTION

CHAPTER IX

ADMINISTRATION OF THE
SCHOOL DISTRICT'S PERSONNEL PROGRAM

The administration of the district's personnel operation is one of the essential tasks of the Logistical Manager. In medium to large sized school districts, the Logistical Manager may delegate the personnel operation to a key person on the logistical staff. This individual may be called the personnel officer (or some other designated title) in some systems. Some smaller systems will directly place the personnel task upon the Logistical Manager.

Foundational support for the school district personnel program will rest with personnel policies. The personnel officer, the Logistical Manager, and the superintendent, periodically need to evaluate present policy, alter policy, terminate policy and construct policy to fit the current needs of the school district. In order that policy becomes legal and binding, it must be passed by the local board of education. This fact alone will provide that the previously mentioned central office administrators will have to build support and prove their cases to the board in their request for policy implementation.

There are certain critical areas in the personnel administration sphere that are in dire need of policy coverage. Those areas are:

1. The philosophy of the school district's personnel program.
2. The table of organization for the personnel administrative corps and its staff.
3. Responsibility factors, areas and boundaries of control concerning the personnel administrative corps and its staff.
4. Responsibility for affirmative action and equal opportunity compliance.
5. Construction of job classifications and descriptions for all positions of employment within the school district.
6. The job recruiting process.
7. Evaluation procedures for job candidates.
8. Selection procedures for job candidates.
9. Salary and salary schedule determination for all employee classifications.
10. Orientation programming.
11. Inservice programming.
12. Termination procedures.

13. Labor-management coordination.
14. Labor-management negotiations.
15. Labor-management liaison.
16. Fringe benefit review and offerings.
17. Personnel assignments.
18. Promotion procedures and assignments.
19. Performance evaluations.
20. Retirement procedures.
21. Resignation procedures.
22. Probationary period and procedures.
23. Tenure.
24. Vacation periods and pay procedures.
25. Holiday periods and pay procedures.
26. Assigned duties other than primary tasks.
27. Substitute employees.
28. Student workers, interns, and apprentices.
29. Paraprofessionals.
30. Computer assisted personnel administration and record keeping.
31. General and specific guidelines to personnel administration tasks.
32. Employment testing procedures of candidates for hiring and promotion.
33. Past employment and criminal record checks.
34. Physical examinations.
35. Grievance coordination (with unions and employee organizations) and procedures.
36. Appeal coordination (with unions and employee organizations) and procedures.
37. Leaves of absence.
38. Overtime (daily, weekend and holiday).
39. Reduction-in-force procedures.
40. Transfer procedures.
41. Union and employee organizational seniority procedures.
42. Security and safety.
43. Assignments.
44. Miscellaneous duties.

The Logistical Manager and his/her personnel team must be the originators of any type of personnel policy formulation. Logistical Managers must be prepared to provide personnel data to the superintendent and/or the local board of education at any given time. The Logistical Manager must be in reach of personnel reference materials from his/her personnel staff at a moment's notice. Computer assistance can greatly enhance the convenience of short notice requests in this area.

DETERMINING PERSONNEL NEEDS

Replacement procedures concerning staff members should go through the planning stages during the last half of the fiscal period. This action would be in preparation of the forthcoming fiscal period. The personnel staff would have collected information concerning:

1. Terminations
2. Resignations
3. Leaves
4. Deaths
5. Retirements
6. Layoffs

of most staff members by the end of the second half of the current fiscal period. Employee separations from the school system could be then classified into:

1. Numbers (grand and specific totals)
2. Job categories.

Fiscal limitations in the budget for labor costs may also have a bearing on whether or not 100% replacement of job vacancies can be maintained. Austerity is readily practiced in the area of labor by boards of education in attempting to achieve some level of fiscal parity (between available financial resources and service).

A view of the opposite employment condition is in order. This is needed to express the creation of new positions of employment to meet the needs of specific units within the school district. Units being unable to accomplish their specific goals may well determine through evaluation that there is a need for additional personnel. Disruption of the planning sequence, stoppages, or bottlenecks created in a particular process may be due to inadequate numbers of specific types of personnel.

Another dimension that must be taken into account is the creation of new positions of employment due to newly established needs within the school district.

Additional requests for personnel replacement or creation of new positions may be forwarded by subordinate administrators and unit leaders to the personnel department.

The personnel staff must also realize that some personnel needs will come late in the fiscal period or even after the new period commences. During the latter stages of the current period the personnel staff should have determined a nearly adequate idea of forthcoming personnel needs. At this point a request for personpower (taking the place of manpower) will be made to the Logistical Manager (for approval) who will forward the request to the superintendent for further study and approval. Final approval will be made by the local board of education at the formal request of the superintendent.

THE JOB DESCRIPTION

Job descriptions provide the administrator with a very detailed account of the primary and secondary duties that are to be performed by the individual employee. A job description should also bring forth the level of supervision that is to be exercised by the position in question (if a supervisory position). Explanation is usually made identifying the immediate superior to the described position of employment. Another feature of an adequate job description is that of clarity in order that all readers (candidate, employee, supervisor administrator) can fully comprehend the presented information (see Figures 20 and 21).

Who is responsible for constructing the job description? The response here will involve a number of individuals. Members of the administrative corps and/or the personnel staff (depending upon school district size) may be involved along with the possibility of using consultants who specialize in this area. Input may also be gained from employees that are currently working in the area under consideration along with immediate supervisory personnel. Additional information or assistance can be gained from union representatives and civil services officers. The intended goal here is to obtain a 360° coverage of a specific position of employment.

Once the job description is complete it should assist central office administrators, the personnel staff, immediate supervisors, and employees concerning:

1. Matching personnel needs with the overall educational program (both logistics and instruction).

2. Development of a sound philosophy concerning the personnel effort.

3. Assistance in promotion matters.

4. Assistance in transfer matters.

5. Providing assistance in job study endeavors.

6. Providing assistance in performance evaluations.

7. Permitting a free flow of information concerning a particular position, and how that position is a segment of a still larger operation.

8. Allows employees to observe their assigned responsibilities and authority (if applicable) that comes with a particular position.

9. Provides data which will inform the employee of requirements for possible promotion.

10. Indicates limitations concerning the spheres of influence and responsibility carried by a certain position.

GLACIER WAY PUBLIC SCHOOLS
GLACIER WAY, COLORADO 80814
JOB DESCRIPTION SHEET

CLASSIFICATION AREA   7.00000--Food Service Operations

JOB DESCRIPTION #   7.00101

JOB INDICATOR(S):   School Cafeteria Manager or Food Preparation Center Manager

QUALIFICATIONS: Graduate of vocational food service program at the high school or
                            community college level and/or graduate of military food service
                            schools. Also included would be experience in mass food prepara-
                            tion and services. Of good health as certified by a licensed
                            physician.

IMMEDIATE SUPERIOR: Director of Food Services

SUBORDINATES: All food services workers assigned to the food preparation unit.

POSITION OBJECTIVES: To manage a food service operation which serves wholesome,
                            appealing, and nuritious foods to students and school personnel
                            in an attractive and clean atmosphere.

RESPONSIBILITIES:

     1. Trains and supervises all food personnel in the safe, proper and authorized manner
of using food service equipment and supplies.
     2. Stresses optimum safety and sanitation in food preparation area concerning
personnel, space, equipment, supplies and foodstuffs.
     3. Supervision of foodstuffs inventory, storage and reordering.
     4. Supervision of supplies inventory, storage and reordering.
     5. Supervises first echelon maintenance (user) and care for food service equipment.
     6. Participation in preparation of master menu.
     7. Determine portion sizes.
     8. Determines total number of persons to be fed.
     9. Keeps records of meals served, monies received, foods requisitioned and received,
supplies requisitioned and received, equipment requisitioned and received.
     10. Oversees storage operations (dry, refrigerated, and frozen).
     11. Oversees personnel operation for the unit.
     12. Coordinates and checks with vendors all foodstuffs, supplies, etc., entering the
food service unit.
     13. Oversees all baking and cooking operations.
     14. Coordinates with central office food services director.
     15. Coordinates with federal state and local governmental agencies (such as health
departments, departments of agriculture, etc.).
     16. Supervision of the daily cleaning and sanitizing of the food preparation area, food
service equipment, and dining areas.
     17. Coordinates computer activities concerning the food service operations.

PERIOD OF EMPLOYMENT: Eleven month year
                            Salary and period of employment determined by the local board of
                            education.

APPRAISAL: Job performance will be evaluated on a yearly basis by the
                            director of food service, principal(s), students, and school
                            staffs.

Figure 20. Sample Job Description for School Cafeteria Manager or Food Preparation Center Manager.

Job descriptions pave the way for personnel staff members to establish a job classification system. The classification of positions prepares a founda-

GLACIER WAY PUBLIC SCHOOLS
GLACIER WAY, COLORADO   80814
JOB DESCRIPTION SHEET

CLASSIFICATION AREA: 8.00000--Custodial Operations

JOB DESCRIPTION #:   8.00102

JOB INDICATOR: Building Custodian

QUALIFICATIONS: 1. Ability to read write and cipher.
                              2. Ability to get along with children.
                              3. Of sound and good moral character.
                              4. Positive work record.
                              5. Ability to operate or be trained to operate various types of
                                  housecleaning equipment.

IMMEDIATE SUPERIOR(S):   Building principal and central office supervisor.

POSITION OBJECTIVES: To maintain a clean, sanitized, safe, attractive and positive
                              atmosphere within the school building, therefore, creating a
                              pleasant place in which to learn and work.

REPONSIBILITIES:

     1. Oversees heating, cooling and ventilating operations within the building.
     2. Carry out general repairs.
     3. Keep first echelon maintenance (user) of all equipment as required.
     4. Maintains the school's grounds.
     5. Snow and ice removal.
     6. Participation in general cleaning and other housekeeping duties.
     7. Responsible for building security.
     8. Responsible for building safety.
     9. Maintains inventories of custodial supplies and equipment plus reorders when
         necessary.
    10. Responsible for storage of custodial supplies and equipment.
    11. Responsible for emergency operations regarding general repairs and housekeeping.
    12. Coordinates with principal and central office supervisor.
    13. Coordinates with local and state fire control officials.
    14. Makes daily morning (before classes) building and grounds inspection.

PERIOD OF EMPLOYMENT: Twelve month year.

                              Salary determined by local board of education.

APPRAISAL: Job performance will be evaluated on a yearly basis by the
                              principal and central office supervisor of custodial services.

Figure 21. Sample Job Description for A Building Custodian.

tion for determining remunerations. Classification of job positions is the keystone to the district's overall personnel program. The primary factors concerned in job classification are:

1. The placing of positions with similar demands into certain categories.

2. The placement of specific titles within a given category.

3. Grouping those assigned duties and areas of responsibilities within a category.

4. To review other jobs that have the same or similar duties and responsibilities, and to place them in a certain or similar category.

5. Establishment of similarity in required qualifications.
6. To use the same of similar evaluation procedures to determine selection.
7. Determine the sphere of supervisory influence in regard to each position.
8. To determine the same or similar amounts of wage payments.

By establishing a classified system concerning all of the job descriptions involved (within the school district), personnel staff members and administrators will be better able to observe the overall personnel requirements. A more panoramic view can be taken into each area of classification providing the observer with the ability to realize the importance that each position places in the total employment picture.

RECRUITING, HIRING, AND ORIENTATION PROCESSES

The recruiting process cannot take place unless there is a source or a pool of employees from which to draw. Employee markets have a tendency to fluctuate with the times. During periods of a high economy, potential employees have the opportunity to be selective concerning job openings. Personpower shortages can be created by wars, excellent economic periods, or bountiful and lucrative job openings in many areas of employment. Situations of this nature can create problems for personnel staff members. This situation may prompt personnel to select less desirous individuals for employment. Recruiting in periods of this nature can be a difficult task. Competition from other organizations could possibly hamper the obtaining of needed personnel.

Negative economic periods and decreased employment opportunities usually lend themselves to creating a surplus employee market. A decreasing number of job openings coupled with an excess of potential employees creates a positive position for personnel staffs. The recruiting process during such periods will allow personnel staff members a numerous supply of applications, and the opportunity to select only the premium candidates for employment.

After information has been gathered from the various units of the school system concerning forthcoming personnel requirements, the personnel staff needs to engage in an active recruiting venture. Sources that have the possibility for yielding potential employees could be:

1. State employment offices
2. School counselors and job placement personnel
3. Community organizations
4. Churches
5. Current employees

Actual recruitment of potential personnel can be derived from a number of means such as:

1. Public notices
2. Direct contact by a personnel representative
3. Radio
4. Television
5. Submitted applications
6. Newspapers

Recruiting guidelines must coincide with affirmative action and Equal Opportunity Compliance dictates. Notice should also be taken of recent court decisions concerning hiring practices. Recruiting practices must include the selling of the school system to potential employees. What are the positive factors being offered by the district? Are competing school districts and industries offering more? Strategy needs to be planned in order to present the school district as an attractive organization. Also, an organization that offers potential employees the opportunity for stable employment, opportunity for advancement, and excellent fringe benefits. Recruiting procedures need to be well planned and established into a final format before being placed into activity.

Recruitment will provide the personnel staff with a selected pool of candidates that will have to be screened for actual hiring. Consideration may be required concerning the applicant's qualifications as related to education, training experience, personality, citizenship, etc. Actions of this nature will open the door wider yet to the final selection for hiring. The collection of background data concerning the candidate is to be studied before a final decision (along with any established examination series) to further analyze the candidate in determining eligibility for the job position in question. Examinations may involve:

1. A written exercise
2. Practical application(s)
3. Training sessions
4. Experience checks
5. Oral responses
6. Standardized written exercises
7. Medical examination
8. Dental examination
9. Strength examination
10. Sociometric examination
11. Psychological examination
12. The interview

Of the previously stated examination methods, the interview is the culminating evaluative measure that should be taken. Here there is a one-to-one relationship which gives the interviewer an opportunity to examine the innermost chambers of the candidate. The interviewer has the final say as to whether or not the candidate is to be hired into the organization. The hiring of an individual must not be taken lightly. Test results and other evaluative measures, plus the interviewing results must be carefully studied before the decision to hire is made.

After the personnel office offers a position of employment to the candidate and acceptance is made, the orientation period should follow. The newly hired employee must be acquainted with both the job and the organization that has employed him/her. He/she also needs to be introduced to the supervisory personnel whose spheres of responsibility and authority cover his/her position of employment.

Orientation programs may be on a one-to-one basis between superior and subordinate, or it (orientation) may be formal in nature and a part of the personnel unit's overall program. The formal detailed orientation program will offer a wider spectrum which may be of greater benefit to the new employee.

A detailed study of the employee's job description (see Figures 20 and 21) needs to be made along with his/her position within the unit. Also the unit's role and its position in the school district. Desired conduct and job performance should be brought out to acquaint the new employee with what is to be expected by the supervisory staff. Identification and the role of the supervisory staff should be made at this time to allow better future interaction of superior-subordinate actions such as delegation, reporting, referring and trouble-shooting procedures. The new employee should be given instruction concerning procedures to be taken in carrying out his/her duties. Direction should also be given concerning the school district's philosophy, its (the school district's) goals and what coordination procedures are to be used with external agencies.

Organizational or school district matters that should be a part of the orientation program would cover the fringe benefit program, employee organization-labor union membership, and participation procedures. Union coordination will most likely involve the union and organizational contract, grievance procedures, termination procedures, dues, and meeting dates. Promotion and transfer policies also need to be addressed along with such items as holiday pay, overtime, etc.

Additional information should be given concerning future inservice training and other requirements concerning new employees. Orientation should be well planned and taken seriously by both the new employee and the personnel staff.

IN-SERVICE EDUCATION AND STAFF DEVELOPMENT

The desired outcome of in-service education is to improve the present performances of employees. Inservice is aimed at negative production on the part of employees, and change (orthodox and unorthodox) that is to be introduced district wide or within a given unit of the district. In-service provides the employee with a dimension beyond that of the beginning orientation program and on-the-job experience. In-service education is custom made to fit specific needs which are of concern to school system administration. Personnel staff members and supervisory personnel should be well aware of the present performance level of employees as individuals and as a team unit. Combined efforts by the employees when evaluated will indicate whether school district standards are being met and if policies are being followed. Another point of interest to observe is whether employees are fully qualified and trained to perform the various required tasks. The culminating point in question form would be — Are the goals of the employees and the school district being met?

A study also needs to be taken to determine the direction of in-service training. This study should explore four avenues of approach to the final selection of an in-service program. These four approaches are:

1. The entire school district operation including its positive and negative features associated with job performance. Also, there should be included a projection of personnel activities beyond current situations.

2. Primary unit operations and personnel projections (within the unit), the in-service record, and a detailed study of all jobs involved within the specific unit.

3. Secondary or subunit operations (within the primary unit) along with job classifications, descriptions and projected needs. Additional review would involve goal reaching outcomes and past in-service activities.

4. A detailed study should be made of each individual worker according to the job held and whether individual goals have been accomplished and standards kept.

Once the review has been made along with determining the areas in which in-service is needed to bring employees up to a desired standard (whether established or new), the groundwork has been established for a program of in-service.

In preparing for the proposed in-service program, there are certain factors that should be taken into consideration by the personnel staff. They are:

1. Listing areas of instruction needed for in-service action.
2. Emphasizing adherence to board policy regarding in-service training.

3. Informing the participants why this particular segment of in-service training is taking place.

4. Outlining standards desired.

5. Outlining goals to be achieved.

6. Deciding whether in-service leaders will be in-house staff members of individuals from outside of the organization.

7. Training aids needed for the in-service presentation.

8. Type of training site needed along with its location.

9. Desired staff improvement along with included changes.

10. Reinforcement of supervisory responsibility to the employee.

11. Actual training procedures to be used.

12. Explanation and reinforcement of each individual employee's and unit's role and contribution to the overall program.

13. Strengthening of established and new lines of communication between superior and subordinate personnel and units.

14. Appraisal of the in-service effort.

In-service training is designed to provide the organization with a form of rejuvenation. This action is designed to reduce those negative actions that have resulted in impairment of operation by the organization. In-service action is programmed to bring the employees up to standard in knowledge and performance.

FRINGE BENEFIT PROGRAMS

Fringe benefits apply to those extra services or financial advantages awarded to an employee in addition to his/her salary. In other words it is a remuneration beyond the services that are required in one's employment with an organization. Items that may be involved are:

1. Free or partially paid insurances (Life, health, dental, annuities)
2. Paid vacations
3. Leaves
   a. Sabbatical
   b. Military
   c. Maternity
   d. Overtime banking
   e. Holiday
4. Stock options
5. Profit sharing and bonuses
6. Longevity pay
7. Jury duty pay
8. Discounts

9. Pension plans
10. Credit union
11. Travel expenses (to seminars and conferences)
12. Recreation facilities
13. Parking facilities
14. Dining facilities
15. Lounges
16. Medical and dental services

Some organizations will offer fringe benefits as an incentive for recruiting premium workers. While others firms are persuaded to do so through collective negotiations with employee unions or organizations. No matter how the school district arrives at its fringe benefit package, it can become a useful tool to the personnel officer in recruiting and maintaining a better quality of workers. In addition to an adequate wage, the employee realizes that he/she has dividends in fringe benefits which provide extra savings, opportunities, services, or a combination thereof.

Opportunities from insurance packages alone can assist the employee in a number of ways. For example:

1. Low premium rates due to group plans.
2. Eligibility for various types of insurances because of group plans.
3. School district's ability to obtain attractive insurance group packages.
4. The school district's option to substitute insurance or other fringe options for elaborate salary increases which may reduce the incentive for tax rebellions by lay citizens.

Any fringe benefit program should be carefully scrutinized by the personnel staff before it is submitted for approval by a board of education. Contemplation should be made along the following lines:

1. Is the fringe benefit package supported by both the union (and/or employee organization) and central office administration?
2. Are the employees (minus their union or organizational leadership) in favor of the fringe benefit package?
3. Can the school district project its affordability to pay for the package from short and long range points of view?
4. Will the package provide an incentive for recruiting and maintaining premium employees?
5. Are the employees (in general) in need of the fringe benefit package?
6. What are the package's maximum opportunities to the employees?
7. What are the package's maximum opportunities to the school system?
8. Will the personnel, accounting, and computer staffs be able to cope with the additional tasks that will be required by the new fringe benefit program?

School districts should realize that in most cases an attractive fringe benefit program will reap dividends for the personnel staff in attracting and obtaining a better type of employee. Premium employees will provide the district with greater reliability, production, quality of performance and economy of operational expense.

LABOR–MANAGEMENT NEGOTIATIONS

Labor-management negotiations involves the coming together and the establishment of a formal agreement by representatives of a certain classification of employees (as epitomized by a particular labor union or employee organization) and of the school administration. The formal agreement is not only the standard between labor and management, but it also provides the guidelines for daily operations and a system of grievance. There are guidelines concerning labor-management negotiations which are represented by federal and state labor law.

The formal agreement or contract which is agreed to by labor and management (usually after periods of great confrontations, but not always) may involve a number of items such as:

1. Wages
2. Fringe benefits
3. Transfer procedures
4. Terminations
5. Reduction in force procedures
6. Seniority methods and privileges
7. Procedures for negotiations
8. Grievance procedures
9. Dues collections
10. Contract interpretation
11. Working hours
12. Lunch periods
13. Coffee breaks
14. Clean-up time
15. Disciplinary reprimands and warnings
16. Working conditions
17. Safety and security procedures
18. Leaves
19. Review of individual personnel records
20. Vacations
21. Overtime
22. Duration of the agreement or contact between labor and management

23. Hiring procedures
24. Union input concerning hiring procedures
25. Retirement
26. Bumping
27. Rehiring
28. Authorizations to attend union conferences
29. Holiday pay
30. Sick leave
31. Union representation at termination and disciplinary hearings
32. Employee probationary status

Before the process of labor-management negotiations gets under way, there is need to establish the bargaining unit. The bargaining unit is a classification or certain classifications of workers that are represented by a particular union or organization. Once the bargaining unit is established its contact with management through the negotiations effort will influence only the classification(s) of workers it represents. If there are competing unions striving for the position of bargaining unit, an election may be held to determine which union will be recognized by management as the sole bargaining unit.

Labor-management negotiations will involve the selection of team members from both labor and management. Team size will have to be determined by both groups, however, one group will not hardly let their opponents overpower them in team size.

In preparing for the forthcoming conflict between labor and management, both sides usually reconnoiter the other's camp to obtain information concerning individual personalities, strengths, weaknesses, mannerisms, ages, liberal views, conservative views, etc. Data regarding past negotiations sessions should be reviewed by both sides in order to prepare for the new negotiations.

If an impasse or deadlock occurs between management and labor it may be resolved through either:

1. Mediation through a third party whose goal is to facilitate negotiations through interaction between both parties combined and through an individual effort. The mediator attempts to resolve the impasse through contact by communicating with both sides.

2. Arbitration is the use of a third party to study the impasse and issue a final and binding decision. The use of an arbitrator is usually a last resort to naturalize an impasse situation.

Once labor and management coincide to the format and the body of the agreement in question, it is normally written and signed by both groups (labor and management). The next procedure usually goes through the process of ratification by the rank and file of the union or organization for final acceptance.

ADMINISTRATION OF THE PAYROLL

Salary procedures within the school district should be guided by board of education policy. Key to policy development is the school district's willingness to pay an adequate or better than adequate wage to its employees. The better the wage system, the better the quality of workers attracted to the organization. Prime factors that are concrete to policy in the salary area are:

1. Local and regional influence upon wage offerings for the various job classifications in the district.

2. Labor union influence upon wage offerings concerning various job classifications within the school system.

3. Entry and maximum salary levels according to local, regional and union influence.

4. The extent of the fringe benefit package.

5. Bonus offerings for longevity of service to the school system.

6. An adequate job evaluation system for all classifications of jobs held in the school system's operation.

7. The pay structure within every job classification and job level.

8. Salary control (regarding budget, overtime, holiday pay, etc.).

9. Pay deductions (taxes, credit union, union dues, parking, retirement, etc.).

10. Pay periods.

11. Pay plans (10 month, 12 month, etc.).

12. Cost of living adjustments.

13. Maintaining equity and fairness of the salary system.

14. Periodic salary reviews.

15. Periodic review of school district's financial ability to maintain or increase salary payments.

16. Adherence to federal and state labor laws regarding salaries.

Other areas that personnel staff members should be involved with regarding salary administration are:

1. The overall budget for labor.

2. Specific budget areas of the various job classifications and job levels.

3. Salary evaluations.

4. Cost of living studies.

5. Examination of individual salary records and job evaluation results.

6. Promotion, transfer, and demotion influences upon individual salary situations.

Overseeing the salary administration operation by the personnel staff is a tremendous undertaking. Regardless of employee and union dissatisfaction regarding salary, the payroll machine must be tuned to a high level of synchronization concerning budget, and yet meet the needs of the workers. Labor-management negotiations many times will threaten to unbalance the salary budget and place a hardship upon the school district. Another fact that is worthy of consideration is the school district's present and/or future ability to pay for increased wages and/or fringe benefits.

TROUBLESHOOTING PERSONNEL PROBLEMS AND TERMINATION PROCEDURES

Problems which arise concerning the work force's input and participation of the organization's daily tasks are the responsibility of the personnel staff. These problems can be divided into the following classifications:

1. Employee vs. management problems
2. Employee vs. employee(s) problems
3. Employee vs. external problems
   (those problems that are outside and not related directly to the job scene, but may have a bearing on employee production and relations with peers and superiors.)
4. Employee mental and physical health.

A prescribed cure-all with which to terminate all employee problems is not to be found, but adequate use of the following tools and specialists by the personnel staff can greatly assist:

1. Conferences between management, and the employee.
2. Conferences between management, the employee and the union representative.
3. Use of the organizational-union grievance procedure.
4. Use of an industrial or personnel guidance counselor.
5. Use of an industrial or personnel psychologist.
6. Assistance from the medical staff.
7. Assistance from the social worker staff.

Personnel staff members and specialists must remember that the authority of managerial staff cannot be displaced in order to solve employee problems. In addition, neither can the labor-management contract nor the established grievance system be violated in order to appease or attempt to neutralize employee issues. Specialists such as counselors, psychologists, medical personnel, and social workers can be of great assistance to personnel staff members concerning employee conflicts.

Disciplinary procedures must be established and carried out by the organization's personnel unit whenever a violation of district policy and/or the labor-management contract exists. Disciplinary measures are necessary if control and order are to exist within the daily operation of the organization.

The school district needs to have policy concerning disciplinary action against its employees. Disciplinary policy action should also be coordinated with labor unions or employee organizations (for contract and grievance purposes) that are sole bargaining agents for the various employee classifications. Another point of consideration is that the disciplinary actions must coincide with state and federal statutes and legal interpretation as brought out in court decisions. Due process needs to be provided to all employees involved in the organization's disciplinary actions.

Employees need to be aware of the organizational disciplinary code through in-service training and actual presentation of a copy of the rules.

Enforcement of the disciplinary code should be done in a fair manner to all employees. Using different degrees of punishment to different individuals involved with similar infractions can only lead to possible conflicts and legal problems.

Procedures for disciplinary actions should follow along the following format:

1. Oral and/or written warnings (to the employee and for his/her record) concerning the violation (depending upon the severity of the infraction).

2. Reference to board policy and/or the union contract which states that the employee has committed a violation.

3. Explanation to the employee of the disciplinary action that can be taken by management.

4. Coordination with labor union representative(s) (if applicable).

5. Explanation to the employee of his/her rights and appeal procedures.

6. Suspensions from position of employment (depending upon severity of infraction).

7. Punishment or termination (also depending upon severity of the employee breach).

New and established employees need to be aware of the school district's disciplinary policies and procedures; union participation in such matters; organizational procedures; and their rights plus appeal procedures.

Summary

The Logistical Manager's responsibility for the school district's personnel program is a very serious undertaking. School district needs for the construction of job classifications, descriptions and employee needs along with budgetary restraints may well produce a climate of complexity to the attempt of meeting the school district's goals.

Recruiting, selecting, and training of employees along with the establishment of an adequate wage is of prime importance to the operation of an organizational personnel unit. These tasks will assist in meeting the needs of the school district.

Once the employee becomes a member of the school district's staff he/she should be trained and kept up to a current level of knowledge through the use of in-service and staff development.

Fringe benefits offer an added indirect income to the employee, and they (fringe benefits) can serve as a recruiting device (especially if there is considerable competition by other school districts and the private business-industrial sector).

The Logistical Manager and the head personnel officer must have a knowledge of labor-management relations if they are to succeed in contract negotiations and grievance procedures with labor unions. The bargaining table is not the place for on-the-job training.

Salary and pay administration is more or less the culminating feature of the personnel effort. The establishment of salary schedules, pay periods, pay plans according to job classifications, coordination with federal and state procedures are some of the duties involved in administration of the school district payroll.

Employee problems and welfare must be placed under the wing of the district's personnel operation. Assistance must be given by personnel in attempting to help solve employee problems, but not at the risk of undermining managerial authority. To do so would eradicate respect and control.

Termination of employees should be used as a last resort. Employee dismissal is dependent upon the severity of the infraction by the employee against board of education policy. Employees that are terminated or punished for disciplinary reasons should also be given the right to appeal.

CHAPTER X

PURCHASING, SUPPLY, AND STORAGE MANAGEMENT

THE PURCHASING PROCESS

Policy

Today's public school district is a multimillion dollar business operation which functions without the profit motive. Instead of operating within a certain margin for profit, the school district's goal is that of offering a service. This service being the providing of education to the public.

The daily carrying out of the educational process will require the use of various types of supplies and equipment. Some supplies are consumed at a rapid rate while the consumption rate of other supply items will be at a much slower pace. In the equipment arena there are certain types of materiel which may be used over a period of several years, while some equipment items will wear out or become obsolete over a shorter period of time.

The current wave of rising costs along with taxpayer revolt and public clamor for accountability has required the use of austerity in the purchasing plan of action.

A system of purchasing (like any other phase of school management) requires the use of specific local board of education policy. It must be remembered that this policy has to be in accordance with the usually broad application of state law.

In order that the school district's purchasing operation function as a well organized and well tuned segment of the logistical program, there must be a key reference point in the form of policy.

Formulation of purchasing policy should be made by the Logistical Manager and the chief purchasing officer. Approval for new or altered policy needs to be obtained by the superintendent and finally by the local board of education.

General areas that should be covered by board purchasing policy are:

1. Responsibility for the purchasing program which includes: (a) direct association by administrative position (involving key central office personnel such as the Logistical Manager and the chief purchasing officer); (b) overall responsibility (as charged to the superintendent); and (c) assigned segmented responsibility (as it concerns lesser specific supervisory person-

nel assigned to the purchasing functions of the school district.

2. Authority, zones of operation, and authority delegation of the various supervisory personnel involved with the district's purchasing operation.

3. Designation of the central office administrator and his/her staff that will be responsible for the district's purchasing functions.

4. Designation of the building level administrator as the purchasing agent at line level.

5. All jobbers and vendors must operate through the central office purchasing administrator.

6. How the purchasing function assists all programs (instructional and logistical) within the school district.

7. The objectives of the overall purchasing function and its various units.

8. A purchasing priority system.

9. Vendor determination and relations.

10. Functions of the purchasing unit.

11. Specification construction.

12. Standardization formulation.

13. Quality control procedures.

14. Supply and equipment economy.

15. A planned purchasing process (from requisition to receipt of and payment for goods or services).

16. Periodic review of purchasing policies.

17. Periodic evaluation of the overall purchasing operation.

18. Bidding procedures.

19. Coordination with local government (if fiscally dependent).

20. Compliance with local, state and federal legal requirements regarding purchasing procedures.

21. Declaration of chief purchasing officer position and selection.

22. Establishment of a two way purchasing communications network.

23. Safety and security procedures.

24. A plan for requisitioning (through a chain of command) supplies and equipment should be formulated by the central office purchasing administrator.

25. The requisitioning plan should be evaluated and reviewed periodically by the central office purchasing administrator and building level principals.

26. Alterations to the school district requisitioning plan should be formulated by the central office purchasing administrator.

27. Bidding procedures must be in line with state law.

28. There is a need for procedures concerning emergency purchasing at both central office and building level.

29. Coordination of the building level inventory systems with the central

office and warehouse inventory function. This would allow for more centralized purchasing at cut rates. A uniform physical inventory should take place twice during the fiscal period.

30. Inspection system for supplies and equipment once they are received by the school district.

31. A system for returning damaged, missing or incorrect supplies and equipment.

32. Establishment and maintenance of a centralized or regionalized warehousing system.

When policy is accepted, passed by the board of education, and recorded in the board's minutes it becomes legal and binding. Administrators (the Logistical Manager and the chief purchasing officer) must enforce policy in order that it be effective. Policy is available to assist the purchasing operation in being more synchronized and tuned to meeting the school system's needs.

Organization of the Purchasing Operation

Purchasing will have a connection with all segments of the school district (whether they are instructional or logistical. All units are in need of supplies and equipment in order to carry out their assigned functions and meet their assigned objectives. There is no standard organizational format for a public school district. School districts differ in geographical size, pupil population, numbers of personnel, philosophies, educational programs, logistical programs and more specifically—the purchasing program. Smaller school districts may not have a chief purchasing officer and such duties may be carried out by the Logistical Manager or the superintendent. Medium to large sized school districts offer the opportunity for more specialization of administrative duties. The Logistical Manager usually delegates the entire purchasing function to the chief purchasing officer and his/her staff. The chief purchasing officer's staff may consist of (according to the district's organizational format and needs) an assistant, a series of buyers, a clerical supervisor, a series of clerical personnel, a warehouse manager, an assistant warehouse manager, a staff of warehouse workers, a warehouse clerical supervisor, and a series of warehouse clerks. As one moves from district to district variations to the above patterns may be found (see Figure 22).

Authority

The authority to operate a purchasing program will come chiefly from state statutes since the state has prime responsibility for public education.

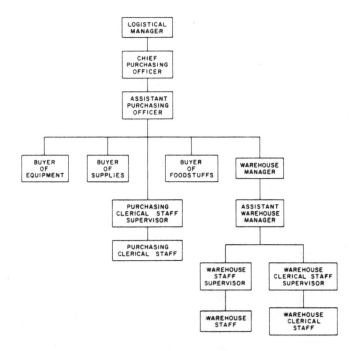

Figure 22. A Typical Medium-to-Large Sized School District Purchasing and Warehouse Unit.

Additional state directions may come from other state agencies such as state departments of education and state boards of education. Fiscal dependence will allow local government (city, county or metropolitan) to have ordinances concerning the purchasing operation that must be adhered to. If a local school district is involved with federal programs, there will most likely be federal guidelines concerning purchasing.

Even though the chief purchasing officer has authority to be in charge of all the purchases of the school district, there is need to coordinate with consumers concerning quality and specifications of a given product or service.

A point concerning purchasing personnel and which bears a considerable amount of elasticity is that of legal interpretation of the various governmental level (federal, state, and local) laws. The chief purchasing office may well have to seek legal assistance in such manners.

Specification Construction

Specifications play a key role in the purchasing process. They (specifications) are the guides in determining a particular item of equipment, a certain supply object, or a certain service that is to be performed by a vendor. Specifications allow for particular standards of quality desired by the consumers (the staff) within the school district. Through the construction of proper specifications for individual types of supplies, equipment, and services, the students and staff will better be able to carry out their tasks and meet their goals. Proper services, equipment, and supplies can also assist in not only of completion in timely fashion, or the satisfactory rendering of a service, but also in the economy of use (which provides considerable savings for the school district).

Specification construction needs to have the following influencing factors incorporated into its process:

1. Consumer input.
2. Name of the manufacturer.
3. Brand name.
4. Model and catalog identification numbers.
5. Performance records and evaluations.
6. Prime features.
7. Primary and secondary functions.
8. Post trial and testing results.
9. Evaluations of specifications.
10. Periodic specification alterations to better meet the needs of consumers.

Specifications when constructed need to be very thorough, and consideration needs to be made concerning the previously listed ten factors. A general description of the desired item needs to be listed along with: (1) brand name, (2) model and catalog number, (3) accompanying features and functions, (4) quantity or size, and (5) alternate items that will provide the same performance level and are of similar or better quality.

Over a considerable period of time consumer and purchasing personnel will formulate data needed for assisting in specification construction. However, elasticity needs to be placed into the system to allow for newly marketed items to be considered for use by the school district.

Specifications requirements in the purchasing process permits established standardization procedures to be fully enacted. The bidding process by various vendors becomes more unique in their (the vendors') quest for a marketing breakthrough. Specification will also permit uniformity and will allow foundation requirements in the bidding process.

The use of specifications opens the door to certain needed factors regarding the desired product or service. These factors are:

1. A detailed description of the standards required for a particular product or service. Also the reasons why particular standards should be described. This is essential for the objectives desired by the use of a particular product or service.

2. A detailed description of the quality desired and why this particular quality is desired. The correlation of quality and usage is essential if the good or service is to meet its objectives.
3. A detailed description of how the product or service will be used by the school system.
4. Research and test information related to the performance standards and/or requirements met by a particular product or service. Also, how this research and test information applies to the needs of the school district.
5. A presentation of warranties required for the product or service.
6. Dunning and financial obligatory procedures.
7. Packaging, delivery and servicing requirements.

Preparation of specifications should be prepared by a committee consisting of a representation of the prime consumers, the school Logistical Manager and the purchasing administrator. Input by the potential users of a product or receivers of a service is essential. Objectives for a particular product or a service should also be established. This provides the school district with a basis to evaluate whether the product or service is economical plus meets the purpose intended. Evaluation concerning the product or service's continuation or termination can be determined at this particular point in time.

Standards of Quality

Specifications provide the foundation for standards of quality concerning services, supplies and equipment. Quality results from the performance and/or durability provided by a good or service. Optimum performance and durability are desired by the lowest cost possible. Sometimes quality can be determined through testing rather than through actual use. At times there may be a combination of both actual use and testing with evaluated results.

Standardization of supplies, equipment and services directs itself to two primary goals. These goals are:

1. Economy
2. Efficient Service

Economy is gained through the funnelling process of adjusting the need of a particular type of good or service to fit the needs of several operating units (school buildings, shops, divisional offices, etc.) throughout the district. For example, the need for a particular type of light bulb for a particular type of desk lamp could be narrowed down to a certain wattage. This particular size of light bulb could offer a certain type of illuminating characteristic which would benefit all users in the school district. Such practice would offer economy in relationship to purchasing large lots of the same lighting device and an efficient type of service to all users of this particular desk lamp bulb.

Obtaining district wide multiuse for a particular item of service will allow for a more convenient flow of the inventory process or the need of a particular service. There will be less over-stocking of inventory items and a precise, scheduled need for nonimpromptu services. Standardization would allow for less friction and more participation in competitive bidding by various vendors. Standardization also allows for additional flexibility permitting the entry of change as it occurs in new products, new methods and new services. The use of a similar method of standardization in the military logistical system has aided the United States to be victorious in past international conflicts.

Standardization is in need of constant review through staff and user participation if it is to be successful. There is also a need for trial or testing periods concerning goods and services. Such trial or testing ventures will allow for evaluation (by the users) of a particular good or service before district-wide implementation. Consideration must also be given to annual and/or semiannual evaluation of standardized goods and services. This action can help determine whether the use of such items meets the specific goals that have been established. If such goals have not been met, there is a great possibility that staff or user consultation (with the purchasing administrator and the business manager) will demand curtailment of a particular good or service.

In summary, standardization involves the determination of universality in product and service usage coupled with economic efficiency.

In order to commence a quality standards program there must be direct coordination with the specifications effort. Elements which need to be included in determining standards of quality are:

1. A general breakdown of the item or service desired.
2. Other items that may have a bearing on a proposed standard of quality.
3. Involved consumer and purchasing personnel.
4. Specification construction for the concerned good or service.
5. Alternative goods and services.
6. Test and actual use results.

Quality standards should be reviewed periodically to determine whether alterations should be made in order to better meet consumer goals. Introductions of new goods and services will push the necessity of constructing new and sometimes initial standards of quality.

Need Determination

Administrative control needs to be exercised in the determination of the need of a particular good or service. There should be an option for administrative approval or denial concerning requisitions made by subordinates. Subordinates should be informed that the need must be bona fide and consideration must be given to cost and staying within budgetary limitations. Therefore, good faith must ride along with the initial requisition for a particular good or service.

Once the need is approved by the administrator at the point of origin and it is forwarded to warehouse or purchasing personnel, there should be a second action concerning determination of need. Warehouse or purchasing personnel should check (through computer if available) concerning similar items previously ordered by the originating unit and when these items were ordered. Financial management's accounting unit also needs to be alerted to determine whether the originating unit is financially able to pay for the item(s) being requested.

Need determination is essential to prevent waste, hoarding, and unwise spending. The requesting unit should be required to prove its need for goods and services.

Analyzing Need

The purchasing process commences with the determination of need in the originating unit. Within the originating unit someone or a computer will discover the need for particular services or goods to assist in task performances. These task performances allow the unit and those associated with the unit to achieve personal and organizational goals.

In the area of need determination, the originating unit spokesperson must be able to:

1. Recognize the need—If there are bottlenecks, shortages, low inventories, lack of performance, difficulties, or the nonachieving of primary and secondary goals—then there is the recognition of a need.

2. Classification of the need—The attachment of specifics reigns supreme once identification is made of a recognized need. A study should also be made on exactly how this newly identified need will assist the originating unit in:
    a. Task performance
    b. Unit goal achievement

3. Defense and support of the established need—The originating unit's supervisor will review need recognition and identification for authenticity and affordability. The subordinate who attempts to declare need must be able to defend his/her position as related to the desired goods or services. If

the originating unit's supervisor favors the need for goods or services, a purchase requisition form or a warehouse storage requisition form will be filled out by the unit for forwarding to the central office purchasing department.

The Purchasing Cycle

The purchasing cycle involves the interaction of both line units (building level units) or other nonteaching divisions in school district. The purchasing cycle will involve either supplies or equipment. Clarification needs to be made at this point regarding the term, supplies, and the term, equipment. Supplies are those items which are:

1. Readily consumed with usage.
2. The item is expendable in nature.
3. Compared to an item of equipment its cost is much lower.
4. Supplies are usually not difficult to replace [1].

Equipment includes those items that are:

1. Usually fixed or semifixed in nature.
2. Equipment is not consumed by usage.
3. Equipment is not expendable.
4. Equipment will depreciate in monetary value over a period of time [2].

The purchasing cycle offers a series of steps which starts out with the original requisition at building or division level to the final receipt of the goods desired. These steps are:

1. Declaration of a bona fide need by the potential user.
2. Preparation of the requisition by the potential user.
3. Examination of the need by the immediate superior.
4. Examination of funds available by the immediate superior (if applicable to the school district's fiscal policies).
5. Examination by the immediate superior for compliance with school district purchasing policies.
6. Approval or denial of the requisition by the immediate superior (at building or unit level).
7. Upon approval of the requisition by the prospective user's immediate superior, it is forwarded to the central office purchasing administrator or agent.
8. The purchasing administrator or agent will examine the requisition and he/she must determine if:
   a. Competitive bidding applies by state law and/or board of education policy.

    b. Availability of the requisitioned item.

    c. Are the item(s) in question needed by other buildings or units?

    d. Are there sufficient funds to cover the cost of the requested items? (This step will depend upon the type of fiscal system used in the school district.)

9. The purchasing administrator's approval or denial of the requisition.

10. Upon approval of the requisition by the central office purchasing administrator, a purchasing order is prepared and sent to the vendor. The approved requisition is filed for record.

11. The vendor (if the requested item is available) will fill and deliver the requested materials to the school district along with an invoice.

12. Upon receipt of the ordered materials, they are checked against the enclosed invoice and the purchase order.

13. The items are then delivered to the school or division where a second receipt and inspection will take place. Comparison here will be made against the invoice and the requisition.

School district inventories will involve each building plus the various units. Overall inventories of this nature will offer the central office purchasing system a massive listing of requests for needed supplies and equipment. In order to prepare for the needs of the next fiscal period, the purchasing cycle will go into operation. However, there will be bidding for large volumes of the particular items requested. Upon receipt and inspection these items will be broken down and distributed to the schools as originally requested. School districts can gain additional savings by purchasing in large lots. If boards of education refrained from various items of supplies and equipment in unusually high quantities by not directly considering each school or unit's specific needs, there would be less waste. In order to acquire and maintain a level of little or no overbuying of supplies and equipment the specific needs of each school and each unit would be met. Additional savings would be gained due to the overall or grand purchase in an extremely large lot. By placing huge quantities of supplies and equipment in schools and units (obtained through unstructured purchasing practices) nonuse, hoarding and waste can become acquired diseases. During inflationary periods, there is no need to allow an antitax and antieducation public additional fuel for their fires of administrative and pedagogical criticism.

Time

Time is a very important element of the purchasing process. There is need to observe the amount of time elapsed from the point that a lower administrative unit (for example, a particular school building or a unit such as transportation or food service, etc.) observes the need for a particular supply or equipment item to the instant that the requested goods are delivered. Between these two extreme poles a number of disorders could occur. For example, problems such as:

1. Strikes
2. Lost orders
3. Stagnation of the ordering process
4. Personnel layoffs
5. Legal entanglements
6. Thefts and hijacking
7. Nonavailability
8. Industrial retooling
9. Obsolescence
10. Employee slowdowns
11. Customer priorities
12. Belated requisitions

In order to combat the time elapsed problem, there must first be a time projected phase. Over a period of considerable years of operating the school district's purchasing process, an average of time consumption could be taken. This consumption would involve the time period from the initial request to that of actual delivery. Time projections would greatly aid in establishing the length of the period which is to be consumed in the purchasing process.

Policy needs to be determined for the establishment of reorder points for constantly used items of supplies and equipment. Constant observance of inventory levels would prompt the requisitioning process. Computers could be programmed to automatically order certain supply items when inventories reach a certain level. Also, each step of the purchasing cycle will require the elapse of a certain amount of time. Purchasing policies should so be established as to require the least amount of bureaucratic red tape and time consumption.

In establishing projections as it relates to time in the purchasing process, the reorder level of supplies and equipment, observance of the school system and vending organization must be at their normal and abnormal paces. Consideration must be made for shortages, supply depletion and mandatory austerity practices. Such action will interrupt the daily operation of the public school program. The establishment of proper lead time is important.

Top priority must be given to emergency purchases. However, projected emergency time tables must be established for every item of supplies and equipment (used by the school district). The purchasing administrator needs to develop through previous experiences, the estimates of how much approximate time will be consumed to obtain various items of supplies and equipment. Such information can greatly assist the planning efforts of school administrators faced with emergency needs of certain supply and equipment items.

The speed with which vendors can or will meet emergency as well as normal purchasing requests will depend greatly upon the public relations efforts of the purchasing administrator. Boards of education and top level school administrators need to face the fact that an excellent public relations program allows for extra goodwill with vendors.

Requested Services

In some situations a service may be requested from an external organization rather than goods. When an organization is selected to perform a service, the work is also inspected to determine conformity with specifications and desired standards. Once the service is completed and approved by the originating and/or the responsible logistical unit, the servicing organization will forward its bill to the accounting unit for payment.

Internal Warehouse Purchases

Originating units may request items that are already stored in school district warehouse facilities. If this approach is carried out, the originating unit is still charged by accounting for the item(s) requested and delivered. The internal warehouse unit will check the items for delivery and send an invoice to accounting (for a charge against the originating unit's account), and a copy to the originating unit for inspection, filing and a check against the requisition.

The Vendor

After the request and purchase order are formulated, the source of supply must be tapped. This particular source of supply is known as the vendor. Vendors are members of the private business sector of our economy and they are, as a rule, highly competitive. The overall goal of the vendor is that of profit after the cost of his/her business operations have been deducted. Some vendors will offer top quality goods or top performance services, yet some vendor offerings are mediocre and yet some are less than desirable. It is up to the purchasing administrator to select the vendor that can best meet the school district's need for a particular good or service. Other benefits such as warranties, guarantees, maintenance, free or prorated replacements, etc., must also be considered.

The purchasing administrator's selection of vendors is well channeled through state law and local board of education policy. In addition, local politics by certain board of education members (overt or covert) with key influential citizens of the community may tighten the freedom of the purchasing administrator in vendor selection. Such actions may also influence the number of vendors participating in the bidding process. However, boards of education and school administrators must realize that today's anti-tax and anti-education public is demanding strict accountability of the public funds expended for education. To be "before the fact" will require the purchasing of goods and services that have the highest quality for the lowest price. Vendors that offer such products and services must be engaged with in order to avoid public persecution and revolt. To obtain top quality at low prices, it may be necessary to work with out-of-town vendors. States and local boards of education should not limit purchasing only to local vendors. Lower prices may be offered by those vendors residing in out-of-town communities. Inflationary situations will demand that economical measures be used in spending from the public purse. Today's citizens have become aware of bureaucratic red tape and nefarious political dealings. Since the Watergate affair, public demands for investigations into suspected unlawful practices by public officials is a common practice. The purchasing administrator must be given the authority to seek out recognized and reputable vendors. Additional assistance to the purchasing administrator in this category would be the establishment of a vendors' directory. Such a directory would be according to classification of goods or services. Once established, the directory would serve as a ready reference and a guide to purchasing.

Vendors should be reviewed and investigated concerning their:

1. Goodwill
2. Years in business
3. Reputation
4. Financial status
5. References (from other school districts)
6. Credit rating
7. Punctuality in delivery
8. Guaranteed service or products
9. Discount programs and procedures
10. Past bidding record
11. Compliance with specifications
12. Service offerings

Additional assistance to the vendors' directory would be that of a rating scale. Vendors could be evaluated by a local school district rating procedure using the above ten factors. Evaluation results could be formed into the following classifications:

1. Superior
2. Excellent
3. Average
4. Marginal

Vendors that have negative ratings would not be listed in the directory. Also, those vendors whose services eventually become unfavorable would be excluded from the directory. Such a review of the directory should be made on an annual basis.

The Vendor Catalog

School districts should maintain a vendor's catalog of various equipment and supply items. This would act as a reference to originating units and also provide assistance to the ordering and bidding process.

Evaluation of potential products could be made through references, other school districts, and the school district's past contact in the purchasing process. Practices such as servicing, warranty abidance, quality of product and service items, costs, attitudes of employees, product duration, and durability should be evaluated before making the final selection.

MANAGING SUPPLIES AND EQUIPMENT

The act of managing delivers control to a particular operation or a series of operations within a given organization. Control will not only effect personnel, but also those features that are the nerve center of purchasing and supply management effort of the school district.

Quality Reinforced

Quality is reached through user evaluation of a product or service that places merit on a particular level of evaluation. Other contributing factors establishing quality could be test results, achieved goals, ease of use or operation, and external input.

In order that quality of a good or service is maintained, the manager must forward to the vendor those specifications that are desired. Mention also needs to be made that quality does not mean the total attachment to a particular product or service in order to maintain certain standards. Users and managers should always be open to the introduction of new services or products that may have better quality offerings.

Once quality is established for a particular product or service, there is need for vendor contact. Vendors will present those items that they think will match the school district's level of desired quality. In addition to quality is the factor of price which has an influence upon quality in relationship to affordability.

Quality data offered by vendors and users should be coordinated because of different interpretations by both groups. Even data supplied by external groups or testing laboratories does not match the user's actual involvement with the product or service.

Standardization Reinforced

Standardization of supplies and equipment allows for flexibility in outfitting and supplying the various units within the school system. District-wide standardization must allow for representative input concerning those supplies and items of equipment that can be readily standardized.

The use of standardization should allow for savings for the district. Purchasing the same goods or services on a large scale can often lead to discounts from vendors. Other factors offered through the standardization process are:

1. Greater ease in need determination.
2. Greater depth in user input.
3. Better vendor input.
4. Easier competitive bidding by vendors.
5. Better warehouse control.
6. Easier inventory maintenance.
7. Obtaining a broader scope through user test results.

There are some items and services that should not be standardized. Allowances and elasticity needs to be made for particular units and school buildings that may call for exclusive goods and services. Such particular needs may not be satisfied by items or services that are purchased on a mass scale. In order for a particular unit or school building to meet its assigned goals, the use of a certain product or service may be necessary. This action would not include those goals or services that are otherwise standardized.

Specifications Reinforced

Specifications act as a medium of control from three points of view. They are:

1. It (the specification) gives a detailed description of the product or service desired by the school system.

2. Specifications inform the vendor of what is desired by the school system, therefore, creating a more detailed input through the school district bidding system or direct nonbidding purchasing system.

3. Provides product or service protection to the consumers within the school setting.

There are certain offerings that should be presented through the use of specifications. These offerings should cover the areas of:

1. Categorizing the product or service desired.
2. Warranty offerings desired.
3. Servicing procedures.
4. Performance standards desired.
5. Payment procedures.
6. Delivery methods, guarantees and requirements.
7. Mechanical or methodological requirements.
8. Average to optimum desired range level of performance.
9. Selected consumer group to be involved.
10. Unit breakdown and containerization methods.

Construction of the specification should be completed with considerable concentration and detail. Knowledge of the product or service is a must if the needs of the consumer or consumer unit are to be met. Consideration must be granted to a number of important factors if the proper construction of the specification is to be accomplished. These factors involve:

1. Consumer and/or consumer unit descriptive input regarding the description of the desired product or service.

2. Catalog and/or consumer periodical material input concerning product or service description.

3. Collection of product or service history (positive and negative views) from other users (including school districts and other organizations).

4. Manufacturer or company input from various firms concerning the desired product or service.

5. Compiling of all data collected and constructing a description of the product or service needed by the school district.

6. Obtaining product or service evaluation by the school district consumer or consumer unit.

Specifications may well be condensed to the brand name level which will reduce the panoramic presentation of product or service description. Elasticity can be allowed through the use of brand name "or equivalent." Such action would then allow for a variety of vendors to contribute to the bidding process or nonbidding purchasing act.

Ethics and Purchasing

A high level of professional ethics must be kept by all school officials involved with the purchasing process. Professional and personal reputations are at stake along with the fact that high standards of conduct must be maintained during contact with vendor personnel. At times intense vendor competition may cause some business representatives to go to extreme methods in attempting to gain marketing control. School officials should adhere to federal and/or state laws along with local board of education policies in working with such matters.

STORAGE AND DISTRIBUTION

The Warehousing Process

As previously mentioned in the purchasing process, there is a point in time which concerns the receipt and inspection of goods. Once this particular task is completed there is a need to store a particular item at a centralized warehouse facility. Or the task may be to ship such an item to building or division level where again it is to be stored at a decentralized facility.

Discussion is in order concerning the centralized or regionalized warehousing and the decentralized warehousing procedures. The organization, its goals and the preference of the school district will determine which plan of warehousing will be used.

Centralized warehousing offers a single or a few very large regionalized facilities at which goods are received, processed and placed in storage areas until their use is required by a lower administrative unit. An organized effort such as the centralized warehouse will demand a very large number of personnel detailed with special assignments and equipment. There is also a need for specialized and strict security measures which may involve additional personnel, anti-crime electronic equipment and security dogs. Other personnel needs will be delivery persons that are required to deliver goods from the warehouse facilities to the district's lower administrative units.

Centralized warehousing offers economy in enabling the school district to purchase large lots of needed supplies and equipment offering possible outstanding discounts. There is also the feature of less complex inventory control of items stored in the warehouse and a better opportunity for a more positive record keeping process. Disbursement of supplies from a centralized warehousing facility offers more accuracy in record keeping by both the warehouse and the receiving unit. Also, inventory control of the receiving units can be overwatched by the centralized warehousing unit. This action is beneficial in preventing waste and hoarding.

Decentralized warehousing gives the lower administrative units (school buildings and divisions) the opportunity to conduct their own warehousing efforts. Decentralization also offers freedom from the dictates of a centralized logistical headquarters. School districts will gain savings from labor expense due to the absence of a mass of central warehousing personnel and equipment. However, security of stored goods in the decentralized warehouse organization will offer the building or division level administrator additional problems. In this age of accelerated criminal activity, normal building level security will not offer the protection of the centralized warehouse. Accuracy of the inventory and record keeping processes may also be lax at the lower administrative levels of the school district. Union organized certificated and non-certificated personnel have the potential for atoning grievances and/or contract differences through disruption of warehousing procedures.

The school district's method of warehousing (whether centralized or decentralized) should be used to its highest potential. The provision of providing safe, adequate and secure storage space for the school district's supplies and equipment should be the district's ultimate goal. Annual evaluations of the existing method of warehousing should be taken to determine whether alterations should be made of the present system. The main question to be asked in such an evaluation is—Does the present warehousing system meet the needs of the school district?

Centralized or Regionalized Storage

In order to have better efficiency and control over the warehousing of purchased items there is need for the school district to maintain central or regionalized storage areas. Goods received, inspected, processed and accounted for at a central or regionalized point allow for a better coverage of the purchasing task. Distribution of the received goods to the originating units can also be better accounted for. Items stored at a central or regionalized lend themselves to better inventory control measures. Centralized warehousing also allows convenience in accounting for the receiving dates of incoming goods, therefore, facilitating the movement of the oldest stock first during the distribution phase.

Centralized or regionalized warehousing offers a number of positive features. They are:

1. Allowing for better control of received items.
2. Allows for better warehouse management through computerization.
3. Greater efficiency in space management.
4. Better management of inventory/accounting procedures and records.

5. More elasticity in distribution to schools and other school district units.

Decentralized Storage Procedures

Some school systems may use a decentralized storage system in which all goods are received and accounted for by the originating unit. The party that is in charge of product receiving must have a knowledge of the incoming items in order to match goods (and the invoice) with the purchase requisition, plus approve the condition of the delivered items. The originating unit will also be in need for adequate space for item storage. In addition, the originating unit will be in charge of accounting for all goods received and distribution to those needed areas within the unit.

Decentralized storage systems allow for certain positive features like:

1. Convenience of the desired product and immediate distribution to the individuals in need.

2. Reduction of the delivery costs from a centralized or regionalized unit to the originating unit.

3. A more direct thrust from the vendor to the originating unit, therefore, eliminating the centralized storage unit as a middle contributor in the purchasing process.

4. Direct accounting (from both inventory and financial management views) of received goods by the originating unit administrator.

Storage Management

Management of the warehousing storage area is the key to an effective supply program for the school district. The prime requirement concerning storage management is that of meticulous planning. Key points in the planning phase will be the projection of: (1) supply and equipment tonnage, (2) volume occupancy in relation to space requirements, (3) rate of flow (including actual storage time) from receiving through distribution to originating unit. Tonnage can be broken down into supply and equipment classifications (including packaging. Volume occupancy (including packaging) will determine space requirements needed. The flow rate which includes the starting time at the reception point and including down storage time, plus distribution to the requesting unit. These three factors along with past and anticipated receiving information will assist the warehouse storage manager in meeting those needs to insure an effective support effort to the school district.

Whether the school district's storage machine is centralized or decentralized, the same principles will apply. In planning for the storage operation, past records will indicate both peak and low periods for warehouse traffic. Also, there must be coordination with the school district's fiscal period and the fiscal periods of other governmental organizations and business organizations.

There is need for enforcing the storage management doctrine of moving the old stock out first. Subordinate managers and workers should be instructed to adhere to this rule in order to prevent waste and the promotion of obsolescence.

Other important factors that will be required if a successful storage program is desired are:

1. Storage area requirements
   a. Dry
   b. Refrigerated
   c. Freezer
   d. Shelves
   e. Bins
   f. Floor storage
   g. Metal, wood, or plastic floor elevations
   h. Temperature control
   i. Moisture control
   j. Hazardous areas (proneness to combustion and explosion)
   k. Rack storage
   l. Vermin control
   m. Fungus control
   n. Rust control
   o. Physical and chemical breakdown
2. Convenience for rapid distribution to requestions units
3. Computer assistance to:
   a. Inventory control procedures
   b. Item location
   c. Item distribution
   d. Financial managerial accounting, billing, and paying procedures
4. Stock numerical bar coding, and color coding schemes
5. Storage policy construction, enforcement, review, alteration, and termination
6. Inservice planning and instruction regarding facilitative and innovative input of the storage system.

The warehousing storage manager needs the cooperation of his/her subordinate managers and the staff workers in order to be successful. Fair, but firm treatment toward all subordinates plus the total adherence to storage policies will assist in creating a positive and productive atmosphere.

Distribution

Distribution involves the movement from the warehouse storage facility to the requesting or originating unit. Items of supplies or equipment to be distributed may come from available stores, or from a vendor's special shipment.

Once an approved requisition has been forwarded by purchasing to warehousing storage unit, the distribution phase commences. Tasks that must be completed by the warehouse team prior to actual delivery to the requesting unit are:

1. Formulation of the requested order and delivery route channelization.

2. Activation of computer product search and position scheme.

3. Activation of computer recording, inventory, billing and shipping systems.

4. Final check, packaging and containerization of product(s) (using the oldest stock) to be shipped to the requesting unit.

5. Merging of containerized product(s) with computerized delivery routing system.

6. Loading of containerized product(s) on delivery trucks.

7. Delivery of containerized product to requesting unit and presentation of the invoice.

If a school system does not have a computer capability, the computerized features listed above must be performed manually. The use of computers in the distribution phase will greatly facilitate and accelerate the task of product movement.

Various points of the calendar year will provide both high and low periods concerning requisition orders. For example, logistical and instructional supplying may peak during the months of June, July and August. Also, the second semester preparation period of December and early January. Logistical supplies such as salts, chemicals, plus ice and snow removal equipment may peak during August, September and October. Warehousing management should be familiar with past fluctuations of the rates of requests.

Prior to routing channelization, as it relate to delivery to the requestion unit, planning should have taken place in the establishment of delivery zones within the school district. A timetable should have been established that would identify a delivery zone with a date of delivery (using a Monday through Friday scheme). For example, schools and other school district units located in zones 2 and 4 will have Monday and Wednesday delivery dates. Schools and units located in zones 1 and 3 will be served on Tuesdays and Thursdays. All schools and units in zones 5 and 6 (smaller area with few schools(will be allowed deliveries on Wednesdays. The previous material presented serves as a hypothetical illustration of staggering schools and units of particular zones with specific delivery dates. The overall size of the school district along with geographical location of specific schools and other district units will better determine the delivery scheme. However, the delivery scheme should be constructed to adequately serve the school district's needs.

Managerial personnel also need to study an establish time consumption patterns to determine average delivery time needed to cover each delivery team's route. The patterns along with established elasticity will benefit both management, the receiving unit, plus the delivery team in their daily route planning.

Other considerations that must be taken into account include deliveries that require special care such as:

1. Temperature control
2. Vertical or horizontal placement
3. Excessive packing requirements
4. Expediency
5. Negative exposure to light
6. Negative exposure to moisture
7. Placement within the receiving unit.

Warehousing managers must also familiarize their staffs with the reverse flow of distribution that comes from product return by the receiving unit. The receiving unit bears the responsibility for proper packing, containerization, and preparation of school district reports concerning the return. Distribution in this situation is reverse in nature with the receiving unit becoming the pick-up point for warehouse delivery personnel. The products are then forwarded to the warehouse for further paperwork and delivery (by warehouse personnel, contracted carrier, or picked up by the vendor or the vendor's contracted carrier). Once received by the vendor, the returned items are either credited to the school district's account, or exchanged for duplicate or similar items. Paper work in this area can be facilitated through the use of the computer.

INVENTORY PROCEDURES

The inventory system operates at two distinct levels. There is a progressive level that functions day by day and is called, the *daily inventory*. The daily inventory is carried out along with the incoming and outgoing stock flow of the warehousing unit. Manual or computer count should be taken of all supply and equipment items going in and out of storage. A computer capability affords the administrator and his/her staff an immediate count of all warehouse items at a moment's notice. The daily tallying will also indicate the numbers of items sent to a specific receiving unit. This would also aid in the total numbers of items received by a specific receiving unit and their rate of consumption of supply type goods. Computer input by the receiving unit would give a more accurate picture of their consumption rate of supply goods, and the inventory picture concerning equipment items.

Previous statements indicate that the daily inventory thrust involves a very frequent association with time. The second distinct level of inventory operation is that of the *formal inventory* which takes place usually once or twice a year. This inventory is designed to give the administration a more accurate account of all supplies and equipment in storage and out in the schools or other field units. Formal inventory action can be carried out through a manual or computerized count. The computerized count will offer a more accelerated and accurate count if there is employee cooperation in carrying out *all* requirements.

Another dimension that is associated with the daily or formal inventory functions is the financial worth which is attached to an inventoried item. This action allows administrators to observe not only the number of goods that are stored or out in field units, but the price tag attached to specific items and the overall total dollar value.

The use of a warehousing or storage ticket could assist both the central warehouse and the receiving unit. Such a ticket would allow a recording of item flow (coming in and going out). Use of the storage of warehouse ticket could be adapted to a manual or computerized inventory system. The dollar figure could also be listed as a matter of record.

A warehousing or storage ticket should have the following features:

1. Should allow the ability for adaptation to the inventory record through manual or computerized systems.
2. Give a complete description of the equipment or supply item.
3. Lot allocation and description.
4. Requisition date and assigned number.
5. Date of warehouse reception.
6. Date of warehouse shipment to requesting unit.
7. Identification of requesting unit.
8. Lot breakdown policy.
9. Warehouse placement.
10. Warehouse storage period.

Proper inventory measures by the central or regional warehousing units and also field units will offer logistical administrators a more accurate picture of equipment in storage and in use along with supply availability and consumption. The school district will also maintain (through the inventory system) a better financial picture as it concerns spending for supply and equipment items.

Use of a computer system will allow for a more facilitated and accelerated inventory function than the manual system. However, the key to success in computerization is complete employee compliance to all required tasks. Employees have to be orientated to the fact that the computer is not a robot which has the ability to accomplish the work of ten persons bent upon human replacement. Proper orientation and infusion into the inventory function can provide for a smooth transition from the manual to computer assistance.

Summary

Policy is necessary if there is to be order an control of the purchasing, supply and storage machine. Policy forms the foundation from which management provides enforcement which allows the assistance of the unit obtaining prescribed goals.

The purchasing function should be administered by one person (the purchasing officer) in order to prevent confusion. There should be a particular scheme from the requesting phase (by the field unit) to that of reception of the good or service (by the field unit). Bidding, vendor selection, quality, specifications, financial management functions, storage and delivery are also part of the purchasing function.

Inventory provides storage managers with both a physical count and a monetary count of all supplies and equipment items that flow through the school district. The school district can then compute its consumption rate of supplies and the use and function rate of equipment along with associated costs. Computerized assistance to the inventory function will allow for greater speed, accuracy, and flexibility than that of a manual system.

CHAPTER XI

ADMINISTERING THE
SCHOOL DISTRICT'S INSURANCE PROGRAM

PROTECTION IN RISK SITUATIONS

Public school districts are in need of a direct protection which places heavy armor in the direction of a variety of assaults. Possible or actual loss of property through disaster or theft will place a responsibility upon the school district to become aware of property values (current and projected along with an inflation factor). The school district also needs to take account of how loss effected property should be replaced, repaired or compensated for.

Another area of protection against possible assaults upon the very fiber of the public school district is that of surety bonds. These bonds cover the possibility of nefarious acts by employees or contractors which could cause financial loss.

Indirect assaults which a school district may be concerned with are in the area of liability coverage. This type of coverage should be placed in force to protect against tort situations involving both employees and those individuals or organizations external to the school system. The common law principle of governmental immunity in the area of torts does not carry the influence that it did a decade or two ago.

Other possible risk areas which includes coverage of school employees are those of fringe benefit insurances. Some school districts pay 100% of employee insurance premiums while others may pay a certain percentage. A number of school districts will leave the option of paying the entire premiums cost to the discretion of the employee.

A school district may also be involved in taking out insurance policies in other minor areas such as title insurance, check forgery and alteration insurance, etc. This statement and the preceding ones point emphatically to the fact that there is need to involve the process of management in overseeing the district's program of insurance. Not only will the risk managerial program be concerned with the insurance company solicitation, coverage, bidding, and selection, but with school district safety programs and procedures. Additional information concerning various types of school district insurances will be mentioned later in the chapter.

An adequate risk management program should be a part of the central office nerve center, and also a part of the Logistical Management operation. In some school districts this may be a direct task of the Logistical Manager, or it may delegated to an individual that has been appointed as the school district's risk manager.

Regardless of the organizational scheme of the logistical machine, there are ground rules that should be established if a successful insurance program (or risk management program) is to function within the school district. They are:

1. The school insurance program should reflect the philosophy of the school district and the surrounding community.

2. There should only be one central office administrator in charge of the insurance program (preferably a member of the logistical machine).

3. A planned, careful, critical and evaluative review should be made of all potential insurance companies and their agents to determine desirability.

4. A determination assessment of the width and depth of coverage needed to adequately protect the school district.

5. Obtaining the coverage as outlined in Item 4 at the lowest possible cost.

6. The establishment, operation and compliance with a more than adequate school district safety program. Remembering the fact that safety cannot be overstressed.

7. An annual review and appraisal of all insurance coverages, policies and premium expenses within the school district.

8. Concentrated action upon appraisal results mentioned in Item 7 which result in one of the following actions:
   a. Continuance
   b. Alteration
   c. Termination

Risk has been marked as the speculation of damage, injury or loss to an individual or organization. As mortals, we can operate at a certain level of expectation and have the possibility of reaching prescribed objectives, however, one must realize that uncertainty will have a place in the best of constructed plans or operations. Such uncertainty can be negative and bring about the chance of loss.

Risk comes in a variety of forms. Disaster and loss are the negative outcomes or risk, can be caused by:

1. Acts of God
2. Individuals
3. Informal groups
4. Formal groups
5. Mishaps

6. Fire
7. Explosions
8. Uncontrolled water and waste water systems
9. National economy
10. Property
11. Liability
12. Personal

Insurance is a buffer against disaster, loss and provides a reduction of the probability of risk. It transfers the established risk to another party. Such a party would be the insurer (or insurance company). Insurance companies will take on an individual's or organization's risk for a fee (which is called the premium). A contract (or policy) is drawn to the satisfaction of the insured and insurer which identifies the conditions of operation. The transferring of risk from the school district to an insurance company relieves the district of the anxiety brought about by the probability of loss.

THE INSURANCE COMPANIES AND THEIR AGENTS

Selection

The insurance business in America is represented by numerous companies in which one may well find variation in rates, coverage, and services offered to the insured. Risk managers representing public school systems should try to seek optimum coverage and services at the lowest premium rates possible. In other words—"The most for one's money." Specifications can be constructed by the risk manager in order to assure that the desired coverage is met by those insurance companies involved in the bidding process. Another point of consideration in this area would be what type of services are offered to the insured by the insurance firm. A question that may be asked is—Will these services be of convenience to the insured? Evaluation is needed here to determine the insurance companies that have positive service programs. The lowest bidder may not necessarily offer the best insurance program for the school district.

As far as insurance business is concerned, contact is usually made between the risk manager representing the school district and an agent representing the insurance company. Insurance agents are usually local people that are owners of an insurance agency which may represent a single insurance company, or a variety of companies.

Before the bidding process takes place, an evaluative yardstick needs to be placed into action. By using such an instrument (constructed by the risk manager) examination is permitted to weigh both the insurance company and the agent. Input in the area of evaluative comments by other school districts; total insurance sales by the company and the local agent; characteristics of insurance policies written by the company and the local agent; the state insurance office's rating of the company; total years of service of both the agent and the company; and the record of service to the insured by both the agent and the company.

The evaluation should be taken of all agents and companies participating in the bidding process.

Characteristics of Insurance Companies

The risk manager of the school district will seek information regarding insurance companies, their coverage and their services through contact with a local agent. The agent may represent a number of insurance companies or he/she may be associated with only one insurance firm. The agent has the duty of writing the policy for a particular insurance company that will then assume the risk for the school district.

There are two major prototypes represented in the classification of insurance companies. They are:

1. Stock companies — These organizations are constructed along similar lines as that of a corporation. There are stockholders who elect a board of directors for policy making and direction. Stock insurance companies that gain a profit during a fiscal period will pay a dividend to the holders of its stock.

In the area of policy holders maintaining stock in the company, explanation is needed to explain further subclassification of the policy holders involved with the holding of the company's stock. Two further subclassifications are presented concerning types of policies.

    a. Participating policy — a stock company's insurance policy which allows the holder to receive apportionment of the company's profits through the dividend process.

    b. Nonparticipating policy — policies of this type taken with a stock company does not permit the holder to share in company dividends.

2. Mutual companies — These type of insurance companies are constructed minus holdings of capital stock. Premium payments by the policy holders are the financial foundation of the company. Losses are charged against the company's reserves. Boards of directors are elected by the policyholders to provide policy and direction for the company.

Another classification of insurance organizational type that is operating in the United States is the Lloyds of London firm (considered by some to be one of the most powerful insurance sources in the world). This organization consists of individual insurance underwriters rather than that of an insurance company. The official seat of Lloyds is in London, England, but its underwriters (who hold membership in Lloyds) are involved in insurance matters throughout various sections of the world.

Another classification of insurance organizations that may work with public school districts is that of the state owned and operated insurance program for public schools. Programs of this nature may involve one of the two methods of organization, administration and operation:

1. The state insurance officer and his/her state department of insurance programs.

2. The state office of public instruction. Programs of this type have the possibility of offering the local school district a definite savings in the area of insurance expense.

Another classification which can be considered somewhat unorthodox to standard insurance company coverage is that of self-insurance by the local school district. Such a system involves the establishment of a reserve fund through periodic contributions. This reserve is never tapped unless a loss occurs. Some school districts favor this type of procedure in order to save on premium expense.

Insurance Agents and Brokers

Insurance agents are individuals that represent insurance companies for the purpose of marketing and offering services to the insured. The agent is a marketing representative for one or more insurance companies and usually receives a salary and commission as compensation.

Some agents are classified as general agents in which the insurance company allows them to hire and supervise lesser agents.

Brokers are somewhat reverse of the insurance agent, because they are representing the insured. Elasticity is presented here in the fact that the broker can arrange for insurance business with any insurance company authorized to operate within the state. A broker will seek the best possible insurance arrangement for his/her client. In regard to the broker's compensation, a commission is paid by the insurance company.

As one will find in any field or profession, their are both good and bad agents and brokers. The question then arises on how to obtain the services of a reputable agent or broker. Certain fixed features that lend themselves to good quality agents and brokers are:

1. A more than adequate knowledge of the insurance business and the needs of prospective policy buyers.

2. Courtesy

3. Evaluation of customer needs (both general and specific).

4. Knowledge of policy coverage.

5. Tries to give his/her customer the best coverage at the lowest premium cost.

6. Provides more than adequate assistance and service to policy holders suffering losses.

7. Maintains a positive atmosphere between himself/herself and the company (or companies) represented.

8. Active in civic and social affairs in the community.

9. Represents only reputable insurance companies.

10. Has goodwill within the local community.

SCHOOL DISTRICT COVERAGE

Before an insurance company and its policy (or policies) are accepted and paid for by the school district, a thorough examination and conference with the agent is in order. This conference should include all aspects of the policy and its intended hedge against specified risks. Areas to be placed under discussion should be:

1. What type of coverage is being offered by the policy to the school district.

2. Is the above mentioned coverage mentioned directly and prime in nature, or is it mentioned indirectly and is secondary in nature?

3. What specific perils are mentioned in the policy?

4. Are there other types of perils associated with those mentioned in Item 3?

5. Are there classifications of perils that are directly rejected?

6. Are there classifications of perils that are indirectly rejected?

7. The period of time that policy will be in force.

8. Extension days allowed beyond policy termination date (which allows for the premium payment to be received by the company).

9. For what reasons (if any) may the policy be revoked?

10. Does coverage extend beyond the school district boundaries? State boundaries? National boundaries?

11. Procedures for settlement of insurance claims.

The type of policy purchased identifies the area of coverage desired by the school district. Common areas of school district coverage can include the following major categories:

1. Property Ownership

2. Vehicular Transportation

3. Surety Bonding
4. Tort Protection
5. Personnel Benefits
6. Diverse Needs

Property Ownership—This particular kind of insurance coverage will include the district's school and auxiliary structures along with their contents. Most insurance companies will allow 100% of value (of structure and contents). In fact there may be escalation clauses which automatically allow for the inflation factor. In the other direction the risk manager may also seek insurance coverage for less than the current value for lower premium rates. In these inflationary times it is recommended that school districts insure their property for current values plus allow for inflationary influences. Possible losses to building structures and their contents may be the result of:

1. Acts of God
2. Fire and smoke damage
3. Explosion
4. Damage by airplanes or vehicles
5. Water or sewer line damage
6. Vandalism
7. Crime
8. Destruction of glass panes

Vehicular Transportation—All motor vehicles (buses, cars, trucks and tractors) should be insured against losses due to:

1. Acts of God
2. Collision
3. Theft
4. Glass breakage
5. Fire
6. Uninsured motorists

Vehicular liability will be mentioned later under the classification of tort protection.

Surety Bonding—School districts like other organizations need protection against the possibility of nefarious actions and noncompliancy of employees and contractors. The best defense against actions of this nature is that of the surety bond. the surety bond allows for a financial guarantee against loss. Bonds of this type include:

1. Performance bond—This type of bond guards against the failure of a contractor to carry out the obligations of a contract. Additional coverage may include materials, quality control and workmanship.

2. Bidding bond—A springboard type of bond, which labels the bidder as

guaranteeing to be able to enter into a contract with the school district, and has the qualifications to be accepted for a performance bond.

3. Fidelity bonds—These bonds may be individual in nature, or there may be the purchase of a blanket bond which covers all personnel involved with the direct handling of money. Coverage may also be extended to those that are in proximity to school district funds. The fidelity bond offers the school district protection against dishonest employees.

Tort protection—involves the use of liability insurance to protect the district against losses due to injuries or damages against others and/or their properties. States where school district tort immunity ("The king can do no wrong" theory) reigned supreme (due to common law principle) have received a serious setback. The United States Supreme Court decision of the Wood v. Strickland case in 1975 [1] ruptured the immunity of school districts and their boards. This case created a serious aftershock as the governmental tort immunity shield was shattered. This action has somewhat opened the door to governmental or school district liability.

Liability insurance allows the school district to be "before the fact" as much as possible to counter possible liability arising from:

1. Vehicular use (owned, leased, or hired)
2. School property use
3. Employee injury on the job (Workmen's Compensation Insurance)
4. Contracts
5. Damage to the property of others
6. Injury to nonschool personnel
7. Liability of all employees (insurance of this type may be also offered by employee organizations and unions)

Personnel benefits—Insurance in this area many times comes under the employee fringe benefit package which is offered by the school district. Premiums may be paid wholly or in part by the employee. In some school districts all premiums may be paid by the school district. Types of personnel benefit insurance policies offered to employees may be:

1. Hospitalization
2. Physicians and surgeons
3. Dental
4. Life
5. Accident
6. Disability
7. Income
8. Major medical
9. Retirement

10. Tax sheltered annuities
11. Body dismemberment

Diverse needs—This category allows the board of education that portion of elasticity which is activated to fill those very specific needs. For example:

1. Earthquake insurance
2. Flood insurance
3. Forgery insurance
4. Boiler insurance
5. Water sprinkler leakage insurance
6. Specified insurances against computer crime
7. Athletic insurance
8. Etc.

School districts should maintain a shield of coverage which meets the needs of the organization and according to its affordability. The risk manager must be able to find and maintain this delicate balance and yet shield the district from financial loss.

Summary

Overall responsibility for the public school district's risk management program falls upon the shoulders of the Logistical Manager. In medium to large sized school districts, there may be delegation to a logistical staff member who is assigned as the school district's risk manager. These should be only one administrator at the central office level in charge of the insurance program. Smaller school districts may attach this task to the already task heavy burden of the superintendent or the Logistical Manager.

The risk manager must evaluate the risk situation within the school district and plan for the transfer of these risks to another party—the insurance company. Another situation facing the central office administrator in charge of risk management is the obtaining of adequate coverage at the lowest price possible. Customer service options by the insurance company must also be considered for possible use if a claim is to be filed. Selection of an agent and insurance company should not be considered only by specifications and the lowest bid.

School district coverage concerns six major categories. They are:

1. Property Ownership
2. Vehicular Transportation
3. Surety Bonding
4. Tort Protection

5. Personnel Benefits
6. Diverse Needs

Policy coverage in these areas should be placed under periodic review (preferably on an annual basis) to appraise coverage, cost, service, and the claim filing process. Evaluative results will move the risk manager to a position for either recommending alteration, continuance, or termination of present insurance policies.

PART SIX
THOSE ROUTINE YET ESSENTIAL TASKS AND TECHNIQUES OF THE SCHOOL LOGISTICIAN

CHAPTER XII

MAINTENANCE AND OPERATIONAL FUNCTIONS OF THE SCHOOL DISTRICT

In order to avoid confusion concerning the terms, *maintenance* and *custodial operations*, a presentation of definitions is in order. The use of the word, *maintenance*, refers to the logistical service involved with a school plant, an auxiliary structure, or an item of equipment in a series of systematized functions. These include actions which are needed to allow for repairs, servicing and replacement procedures. Repair, servicing and replacement may directly concern the facility, or an equipment item which has been integrated into the overall daily execution of the building and the programs it houses.

Custodial operations are involved with those daily services which are needed to keep a building open and functioning for its intended purpose. For example heating, cooling, housekeeping, ventilation, sanitizing, etc.

Both of the above tasks can be part of the school district's internal logistical functions of maintenance and custodial operations. It should also be noted that wholly or partially contracted maintenance or custodial operations can be issued out to external organizations. Regardless of the method used, school districts should still require high standards of performance.

Administration of Maintenance and Custodial Operations

The major direction for the school district's maintenance and custodial operations tasks will come from central office and under the direction of the Logistical Manager. Another possibility is that an administrator (at the director's level) may be delegated the authority by the Logistical Manager to administer the district's maintenance and/or custodial programs. Central office personnel that are involved in maintenance and operations usually assist their subordinate staff members in:

1. The needed logistical support.
2. Validating maintenance and custodial requests.
3. Training (on-the-job and inservice).
4. Scheduling.
5. Assignments.

6. Supervision.
7. Troubleshooting.
8. Priority establishment.
9. Planning.
10. Budgeting and financial management.
11. Personnel administration.

Contracting maintenance and/or custodial services will greatly reduce the above items, especially in the areas of logistical support. This is due to employees being administratively covered by the contracting organization. Other administrative duties (validation, scheduling, assignment, priority and planning) that involve placing the contractor in the facility will continue along with troubleshooting and supervision.

Another administrative direction for the maintenance and custodial operations tasks will be the input of the building level or line administrator. The principal or administrator (if an auxiliary building) in charge of the facility has a close contact to determine what functions are needed to keep his/her building operational and well maintained. Definite coordination of the maintenance and custodial procedures should be carried out between the central office maintenance and operations administrators, the building principal or auxiliary administrator, and the workers. Policy should be strictly adhered to along with any union contracts and procedures (if applicable). Maintenance and custodial policy should contain not only guideline, but the establishment of administrative lines and zones of control (central office and building level).

Facility administrators (principals and other central office administrators charged with the responsibility of a board of education housing unit) should definitely have the right to supervision of maintenance and/or custodial work in their buildings. Work that is not being completed up to a specified standard, or places building occupants into situations that are unhealthful and/or dangerous, must be brought to the immediate attention of central office administration. From this particular point onward, corrective measures must be coordinated and taken to administrators (at both building and central office levels) and the concerned staffs.

Another level of supervision that should be brought out are those members of the maintenance and custodial teams that are in the capacities of foremen or senior team members. These individuals are in direct contact with the maintenance or custodial staffs and the assigned tasks that are being undertaken. Foremen or senior team members should receive both central office and building level administrative input concerning assigned task situations. However, a great deal of initiative, experience, and skill is exercise in allowing these individuals (foremen and senior team members) to direct and complete their assignments.

All levels of custodial and maintenance supervisory control should be built upon and reinforced through policy. All policy must be adhered to if there are to be successful completions of task assignments. At the foundation of the policy structure, there are some dominant keystones which individually bonds the maintenance and custodial programs. These keystones are:

1. Primary and secondary goals of each individual program.
2. Primary and secondary goals of the maintenance and custodial programs as they each concern equipment, school plants, or facilities.
3. Creation of a satisfactory condition in which the facility, plant or equipment item can reach its prescribed goal(s).
4. Explanation of supervisory lines.
5. Explanation of authority zones.
6. Explanation of responsibility zones.
7. Format for training and inservice programs.
8. Personnel administration guidelines.
9. Appraisal systems.
10. Review procedures.
11. Policy alteration and termination procedures.

MAINTENANCE—THE REPAIR, REPLACEMENT, AND SERVICE FUNCTION

Intent

One may ask—What is the school district's intent through the action of conducting a district wide program of maintenance? Responses could possibly come in the form of:

1. Keeping school district buildings and equipment in first-rate order. The goals here being:
   a. Preservation in state
   b. Longevity in operation
2. The second point will take us back to the fact that, "safety cannot be overstressed." Therefore, as program in maintenance cannot be overstressed because good maintenance promotes safety.
3. Through the operation of a satisfactory maintenance program, the school district can achieve a future reduction of major repair and replacement costs of facilities and equipment.
· 4. The upkeep element associated with the maintenance program may come from internal or external (contracted) services. Upkeeping procedures

are usually assigned to keep the building or an item of equipment in prime order (to be able to proceed with its assigned duty to the facility).

The Repair, Replacement and Service Tasks

Maintenance is concerned with a trident approach toward keeping the school district's machine in a synchronized and working order. An analytical breakdown of the above mentioned trident approach includes the elements of:

1. Repair—This task includes the returning of an equipment item or a facility (or a segment thereof) to its original state or working order.

2. Replacement—There are times in which an article of equipment or a facility will have to be wholly or partially rebuilt or restored on a singular or multifarious level.

3. Service—This task involves those prescribed steps suggested or required by a manufacturer (for warranty and/or longevity purposes). Service requirements may also be a part of school district policy in order to assure as much time as possible for satisfactory operation and product life.

The Echelons of Maintenance

A school district's maintenance program should be stratified according to levels of performance responsibility. Explanation is needed to explain that the entire maintenance program for a particular item may be contracted to external sources. The other polar extreme would be that another item may be fully maintained by the school district's internal maintenance system.

Stratification of the maintenance program could involve the following:

1. First echelon maintenance—This program involves the basic maintenance functions or troubleshooting performed by the user or those individuals assigned (such as custodians) to assure function or incorporation of the item's function into a larger complex unit. Minor operations such as fluid level checks, minor replacement, performance, visible points of wear, etc. are monitored, serviced or reported (to the second echelon) at this particular level.

2. Second echelon maintenance—The maintenance program at this particular level requires the input of a specialist to correct, repair or possibly provide an advanced service requirement to a particular item or facility. The specialist may be a mechanic, an electrician, carpenter, a heating and air conditioning person, etc. The maintenance act will involve a person with the training and experience to engage in the required task. Second echelon maintenance is more detailed and advanced, plus it calls for assistance beyond the user or assignee.

3. Third echelon maintenance—Concerns the highest level of maintenance provided by the local school district. Repair, replacement, and service functions at this level would be strictly performed by specialists and would definitely be at the advanced level.

4. Fourth echelon maintenance—Any repair, service, and replacement function that cannot be performed at school district level, would be forwarded to external organizations. Such as specialized repair shops, dealers, or back to the manufacturer. Such involvement by these external organizations may involve their coming to the school site in order to carry out their duties.

Characteristics of Maintenance

The maintenance function can take on a number of faces with relation to its particular traits. These traits are determined according to the purpose involved with a specific maintenance goal. The categories that are in need of explanation include the following:

1. The Preventative Maintenance Program—This type of program includes those features of maintenance that are involved with both equipment and facilities. Directives as to the particular care (lubrication, changing parts, application of coatings, etc.) of specific items may come from the manufacturer and/or board policy. The primary goal of preventative maintenance is to provide that care which is needed to maintain operation or to preserve the object for a longer duration without costly repairs or lost person-hours.

Preventative maintenance is usually projected and it operates mainly at the first and second echelon levels.

2. Systematic Maintenance—Maintenance carried out in this category involves detailed planning. Replacements, rebuilding, repairing, or servicing will take place at a certain specified time (which may be measured in time consumed in operation, mileage, chronological age, cyclical segmentation, etc.). Maintenance of this type features programmed tasks which are to greatly reduce overall time loss, financial loss, labor inactivity, and production down time.

3. Setup Maintenance—Maintenance of this nature works on the same principle as that of the setup person on the factory or industrial scene. The setup person is a maintenance person whose duty station is within the factory site. He/she immediately goes into action (repairing and replacing) if a breakdown or stoppage occurs. The setup person also facilitates the operation of function of equipment, or a work task.

Similar proceedings could be applied to heating, air conditioning, freezer and refrigeration service persons placed on call by the school district's maintenance office. The same can be said of plumbers, glaziers, computer service personnel and others.

4. Crisis Maintenance—Equipment items or facilities that have the need for repair, replacement, or rebuilding at a moment's notice (along with the item being in demand or creating a dangerous situation) will prompt maintenance personnel to immediately correct the problem at hand. A prime example could be that of a damaged water or sewer line; a damaged roof; broken natural gas line; etc.

Maintenance Recording

Maintenance requests; trips to and from the site; method of correcting, repairing, servicing, replacing, or rebuilding; supplies, equipment and parts used; person hours involved; dates and times; plus the evaluation of the finished task should all be kept on record.

School districts that are on computer systems can store such information in their data bank from standard hand written forms. Information of this type can readily be retrieved at a moment's notice if an inquiry situation arises.

Those school districts that must rely on manually prepared records also need to develop a storage and retrieval system. The use of microfilm may well cut down on precious space.

Records need to be kept not only for an informative reason, but also for cost analysis studies which would allow maintenance administrators to cut costs in any areas or potential areas of waste. Record information would also allow the maintenance section to better plan its future operations. The past can offer some vital information on how to prepare for the future.

The Maintenance Staff

A school district's maintenance staff will consist of a variety of workers that are involved in keeping the system's equipment and facilities in top working condition. Consideration must be given to school systems that contract a portion or all of their maintenance needs with external organizations. Reasons for the contracting situation may be varied. For example:

1. Reduction in cost.
2. Elimination of management-union strife.
3. Better quality control.
4. Elimination of fringe benefit packages.
5. Decrease in task time consumption (due to additional worker involve-

ment than standard internal crew organizations).

6. Decrease in supervisory costs.
7. Decrease in cost for supplies and equipment.

A general classification list of internal or contracted maintenance personnel that are most likely to be involved in the maintenance duties of the typical school district are:

1. Waste systems and removal personnel.
2. Refrigeration, freezer and air conditioning mechanics.
3. Heating and ventilating personnel.
4. Sheet metal and air duct workers.
5. Fire control and fire extinguisher staff.
6. Roofers.
7. Glaziers.
8. Carpenters.
9. Plumbers.
10. Electrical motor mechanics.
11. Automotive mechanics and service persons.
12. Automotive body repair persons.
13. Electronic service personnel.
14. Computer service personnel.
15. Boilermakers.
16. Pest control service personnel.
17. Street, sidewalk and driveway installers and repair persons (concrete and asphalt).
18. Fence installers and repair persons.
19. Carpet repair and cleaning personnel.
20. Elevator service persons.
21. Electricians.
22. Small engine service and repair persons.
23. Painters.
24. Sandblasters.
25. Roof drainage installers and repair persons.
26. Robot service and repair persons.
27. Security system installers and service persons.

CUSTODIAL OPERATIONS—THE DAILY CARE OF THE FACILITY

Custodial programs may be internal to the school organization or they may be contracted with outside organizations. Regardless of the system used need is required for the administration of the custodial program. Administrative direction to meet the needs of the facility operations effort can result in proper goal construction and achievement. This situation prevails in either a school district conducted or contracted custodial program.

The Housekeeping Endeavor

School districts should maintain general programs for the housekeeping of facilities within its boundaries. Policy conducting the duties of disinfecting, purifying, warehousing, equipment movement and placement, plus performing minor repair, replacement and servicing will apply to all facilities of the district. However, some consideration has to be given to individual facilities and their rate of use. Some buildings will be involved with programs lasting beyond the normal school day. Excessive use of this type can place extra wear and tear upon the facility. Also, extra activities of this type can place a possible alteration to normal custodial hours (in order that the unit is kept operational). Facilities housing security, transportation, or centralized or regional food service units will be engaged in unorthodox working hours, therefore, requiring varied hours for custodial assistance. Overall there should be elasticity in the custodial program in order to meet the district's needs which is concerned with keeping all of its facilities at 100% operating efficiency.

Housekeeping will involve a number obligations on the part of the custodial staff. Some are:

1. Sweeping.
2. Dry mopping.
3. Wet mopping.
4. Scrubbing.
5. Scraping.
6. Wax application and polishing.
7. Wax removal.
8. Dusting.
9. Washing.
10. Disinfecting.
11. Refilling dispensers.
12. Waste collection.
13. Waste removal.
14. Liquid or wet cleaning.
15. Vacuum cleaning.
16. Fuse exchanging.
17. Light bulb exchanging.
18. Temperature setting (manual or computer).
19. General cleaning.

20. Sanding.
21. Refinishing.
22. Carpet shampooing.
23. Metal polishing.
24. Mirror polishing.
25. Glass polishing or cleaning.
26. Application of coatings to equipment.

The above mentioned custodial duties must be further programmed according to frequencies of periodic activity. Segments of time concerned with the carrying out of housekeeping duties are:

1. Annually
2. Biannually
3. Quarterly
4. Monthly
5. Biweekly
6. Weekly
7. Daily
8. Frequently or as needed within the segment of a day.

Internal sections and needs of a typical school building that are in need of custodial attention are:

1. Foyers and hallways
2. Offices
3. Classrooms and laboratories
4. Gymnasium
5. Auditorium
6. Restrooms
7. Dining hall
8. Water fountains
9. Locker rooms
10. Shower areas
11. Floors
12. Stairways
13. Chalkboards
14. Walls and ceilings
15. Restroom plumbing fixtures
16. Windows, mirrors, and glass fixtures
17. Storage rooms
18. Illumination fixtures
19. Heating, cooling, and ventilating control
20. Metal fixtures

21. Control and assistance to security and fire systems
22. Pest control assistance
23. General supply replenishment and reorder
24. Woodwork and window sills.

The external area which surrounds the school house or board of education facility will require:

1. Lawn care.
   a. Cutting
   b. Fertilizing
   c. Watering
   d. Trimming
2. Leaf raking and removal.
3. Shrub care.
4. Planting and care of flower beds.
5. Parking lot maintenance.
6. Maintenance of bus mounting and dismounting areas.
7. Policing of school grounds.
8. External window cleaning.
9. External building care.
10. Snow and ice removal.
11. Care of campus trees.

Custodial Standards

Optimum standards concerning custodial care should be developed by the Logistical Manager and the director of custodial services. These standards should then be formulated into the custodial operations policy for the school district. Once these standards are incorporated into policy they must be enforced by administrative and supervisory staff members. Custodians also need to realize that it is the following of these policies which establishes the standards of custodial care. Adherence to policy should be placed within the custodial zones of responsibility.

Custodial standards should include all facility areas. In addition, these desired levels of workmanship and quality performance should be placed in the above average category. Mediocre performance should not be tolerated by supervisory personnel.

Primary areas of custodial standards should include:

1. The creating and maintaining of a healthy sanitized environment for students and the instructional staff.

2. The creating and maintaining of a safe facility for students and school personnel.

3. Development and enforcement of a quality control program.

4. Maintaining a quality assurance program.
5. The hiring of qualified and dependable individuals.
6. Requiring skillful and precise handling of custodial tasks.

QUALIFICATIONS PLUS SELECTION OF MAINTENANCE AND CUSTODIAL EMPLOYEES

In order to uphold standards, quality and policy there is need to hire individuals with the ability to comprehend what is required of them. Also, they (the hired personnel) must be able to carry out in an acceptable manner the tasks that are required of them.

To select competent personnel from the labor pool, a series of examinations should be used to reduce the applicants to an acceptable lot. These appraisal procedures could be:

1. An evaluation of how the applicant completed the application form.
2. Use of an examination to test knowledge and intelligence.
3. A physical examination by a licensed physician.
4. The interview process.
5. Law enforcement check for past criminal record (if any).
6. Credit office check to determine financial solvency.

Other items that should be considered in the selection process are:

1. Age.
2. Union participation.
3. Location of residence.
4. Personal appearance.
5. Personal hygiene.
6. Schooling.
7. Advanced schooling beyond high school.
8. Specialized training.
9. Military service and type of discharge.
10. Military training.
11. Character references.
12. Past experience.
13. Marital status.
14. Organizational membership(s).
15. Past diseases (through medical examination by a licensed physician).
16. Past work record.

Once the examinations have been given and the above items have been considered, plus the selection and hiring carried out, further appraisal can be made through:

1. Training sessions and inservice.
2. On-the-job training.
3. A probationary period.

Satisfactory evaluative marks during the above mentioned periods will enable administrative and supervisory personnel the opportunity to either release or maintain the selectee in a position of employment. Additional appraisal of the employee can be gathered throughout his/her career by individual and work performance grading. Evaluation can also be used in advanced inservice training which is usually given numerous times during an individual employment period.

Summary

Custodial operations concerns those support services that must be carried out to keep the school building or other school district facilities operational. When a building is in a condition to allow a particular program or programs to function within its confines, there is an attempt by those in charge to reach their assigned program goals. A properly functioning custodial team will make sure that a building and its contents are in prime order to assist the program and program personnel to achieve such goals.

Maintenance as it concerns the school plant or other board of education buildings, involves those steps needed to preserve or elongate structural life. Maintenance also encompasses the steps that add life to the various items of equipment. The question may arise as to the identity of the previously mentioned steps. They are:

1. Repair
2. Replacement
3. Service

These steps have to be taken as a result of:

1. Fair wear and tear
2. Time use
3. Acts of God (storms, lightning, floods, etc.)
4. Unexpected incidents (due to explosions, poor quality, poor workmanship, etc.)
5. Planned change (remodeling, expansion, etc.)
6. Mechanical breakdowns
7. Unfair wear and tear (misuse, abuse, unawareness, etc.)

Maintenance and custodial services may be a direct internal segment of the logistical effort and/or it may be contracted out to external organizations.

If contracting takes place, there is still need for direct supervision by internal central office and building level administrators.

The Logistical Manager and those lesser administrators in charge of custodial and maintenance functions (if the school organization plan allows for lesser administrators in these areas) must assure the school district that buildings and equipment are kept in proper order to allow the instructional or other school district programs to operate in a positive and meaningful environment.

CHAPTER XIII

TRANSPORTATION SERVICES

Today's school district is involved with a set of dual objectives. One objective is that of instruction which is primary in classification. Such reasoning exists because instruction is the vehicle by which the populace is educated. The other objective is that of logistical services which support the primary instructional program. One must realize that without logistical support, the instructional program would be doomed to failure. This particular line of thought points to the definite need of a school district to maintain a properly administered program of support services.

An important logistical service that will be focused upon at this time is that of pupil transportation. The typical school district is dependent upon transportation for its daily movements between the home and the school. There is also dependence upon motor vehicle use in transporting pupils for extracurricular programs.

In more recent times, a considerable amount of demand has been place upon the transportation function because of:

1. Consolidation of smaller school districts
2. Court ordered busing for desegregation purposes
3. Suburban growth and the urban to rural movement
4. Grade level clustering practices
5. Special educational programs

Such demands as these particular factors along with rising costs and energy shortages has created a need for a properly administered economical program of transportation. In order that a program of this intensity operate at top level efficiency, there is need for adequate policy and capable administration.

Both large and small school districts need to formulate transportation policies and establish an administrative position for directing the district's transportation program. Smaller school districts may place the duty of directing the pupil transportation program as an additional obligation of the superintendent. However, it must be taken into account that rising costs, transportation budgetary problems, energy problems, transportation personnel obligations (in-service, collective negotiations, grievances, hiring, firing, etc.), vehicular purchases, and vehicle maintenance are part of transportation administration. A small school district needs to determine whether these additional duties are too strenuous for the superintendent. Administrative overload may necessitate the creation of a transportation administrator's position. There is also the need for a transportation staff if the vehicle units are board-owned.

Medium and large school districts are automatically in need of an administrator for the transportation program. Districts of this caliber will definitely require an adequate transportation staff if the vehicle units are publicly-owned.

A school district's transportation service assists the instructional program by:

1. Transporting pupils to and from the various learning centers internally and externally (in regard to the school district).
2. Transporting pupils to and from extracurricular activities.
3. Transporting pupils to and from instructionally related field trips.
4. Providing transportation services to school-community related activities.
5. Providing transportation services to the school district's guests and visiting dignitaries.
6. Transporting special education pupils to and from the center of learning.

ADMINISTRATION OF THE
DISTRICT LEVEL TRANSPORTATION PROGRAM

The Director of Transportation: A Central Office Administrator

Transportation is indeed a needed service to the school district, however, it must be properly managed and operated according to an adequate system of policy. Management of a school district's transportation services will vary according to size. As previously stated, small school districts may place the duty of their in-house transportation administration as another duty of the superintendent. However, the demands of directing a transportation program may necessitate the delegation of such duties to another central office administrator of lesser rank.

Medium to large school districts will usually maintain a table of organization slot for a Transportation Director at the central office level.

The Director of Transportation will have the responsibility for administration of the district's overall transportation program. This particular situation is mandatory whether this school district is operating with its own organic transportation units or units under contract with private owners. However, school systems that maintain contracts with private carriers will have a less complex administrative role for the Director of Transportation. This will be due to a greater portion of the administrative and maintenance duties being carried out by the private carrier.

Administrative duties carried out by the Director of Transportation are:

1. Formulation of transportation policy. Also, evaluation, alteration and possible termination of existing policy.
2. Liaison with building level administrators concerning:
   a. Pickup and release points
   b. Time schedules
   c. Routing procedures
   d. Pupil transportation accounting
   e. Pupil mounting and dismounting procedures
   f. On-campus pupil staging areas
   g. Transfer assembly points
   h. Building level supervision of transportation activities
   i. Driver-pupil relationships
   j. Pupil discipline and control
   k. A transportation safety program
3. Liaison with external agencies such as governmental (state and local) highway departments; law enforcement agencies; United States Weather Bureau (road conditions); and the news media (daily newspapers, radio, and television).
4. Hiring and training of driver personnel.
5. School bus maintenance program (if busses are board-owned).
6. Establishment of policy concerning the procurement of replacement parts and supplies (including gasoline and other lubricants) for the operation of transportation units (if buses are board-owned).
7. Budget preparation, implementation and evaluation for the transportation operation.
8. Maintaining an effective energy conservation program.
9. Maintaining an adequate public relations program.
10. Maintaining an adequate program of evaluation.
11. Developing and maintaining leadership in administering the transportation safety program.
12. Establishment of policy regarding the procurement of new vehicles (specifically for the local operation beyond federal and state mandates).

Administrative Coordination with Internal Agencies

Within the school organization, the Director of Transportation must keep a positive and active liaison with:

1. The Board of Education
2. The Superintendent

3. Central Office Administrative Staff
4. Building Principals
5. Subordinate Leaders of the Transportation Staff

Boards of education have the responsibility of determining and examining the extent of the school district's policies. This action also includes those policies as they relate to the service of transportation. However, these policies must be within the guidelines as dictated by the state and federal governments. The boards' enactment of the transportation policy gives the superintendent and the Director of Transportation proper authority to enforce those rules and regulations which are needed in order to have a proper and efficient operation of the transportation service at the local district level. Board enacted policy allows a firm foundation from which to launch the proper authority, which is needed in the operational phase. Reinforcement is required here to state that the overall responsibility for the transportation program will rest upon the shoulders of the superintendent's overall responsibility of the district's general education program. However, direct authority and direct responsibility for the providing of transportation services to the children of the school district will rest with the Director of Transportation.

Boards of education are usually not directly active in the districts transportation program, but are more involved in policy formulation, policy enforcement, and policy enactment (as it relates to transportation).

The Superintendent of Schools, along with the Director of Transportation's recommendations, will determine the requirements of a transportation program. These requirements include monies, time, personnel and matériel. In addition, the superintendent may also be involved with the communication and public relations aspect of the district's transportation service.

By having an overall responsibility (which covers the transportation program) the superintendent should have an interest in the operational aspect of the service. Such an interest may involve periodic reportings and briefings by the Director of Transportation. These periodic contacts will keep the Superintendent aware of any current or possible problems which may occur. Keeping the Superintendent and his/her staff informed will greatly assist in being "before the fact" concerning possible negative issues. These actions will also provide for a more correct prescription in the troubleshooting phase as it relates to pupil transportation.

The building level administrator must keep an open and active liaison with the Transportation Office. Transportation personnel who will have a direct contact with school principals are:

1. Director of Transportation
2. Route Master

3. Dispatcher
4. Bus Drivers

The Director of Transportation and the principal will coordinate concerning the overall transportation program as it effects the operation of the principal's building. More specific interaction will involve the principal with the Route Master concerning route alterations which may be periodical or impromptu. Also such changes of the routing procedure may be temporary, semipermanent or permanent.

The principal's contact with the Dispatcher will derive itself from the standpoint of time (as it relates to pupil pickup, arrivals and pupil home drops). Time is of essence in coordinating transportation services with the schedule of the school building instruction program. Problems disturbing the time element can disrupt the timing of the curriculum schedule, and the school building's relationship with its community.

The building administrator's coordination with the Dispatcher will involve (1) the element of time, (2) pupil inconvenience and (3) pupil awareness as it relates to the transportation unit (the school bus and its driver) being operational. Principal-Dispatcher liaison will include whether a substitute transportation unit or other transportation measures will be used to fill the void of sometimes interrupted service.

The school bus driver and the principal will confer on (1) matters of pupil conduct and discipline, (2) pupil safety on buses and (3) driver-pupil relations. It is very necessary that the principal, his/her administrative staff and the faculty to undertake a team effort in reducing pupil-pupil and pupil-driver conflicts on board transportation units. A well-disciplined group of pupil passengers enhances a more sane and safe atmosphere during bus trips.

The school district and the principal will find that strong policies (district-wide and building level) are needed in order to administer an effective program of pupil discipline and control on board transportation units.

Other transportation matters that the building level administrator needs to consider are:

1. A program of pupil supervision at:
   a. Mounting and dismounting points
   b. Pupil holding areas (which are located on school property)
   c. Pupil transfer points (This involves pupils not in attendance at your school, but will transfer from one transportation unit to another on your school's property.)
   d. Bus stops located in your school's area of attendance (Such supervisory practices in this are should be clandestine, periodic and sometimes impromptu in nature.)
2. Pupil bus safety orientation programs should be provided periodically

through the academic year. Such programs need to be coordinated through a joint effort of the Transportation Department and building's administrative staff.

3. A building level pupil accounting system as it concerns the school district's transportation service (with daily, weekly and monthly reports).
4. The establishment of a procedure for school bus routing on the school's campus.
5. The establishment of school bus parking zones on the school's campus.
6. The establishment of pupil mounting and dismounting points.

Concerning coordination with the central office, the Director of Transportation needs to have an open line of communication between his office and other central office administrators. For example, central office curriculum specialists may desire the aid of the Transportation Department to assist in providing transporting services to facilitate the instructional process. Field trips and field based practical instruction are of great importance to the curriculum effort.

Transportation services could greatly aid central office administrators involved in community and public relations. Providing transportation to community members for school related events can induce positive relations between the schools and the populace.

The Director of Transportation needs to have a very close contact with the school business manager. Budget and logistical concerns related to transportation operation will be reviewed by the business manager. Decisions made at this particular level will have a considerable affect on the quality of operation concerning the school district's transportation program.

Subordinate leaders in the Transportation Department should consist of all or a part of the following personnel:

1. Assistant Director of Transportation (in medium to large school systems)
2. Route Master (in medium to large school systems)
3. Dispatcher
4. Maintenance Foreman

The Director of Transportation should have a close relationship with his/her Assistant Director. The Assistant Director should always be kept aware of current and possible future transportation situations. In fact, daily briefings should take place to inform both the Director and Assistant Director. The Assistant Director should be able to take over and operate transportation program at any time. The Director of Transportation needs to coordinate the various transportation functions with his/her Assistant Director.

The Transportation Director's relationship with the Route Master will be that of coordination concerning route planning, route alteration, and route deletion. The Route Master should keep the Director aware of all situations in the community which affects the routing system of school transportation units. The Route Master needs to brief the Transportation Director daily concerning the routing situation.

The Director of Transportation's relationship with the Dispatcher should be that of a daily briefing of the bus driver and bus unit situation. This should include (1) units in operation, (2) units undergoing servicing and repairs, (3) units held in reserve and (4) the availability of substitute drivers.

Coordination between the Maintenance Foreman and that of the Director of Transportation should be along the service and repair status of the entire bus fleet. In addition, the Maintenance Foreman should keep the Director aware of supply and equipment stocks concerning petroleum products, spare parts and other items necessary for vehicular operation.

All of the above mentioned subordinate leaders need to coordinate the following duties of their sections with the Director of Transportation:

1. Budgetary matters
2. Personnel needs
3. Evaluations
4. Orders (concerning supplies and equipment requisitions and purchases)
5. Inservice training

Administrative Coordination with External Agencies

In order to have a smooth and efficient transportation operation, there is a need for the Transportation Director to coordinate with various external agencies. External agencies that could be involved with a public school system's transportation department are:

1. United States Weather Bureau
2. Local and State Governmental Highway and Street Departments
3. Local and State Law Enforcement Agencies
4. Vehicle Dealerships
5. Local, State and Federal Energy Departments
6. Petroleum Industry
7. Labor Unions
8. The Media
9. State and National School Bus Transportation Agencies
10. Insurance Companies

U.S. Weather Bureau

Liaison is needed with the Weather Bureau concerning both long and short range forecasts. Weather has a definite affect on the operation of a school system's transportation program. Conditions such as rain, snow, fog, ice, high winds, and both extremely high and low temperatures can disrupt, delay or terminate school bus operations. Also, the safety factor can be added to the inclement weather operation of school buses.

A detailed study of seasonal, monthly, weekly, daily forecasts by the Director of Transportation (or a subordinate to which the task has been delegated) should take place, especially during the late fall, winter, and early spring seasons. Certain sections of the United States may begin and end their snow seasons at earlier or later dates. In areas where snows can curtail transportation operations, the daily weather forecast along with hourly (both day and night) observations throughout the school district are needed to furnish weather data to the superintendent. Usually the superintendent will depend heavily upon the Transportation Director's input regarding the decision whether or not to operate school buses in inclement weather. The Superintendent's action (depending upon the weather data received) may be to terminate both bus and instructional operations for a given period of time.

Other weather conditions which may require hourly watches are rains (in relation to flooding and freezing problems). Icy conditions (from rain, slush, or packed snow); fog and visibility hazards; high winds (storms, gales, tornadoes); and extremely hot or cold temperatures (which can hamper bus operation and the health and safety of pupils).

Local and State Governmental Highway and Street Departments

Governmental street and highway departments should be contacted daily by the Transportation Director (or a subordinate who has been delegated the authority to do so). Governmental departments of this type can give the Transportation Department information concerning:

1. Detours
2. Street and highway repair points (plus estimated time or repairs)
3. Road closings
4. Reasons for road closings
5. Street and highway construction
6. Street and highway planning
7. Data concerning railroads, rapid urban transit systems, local plus interstate bus and truck routes, bridges (and boat traffic), interstate and expressway systems and their effect upon streets and highways within the school district.

The above mentioned factors may cause the altering of established school bus routes, scheduling times, pick up and release points, and extra emphasis on safety practices and procedures.

Local and State Law Enforcement Agencies

Local and state police can greatly assist in keeping the Transportation Department up-to-date concerning road conditions and road hazards. These agencies are usually the first contacted when negative conditions arise concerning roads and traffic. Law enforcement personnel can also assist in emergency situations. All transportation personnel, whether based or mobile, should have the ability to communicate electronically by radio and/or telephone with law enforcement agencies.

Vehicle Dealerships

Buses will be purchased from dealerships at various times for replacement purposes. In some states the replacing of transportation units may involve a bidding process at state level rather than at the school district level. Whenever buses are to be purchased, state bidding rules and regulations should be followed to the letter. Once a dealer's bid had been accepted and the buses purchased, there needs to be coordination between the Transportation Department's maintenance personnel and the maintenance personnel of the dealership. This coordination will concern compliance with warranty requirements for the period of warranty only. After the warranty period, dealer maintenance services should only be requested when the organic maintenance group is unable to perform a particular service.

The Transportation Department's parts section may order replacement parts from a local dealership or a wholesale parts firm. Bidding and possible contracts could be involved here. This will depend upon board and/or state regulations.

Local, State, and Federal Energy Departments

Local, state and federal governments may make requests or impose rules and regulations concerning matters relating to energy consumption. The Transportation Director should follow the train of thought that the local school board and the local school district legally belong to the state and are considered governmental agencies. Compliance with local, state and federal agencies concerning energy matters would be a means of setting the example for the public.

The staff of the Transportation Department through inservice training should be made aware of governmental requests, rules and regulations concerning energy matters. There is also a need for an organic departmental policy concerning energy conservation.

Petroleum Industry

A school district's Transportation Department will find it a must to maintain a constant liaison with the petroleum industry which supplies petroleum products to the district. Contracts are usually made with individual oil companies on a bidding and contracting basis.

Care needs to be taken when bids are opened each fiscal period concerning the supply of petroleum products. Caution should also be taken while establishing contracts with oil companies due to the frequent price increases during past fiscal periods. Possible future embargoes by oil exporting nations could have devastating effects upon the transportation operations of a local school district. Therefore, transportation administrators need to maintain contact with petroleum companies concerning availability of products and forecasts of any possible delays (of production caused by strikes, international-political strife and production priorities).

Transportation administrators should consider the use of constructing long term storage facilities for petroleum products to act as a reserve against the negative actions of oil exporting nations and domestic refiners. Such storage facilities could be used to store a 3–12 months supply of gasoline and lubricants. A first in first out policy concerning inventories could be put into operation in order that the petroleum products be kept as refinery fresh as possible.

Labor Unions

If the school district is operating in a situation where bus drivers and other transportation personnel are unionized, administrative care must be taken if the department's organizational goals are to be reached.

Contract negotiations should be handled with expertise. If such expertise does not exist in the Transportation Department and/or school district level plus experience concerning negotiations has not been gained, there is a need for consulting services in this area.

Once a contract has been negotiated and signed by both union and administrative personnel, it will be binding. Any negotiable item(s), short or long ranged, that will negatively effect the transportation operation should not be agreed to.

One item that should be agreed upon by both bus drivers and other transportation personnel is that of hiring, training and terminating personnel. The Transportation Department's goals must be achieved by the interaction of both the administration and labor.

Care needs to be taken concerning the daily interaction between administrative personnel and the union membership. The contract as it relates to daily duties should be definitely adhered to. Collective bargaining resulting in adequate wages and fringe benefits can offer administrative personnel the opportunity to be more selective in the hiring process. Excellent salaries coupled with outstanding fringe benefits can attract top-rate job applicants. Also, top-flight wage and benefit packages have the possibility for creating high morale, motivation, better labor-administrative relations and a sound base for future supervisory selection.

The Media

The transportation Department needs to maintain contact with local newspapers, radio and television stations. Such media units can assist in presenting the purposes of the overall transportation program to the public. Items concerning routes and scheduling can be offered by the media to the community. Radio and television stations can bring more up-to-date versions of routing and scheduling changes to parents and students on a daily basis. Maintaining good relations with local media can reap dividends to the transportation program.

State and National School Bus Transportation Agencies

All transportation personnel must strictly adhere to both state and federal regulations regarding the operating of a school transportation program. Federal regulations reign supreme with state regulations being sometimes more specific and closely following federal rules to the letter. Such rules and regulations by federal and state agencies will cover:

1. School Bus Operation
2. School Bus Operations—Annual Inservice Programs, Training Sites and Facilities
3. Operation Standards
4. Rebuilding of Transportation Units
5. Transporting Handicapped Children
6. School Bus Construction
   a. Chassis
   b. Body
   c. Required Accessories
7. Maintenance Standards

Insurance Companies

State regulations will dictate the types and amount of insurance needed fleet coverage of the school district's transportation units. Areas covered by insurance companies in regard to pupil transportation operations are:

1. Liability
   a. Personal
   b. Property Damage
2. Medical Payment (Not involved with tort situations)
3. Collision
4. Comprehensive
   a. Fire
   b. Theft

States will usually determine the minimum amounts of insurance for the above mentioned areas. However, in viewing inflation and rising costs, a school district may wish to insure its transportation units in access of state minimums.

Administrative Authority: A Combined Effort
or Leadership and Management of Public School Transportation Services

Responsibility for the management of the transportation program will probably rest with the Transportation Director in medium to large school districts. Such responsibility in smaller districts will most likely be an additional obligation of the Superintendent. Areas to which management skills will be directed are:

1. Drivers
2. Maintenance Personnel
3. Subordinate Transportation Administrators (In medium and large school systems.)
4. Transportation Support Staff

Before discussing management as it relates to the previously mentioned areas, there are some directions that are in need of explanation. First, administrative authority for the district transportation program will rest with the Director of Transportation. In addition to being responsible for the transportation program, the Director has the authority to operate (within policy guidelines) such a program in the manner he/she see fit to accomplish the districts' established goals. The primary goal of a school transportation program is to provide a transportation service to the school children of the school district. Secondary goals of the transportation program will encompass safety, efficiency and economy in operation of the transportation service.

The second direction for discussion is that of authority which has been granted to the Transportation Director (by board of education policy) and may be delegated to subordinate administrative personnel involved in the school district transportation program. Such subordinate administrative personnel are part of the overall transportation team which must accomplish its predetermined primary and secondary goals. In other words, subordinate transportation administrators as the: (1) Assistant Director; (2) Route Master; (3) Dispatcher; (4) Maintenance Foreman will be functioning to meet their individual secondary goals in the name of the Director of Transportation.

A third general topic for direction is that of leadership as it concerns a school system's program of transportation. Leadership can be called a particular process through which subordinates are influenced to accomplish a goal. In this particular instance the leader or superior has a direct and close effect upon subordinate personnel. Leadership surrounds a personal connection of superior to subordinate. In a situation of this kind the superior will use his/her ability to aspire a subordinate to obtain a goal. The Transportation Director will, through personal influence, attempt to create such a desire within his/her staff to accomplish the overall goal of providing a service of transportation to the school district.

The final topic is that of management which is the process of detailed organizing and the use of available means to accomplish a goal. Management has an indirect influence on subordinate personnel. It is the opposite of the direct personal effect found upon subordinates as in leadership. Management involves the administration of logistical support which is required in accomplishing goals. This logistical support present itself in the certain prime sources which are:

1. Time projected and time elapsed (the fiscal year, academic year, calendar year, past years, projections, etc.).
2. Supplies and equipment (petroleum products, buses, parts, etc.).
3. Budgetary and fiscal matters.
4. Personnel (drivers, mechanics, clerical support, administrators, etc.).

A Director of Transportation is definitely involved in the administration of the previously mentioned sources which are so necessary to accomplish the goal of providing a transportation service to the school district's children. The Transportation Director will find that (1) time projected and elapsed has a bearing on the finances expended or about to be expended during the yearly fiscal period. Time also can be associated with the accomplishing of goals. (2) Supplies and equipment must be available on hand or easily obtained after requisition. This is necessary if the transportation units (buses) are to operate in an efficient and dependable manner. Also, personnel must be indoctrinated with supply economy in order to reduce waste, deterioration, and theft. (3) Personnel which make up the Transportation Team must be present in order that the transportation function be carried out, and replacement personnel must be available. The transportation program cannot afford to terminate itself if certain members of the team are no longer available. (4) Budgetary and fiscal matters are the key to the entire transportation operation. Without funds, the service could not be offered to the community's school children. Budget and fiscal matters create the possibility of the school system being able to acquire supplies and equipment and personnel.

Accomplishing transportation goals has been discussed throughout this section. The Transportation Director and his/her Transportation Team should use the following steps in reaching the goals presented to them:

1. Establish and define the goal.
2. Establish how the Transportation Team and/or segments of the Team will attack the problem of meeting the goal in question plus an examination of available alternatives.
3. The Transportation Director will assign certain subordinate leaders and/or key personnel the authority to carry out the goal reaching plan.
4. Establishment of the logistical requirements and time projections needed to accomplish the goal.

Maintenance Personnel

The Maintenance Foreman is in charge of the overall program of keeping the buses operating in a safe and efficient manner. He/she is also charged with maintaining each transportation unit so that it is dependable, operates at a peak performance level and that the unit has the possibility to obtain the maximum life allowed by federal and state regulations.

Also, the Maintenance Foreman will be in charge of operating a more-than-adequate program of maintenance and preventive maintenance to be followed by both his/her section mechanics and bus drivers. Excellent leadership and management must be demonstrated by the Maintenance Foreman in order to present a successful program and meet the secondary goals of the transportation operation.

Transportation Unit Operators (Bus Drivers)

The bus drivers are the heartbeat of the transportation operation. However, without proper leadership and management procedures, the heartbeat can cease. It is important that morale be high among all transportation personnel, but especially the drivers. Proper leadership and management as it concerns drivers will come primarily from the Dispatcher and also from the Route Master, the Assistant Director and the Director.

Drivers also need to cooperate with the mechanics concerning vehicle maintenance problems and servicing. Cooperation is needed concerning the Dispatcher's assignment to vehicles and routes. Coordination and cooperation is needed with the route master concerning route changes, deletions, hazards, etc.

The Assistant Director of Transportation

This particular administrator (recommended for large systems) should have the same qualifications as that of the Director and also be knowledgeable of the entire transportation operation. The Assistant Director needs to have the authority to:

1. Act as Chief of Staff for the Transportation Administrative Team and provide guidance and direction to the group. This should be done in accomplishing of the team's secondary goals and its overall goal.
2. The Assistant Director, in addition to serving as the Chief of Staff for departmental administrative team, should supervise the maintenance and parts sections. Involvement in these duties would free the Transportation Director to more adequately oversee the dispatching and routing operations. Such action would allow the Director to carry out a more effective liaison with the superintendent, central office personnel, and the community.

The Routing Process

The route is considered to be an established or previously selected course of travel. In relationship to pupil transportation, the action of prior establishment or preselection of bus routes should be guided by board of education policy. However, if the local board of education has no policy concerning transportation routing, then it is imperative that such policy be established.

Overall objectives should be presented in the local policy as it relates to the routing process. There is a need for a determined effort to be demonstrated in the attempt to accomplish the overall objectives. These overall objectives or goals should encompass the following:

1. An Adequate Program of Time Conservation
   The conserving of time will allow for minimum driving time on planned routes and less frequency of established stops. Time must also be considered in allowing the student minimum riding time to and

from school. Time is also thought of when maximum load is achieved on the shortest distance possible.

The conserving of time can lead to the reduction of costs in the operation of school district's transportation operation. The master plan of Director of Transportation is to provide an economical and a minimum time consumption service of bus transport. A routing plan that offers pupils the quickest routes from home to school and from school to home will most likely be the most economical plan.

2. The Offering of a Quality Service

Quality service is brought about by the adequacy of transportation units (buses) available and on reserve. Transportation units should be adequate in number to meet the demands brought about by pupil loads; pupil residential location; time spent in transit; and an adequate number of seats so that *no child* stands enroute to his/her destination.

3. Maximum Safety of the Transportation Program

The establishment of a bus routing system should also be a part of the overall safety program. External input from law enforcement agencies; county, municipal and state road agencies; and daily weather reports as they relate to projected and actual road conditions can play a definite role in the establishment of routing systems. These factors can also call for route alterations that are temporary or permanent in nature.

Minimum Cost Operation

Minimum cost operation is one of the primary goals of the Transportation Director. The routing process can play a very important role here by providing the proper asphalt or concrete carpet for a quick and efficient flow of the pupil home-school-home transporting effort. The placing of bus stops on the route can be a determining factor in the amount and cost of gasoline consumption. The further between stopping points the greater the amount of gasoline saved which in turn saves money in the overall transportation budget.

Route Establishment

The establishment of the transportation routing system is guided by the following factors:

1. Pupil Population Patterns
2. Pupil Stratification as Determined by Grade Level
3. Number of School Buildings to be Served

 4. School Building Stratification as Determined by Grade Level
 5. Placement of Bus Stops as Required for Efficient, Quality and Timely Service

Pupil population patterns can be determined on a plastic overlay of the school district's map. Aids in establishing pupil records can be offered by pupil records or a computer printout concerning pupil residence. Records or computer printouts will also give the Transportation Director's staff information concerning the pupil's grade level and school of attendance. This information will allow the transportation staff to establish color codes for pupils, their grade level, and school of attendance. Manual determination can also be made on an overlay to concerning the residence, grade level status, school of attendance, bus stops and determination of the best and most efficient route to be used. The manual system can allow for alterations to meet any future challenges of the overall transportation system.

Computer systems can be programmed to establish the school district's routing system with its series of bus stops. The computerization of student records would allow for:

 1. Pupil identification
 2. Pupil residence
 3. Pupil grade level
 4. Pupil's school of attendance

Input can be placed concerning the selection of the most qualified routes and stops needed to provide the best service. If properly programmed by qualified personnel, route adjustments could also be made. School districts that are fortunate enough to have computer service should utilize it in their routing system. The computer could also aid in the scheduling process. Whether manual or computerized routing procedures are used, the establishment and maintaining of a routing map with overlay is needed to illustrate: (1) the overall routing system; (2) pupil population; (3) bus stops; and (4) schools of attendance.

 Other items to be considered in the selection of routes (whether manual or electronic) are:

 1. Consumption of time for pupil mounting and transit
 2. Traffic volume on proposed routes
 3. Population density
 4. Number of bus units available

Bus Stops

In regard to bus stop placement, care should be taken concerning two major points. They are:

1. Safety
2. Adequate distance between stops

Safety cannot be overstressed in the establishment of the bus stop. Pupils should congregate at a stop area than not only offers motorists a clear view of the area, but also clear views for observation of the area by residents. Observation by residents of the area can help minimize possible assaults on school children.

Adequate distance needs to be maintained between stops to allow savings in the area of fuel consumption, transmission, clutch and brake wear and tear. Adequate distance between stops will also allow savings in time. This action promotes a more adequate schedule of bus operation.

Scheduling

The act of scheduling involves two overall segments of the school transportation program. They are:

1. Time from dispatching to completion of service.
2. The physical position of a school bus on its particular route.

From the time the school bus is dispatched from the terminal to the completion of that particular bus' route, the scheduling process is in effect. During any given time while the dispatched bus is servicing its route, the bus should be at a particular point at a particular time. Adherence to the time schedule is a must for every driver. By multiplying the strict time adherence of each bus in the school district (to its particular route) allows for a product of overall efficiency in the transportation system. Such a synchronized operation allows the school district's transportation operation to reach a segment of its overall goal—the providing of an *effective service* of transportation.

Once a route has been established and the pick-up points have been determined, scheduling becomes more or less noncomplex in nature. There may be minor adjustments from one academic year to another. However, new routes or established routes with major adjustments are more complex in the process of establishing a time schedule. Before the beginning of the new academic year trial runs (outbound and inbound) at both morning and afternoon time periods should be carried out. These trial runs need to involve the actual stopping at the projected pupil pick-up points. A series of three trial runs should allow for an average to be established from (1) dispatching point; (2) to the various pupil points; and (3) the actual return to the bus terminal. Additional allowance in time should be made to compensate for projected inclement weather and unusually heavy traffic conditions.

Before the fall opening of the school year, parents of school children should receive a copy of their child's (or children's) bus schedule(s). Once the new school year commences, the schedule and the bus driver's log should be checked for adherence and adjustment if necessary. The driver needs to record the times of the various stops and return to the terminal over the first two weeks of school. This period of time will allow for constructing an average to compare with the schedule determined before the school term. The results of the first two weeks' actual operation will give the Transportation Director elasticity to make any needed adjustments. Parents and students must be notified concerning any schedule adjustments.

Once the schedule for each route has been established for the current year, the original copy should be filed with the Transportation Director, the driver, the dispatcher and the route master.

There is a need for policy to be formulated concerning the process of scheduling and the maintenance of the schedule one it is established. Such a policy would be the basis of referral. Maintenance of the schedule involves a dual obligation on both the part of the transportation department and the students who are the recipients of the service. A faithful attachment to the time schedule must be carried out by both parties (the transportation department and the student). Board of education policy should be formed concerning both transportation department and the student's obligation in regard to the time schedule.

MANAGING DRIVER PERSONNEL

Driver Selection

In the selection of school bus drivers, policy needs to be established concerning the following points:

1. A thorough examination of the applicant's driving record.
2. A police check to determine if any past criminal record exists.
3. A thorough examination of the applicant's references.
4. A medical examination of the applicant.
5. Maturity and judgment of the applicant.
6. Ability of the applicant to get along with children.
7. The ability of the applicant to satisfactorily drive a school bus during the training period.
8. The applicant's possession of proper driving license which allows school bus operation (this may vary from state to state).
9. The applicant must possess emotional stability and the ability to work with children.

Once the driver is hired, he/she needs to follow board policy that has been established concerning:

1. A neat and clean personal appearance.
2. No smoking on the bus or while carrying out transportation functions.
3. Dependability.
4. Refrain from profanity.
5. Refrain from alcohol, medication or drugs which may effect the driving process.

Transportation administrators must be very careful in the selection of driver personnel. The safety of the district's school children will heavily depend upon their judgments.

Driver Procedures

The driver is responsible for the bus assigned to him/her. As previously mentioned, policies which govern operation, maintenance, and specifications are controlled at three governmental levels:

1. Federal
2. State
3. Local Board of Education

Before operation of the vehicle, the driver needs to inspect the following items:

1. All mirrors for proper position. Adjust if necessary.
2. All fluid levels
   a. Engine oil
   b. Transmission—if automatic. Manual transmissions should be checked periodically by maintenance personnel and according to manufacturer's instructions
   c. Battery water level
   d. Brake fluid in master cylinder
3. Tire pressure
4. Tire wear
5. Lugs
6. Front door and door operation
7. Emergency doors and door operation
8. Tension of all belts
9. Ignition system
10. All lights and their various functions
11. Cleanliness (exterior and interior)
12. Horn

13. Windshield washers and wipers
14. Heaters, air conditioners and defrosters
15. Steering
16. Air pressure (if bus has air brakes)
17. Instrument panel
18. Emergency equipment
19. Leakages under the bus
20. Hood latch
21. Braking system (primary and emergency)

Any problems or defects should be written up and reported to the maintenance section of the Transportation Department. Coordination between the driver the maintenance section is a must. Driver-discovered problems should be taken care of immediately. The maintenance section should present the driver with a timetable and/or mileage check for services such as:

1. Filter changes
2. Oil change and chassis lubrication
3. Tune-ups
4. Tire rotation
5. Alignment
6. Coolant changes
7. Brake service
8. Manual transmission oil check and change
9. Differential oil check and change
10. Lubricant packings of wheel bearings

Everyday operation of the vehicle must be done in the right manner. Proper operation of manual and automatic transmissions is necessary. There is also a need for the correct procedures in engine operation at required revolutions-per-minute. Consultation of the manufacturer's owner's manual is needed to insure the correct r.p.m.'s at various shift levels.

Pupil Control on Buses

The bus driver must be the master of the vehicle and be given the authority to keep order. However, the bus driver should not be given the authority to punish children. The bus driver's zone of authority covers only the vehicle and its operation. He/she (the bus driver) is concerned only with the safe and efficient operation of the vehicle in question, plus the safety of the passengers. There is a need for coordination between the bus driver and the principal concerning pupil control. The driver should be given a Bus Conduct Report to fill out concerning individual pupil offenses, along with principal disposition of the cases concerned. Parents and pupils must be made to realize that the school transportation service is a privilege and not a right.

Driver coordination with the passengers can help with passenger control. However, we must realize that it is not a panacea. Driver-passenger coordination can be effective through:

1. Emphasis on safety.
2. The presenting of a positive image by the driver to his/her passengers.
3. Emphasizing the importance to abide by rules and regulations (both the driver and his/her passengers).
4. Making sure that all passengers follow the rules and regulations. Do not make exceptions.
5. Keeping your passengers up-to-date concerning rules, regulations and vehicle policies.
6. Direct action with trouble-makers on a private and one-to-one basis.
7. Be firm, but fair in the handling of all cases concerning passenger conflict.

Driver-Principal Coordination

The bus driver and the principal must coordinate not only concerning passenger control, but other areas concerning:

1. Bus routing on the school campus
2. Bus parking on the school campus
3. Bus mounting and dismounting procedures
4. Bus safety training

There is a need for a cooperative effort between the driver and the building administrator. Such action promotes a more safe and efficient service.

Radio Communication as a Means of Monitoring Vehicles and Passengers

The use of a two-way mobile radio with the school bus is a current operation in some school systems. The convenience of this operation allows a closer tie between the bus driver and his/her dispatcher. With the increasing number of vehicles on the highways along with larger trucks, there is greater susceptibility toward accidents. Couple this situation with increased crime, terror and drug addiction in our schools, there is a need for maintaining a close electronic link between the driver, medical and law enforcement agencies. Another advantage of the use of radio in the school transportation system is that of allowing the dispatcher and route master to be aware (on a constant basis) of the time schedule keeping process. Through radio contact transportation administrators are able to find out the physical location of a particular bus at a moment's notice. Another benefit of the two-way radio is that the driver can be readily made aware to maintain the schedule.

In the process of selecting two-way mobile radios for the buses and the base unit for bus terminal use, adequate equipment should be obtained. The radio system selected must have the range to receive and transmit from and to the furthest point in the school district. Consideration must also be given to the climate and terrain of the school district.

Policy must be established along with FCC (Federal Communications Commission) guidelines concerning the use of radio equipment. Driver-radio operations must be informed that the FCC monitors the various circuits. Improper use of the radio can result in fines and penalties.

If radios are introduced into your transportation program, there will be a need for inservice training of all transportation personnel. Once radio procedural knowledge is gained by the transportation section as a whole, new employees will have to be trained.

Local board of education policy concerning radio operation within the transportation department should include the following areas:

1. Remember the bus drivers must share the air waves with others. Transmissions must be for official business only.
2. No personal messages will be allowed for transmission.
3. No profanity can be used on the air waves.
4. Mobile radios will be connected so that they will have the ability to receive and transmit whether the master ignition is on or off (use of a radio master power switch).
5. Drivers must turn off all power switches on bus radios at the end of operation.
6. Do not operate the radio when the bus is in motion. Both hands are needed on the wheel.
7. All transmissions are to be impersonal in nature. Codes should be used for each transportation unit (bus and driver).
8. All drivers and radio operators at the bus terminal will have a knowledge of the phonetic alphabet.
9. The school system and its personnel will have the proper federal licensing for radio operation.

Another electronic device that is available is the radio controlled bus arrival system. A transmitter is placed upon the bus which sends out an electronic signal which activates a receiver signal system within the home. This signal notifies parents and students that the bus is located within a certain distance and traveling time to their particular bus stop.

The mobile radio and the school bus make an effective and important team, therefore, giving the transportation staff convenience of operation. There is a need for the school district to enhance its effectiveness through electronic communication.

THE SCHOOL BUS MAINTENANCE PROGRAM

In administration of the board of education's transportation department's maintenance program, the overall goal of the program is:

> To provide that mechanical service which is needed to keep all vehicles operational at top level efficiency. Also, to establish a secondary program of preventive maintenance (which involves those periodic services to the vehicular stock which will minimize future problems in mechanical operation).

In order that a maintenance program be carried out properly, there must be a line of two-way communication between supervisory personnel, drivers, and mechanics. Each employee involved with the vehicular stocks must follow the maintenance policy and coordinate with others involved.

The Director of Transportation must observe the following elements of the transportation department's maintenance section and correct any deficiencies which may arise.

1. The Maintenance Foreman — This individual should be considered the top administrator of the maintenance section. He/she needs to coordinate with the Director of Transportation concerning the objective and the needs of the maintenance program. He/she will assist the Director of Transportation in formulating and adjusting maintenance policy. The Maintenance Foreman must classify the vehicular stock according to age and condition. The Maintenance Foreman needs to have knowledge of how the previously mentioned factors relate to the assignment of the number of vehicles to each mechanic. Newer buses will usually require less mechanical attention than transportation units with considerable age and mileage. The total number of buses plus their condition (according to age and mileage) will determine the overall number of mechanics to keep the vehicles in running order. Experience is the major factor here concerning the mechanic to buses ratio.

2. Another element is that of the quality of maintenance personnel. Some boards of education have been guilty of hiring unqualified "shade tree" type mechanics to service their transportation stock. Such practice may save money in early returns, but could possibly have grave and delayed repercussions at future dates. A mechanic that is not properly trained to meet the challenges and skills required to service the everchanging internal combustion engine, electrical systems, and gearing systems could well be a liability.

The transportation department must seek properly trained mechanics and be willing to pay the wages required for that particular skill. Additional inservice training must be offered to the maintenance staff to keep abreast of annual model changes. These changes will require internal mechanical servicing once the manufacturer's warranties expire.

Other personnel involved in the maintenance section are tool parts and supply clerks. These individuals must be masters in inventory procedures, inventory control, requisitions, purchases and record keeping.

Mechanic's helpers are individuals that are assigned non-mechanical tasks such as oil changing, lubrication, tire changes and repair, gas pump service, etc. These individuals should receive additional training to later become mechanics.

3. Time is a critical element which makes demands in its consumption concerning the taking of transportation units out of service, repairing them and placing them back into service. Improper use of time can cause backlogging and a shortage of operational units. Time must also be considered in pulling in buses for periodically scheduled maintenance without creating a shortage of operational units.

4. Repair parts—The parts clerk is the key person in providing the maintenance section with adequate reserves of various types of parts that are needed to keep the buses operational. He/she (the parts clerk) must work with an established system for inventory control (through policy) to make sure that an adequate number of parts are always available. The parts clerk must also establish a system of security through inventory (created by policy) and security devices to prevent theft of various parts by internal and external personnel.

5. Tools and equipment—The tool clerks must have an established system (through policy) for the recording of tool and equipment dispensing to mechanical personnel. Here again a system (through policy) is needed to allow for security measures. The cost of tools and equipment are in the high bracket range, and care must be taken against losses and theft.

6. Adequate sized repair shops are needed to house repair and servicing operations of the maintenance staff. The size of such a facility will depend upon the number of buses owned by the school board, and the projected number of buses to be used in future years. Such facilities must meet the needs not only of the buses, but of the personnel working in the facility.

7. The keeping of maintenance publications (manufacturers' publications and internal transportation department publications) is a necessity. Such publications must be kept current and obsolete materials removed on a periodic basis. Manufacturers' publications (General Motors, Ford Motor Company, Chrysler Corporation, International Harvester, Inc., etc.) are usually issued annually or when alterations are made within a model year.

Board of education transportation publications regarding maintenance may also change at any time.

8. Record keeping—Maintenance and driver personnel must be instructed to be knowledgeable of record keeping and of its importance. Records must be kept concerning vehicle inspection (daily) by the drivers and periodically by the maintenance staff. Records must be kept regarding periodic services, troubleshooting and actual services and repairs.

A top flight program of maintenance involves the entire transportation department. The Transportation Director and his/her administrative staff plus the drivers and mechanics must adhere to the various record forms and record-keeping procedures. Records are a basis and a means of referral upon which the transportation department's maintenance program operates.

The maintenance program of the transportation department should operate on three distinct levels. They are:

1. Level 1 Vehicle Maintenance—Which involves the maintenance and preventive maintenance functions performed by the driver. These include the checking of all fluid levels; tire and tire pressure; instrument panel operation; mirror focusing; operation of all doors; light operation; braking operations; and odometer readings. Any other mechanical malfunctions will also be reported at this level to the maintenance section.

2. Level 2 Vehicle Maintenance—This particular level of maintenance and preventive maintenance such as oil changes, lubrication, tune-ups and the repairing of various mechanical functions of the vehicle performed at transportation department level.

3. Level 3 Vehicle Maintenance—Maintenance and preventive maintenance at this level is performed by agencies external to the board of education. Reason here may be the transportation department's inability to handle a particular phase of maintenance or the desire to contract a particular phase to external organizations.

Evaluation of the School Transportation Program

Once a particular program is established, evaluation becomes a constant process. It allows the administration to study the program's effectiveness. The transportation program is a service offered to the students of the district. Primary factors that must be observed in the operation of the transportation program are:

1. Efficiency of operation
2. Economy of operation
3. Safety record of the transportation operation

4. Proper coordination of the transportation service within the district's overall program of instruction.

Operating an economical transportation program that is also efficient is not an easy undertaking. The coupling the previously mentioned items along with safety and proper coordination with the school district's curricular obligation is indeed a task to be reckoned with. However, it is not impossible and should be the aim of every board of education operated program of transportation.

Economy of operation will be reflected in the cost per pupil per mile computation. Other segments of the evaluation of the organization and its operation can be derived from an evaluation of the transportation department's service and its personnel. Evaluations made by the following segments can readily present an overall view of the transportation operation. Evaluation can be made of the transportation operation by the:

1. Superintendent
2. Central Office Staff (Including the Director of Instruction)
3. Building Level Administrators
4. The Transportation Director
5. Students
6. The Community
7. The Transportation Staff

The sum total of the above-mentioned segments would provide a respectable view of the status of the overall transportation operation.

Evaluation of transportation personnel could be made on a trident approach toward each member of the transportation department. A trident-like evaluation would be made by each transportation employee's:

1. Superior
2. Peers
3. Subordinates

An evaluation of this nature would give a 360° coverage of each transportation employee. This type of an evaluation shows the employee a portrayal of his/her work as perceived by employees assigned to three different levels.

Periodic presentation of evaluations of the transportation program should be given monthly, quarterly and annually concerning cost and organization of program operations. Periodic evaluation concerning transportation personnel should be given once a year. An overall evaluation of the transportation service should also be given once a year.

A study of the various transportation evaluations will allow the Superintendent and the Transportation Director to make adjustments. These adjustments will add to or delete from the current method of operation. Adjustments will involve cost of operation, personnel and organization.

Evaluations of the board of education's transportation service are essential. Such evaluation must be used to insure a service that has both quality and low cost operation.

Summary

A properly maintained pupil transportation program is of necessity to many school districts. This particular need is magnified in rural and suburban school districts. City and metropolitan school districts also have a need for the transporting of pupils when there is considerable distance from student residences to the school. The transporting of the handicapped to and from the school (whether rural, urban or suburban) places a need for special transportation equipment in order to provide for an efficient service. An economical and quality transportation service is an essential aid to the instructional program.

Key central office administrators that are usually involved in the district level transportation program are the:

1. Director of Transportation
2. Route Master
3. Dispatcher (Driver Supervisor)
4. Maintenance Foreman

Smaller school districts may require less administrative personnel to direct a program of transportation. Therefore, transportation business is usually carried on with fewer administrators, and it may well be an additional duty of the superintendent.

Coordination has to be maintained between the transportation office (through its driver personnel) and individual school principals regarding pupil discipline and control aboard the buses. Safety cannot be sacrificed for student disruption.

Another point of administrative concern surrounding the school transportation program is the maintenance of school buses. Three goals are sighted here. They are:

1. Safety.
2. Proper operation.
3. Extending the life of the school bus unit.

Drivers and maintenance personnel must cooperate and take part in an established bus maintenance program.

CHAPTER XIV.

FOOD PREPARATION AND MASS FEEDING

SUPERVISION OF THE FOOD SERVICE OPERATION

One will find that school lunch programs are divided into two distinct methods of operations. One such method of operation if the contracted food service program in which the breakfast and/or lunch offering is prepared and transported to the schools by a private catering firm (or the preparation phase will take place on school property). Realization must be made here that such a food contracting organization operates by the profit motive. Also, there is a preset margin of profit which can cause frequent and/or great escalations (as allowed by contract and negotiations for new contracts) in breakfast and lunch serving unit prices. Another method of operation is the lunch and breakfast program—offering by a food service unit organic to the public school district. Food servicing operations of this type are not operated for a profit. The goal of the organic food operation is nonprofit with only a revenue adequate to meet expenses.

Guidance for the administration of the school district's food service program will be that of policy formulated by:

1. The local board of education
2. The state department of education
3. The local department of health
4. The state department of health
5. The United States Department of Agriculture

The overall goals of the school district's food serving program (reinforced by policy) should be:

1. To offer both a breakfast and lunch service to every child (regardless of socioeconomic class) of the school district.
2. Sole and direct responsibility for the school food service operation should be given to a central office administrator (Director of Cafeteria Services).
3. The school district food service program must promote nutrition and health for its students.
4. The food service operation should offer both attractive and nutritional meals.

5. Menu planning duties should be carried out by the Director of Cafeteria Services and a food service committee (consisting of students, teachers, administrators and food service personnel).
6. All sanitation procedures and health department regulations concerning food serving facilities and personnel will be strictly adhered to.
7. All financial procedures regarding food service operations will be strictly adhered to.
8. Classification and formulation of school district recipe and menu directory.
9. Adherence to school district recipe directory.
10. Development and compliance with a covert (so as not to embarrass needy school children) free breakfast and lunch procedure.
11. Compliance with food purchasing procedures.

The Director of Cafeteria Services

All school districts are in need of an administrator to operate their food service programs. Regardless of organizational format as it concerns food service, there are certain responsibilities that must be carried out. Policy formulated at the local, state and federal levels will form the foundation from which to operate.

Qualifications of the Director of Cafeteria Services should involve the following factors:

1. Being a trained dietitian.
2. Having knowledge and experience in the establishment of a master menu for large organizations.
3. Having a knowledge of food service equipment, its upkeep and purchasing procedures.
4. Having a knowledge of food classification, purchasing and preparation procedures.
5. Ability to project food costs and food inflation.
6. Having a knowledge and experience of mass food preparation and feeding procedures.
7. Having the ability to train and work with food service personnel.
8. Having the knowledge to deal with food service unions, grievances and collective negotiations.

Duties of the Director of Cafeteria Services will include:

1. Review, alteration and the construction of a food service policy.
2. Evaluation of the overall and individual school dining operations.
3. Supervises the maintenance and purchasing of kitchen equipment and purchasing of needed supplies.

4. Supervises the fiscal and record keeping operation of the overall food service operation.
5. Supervises the purchases of all foodstuffs.
6. Develops procedures to eliminate overages and waste of foodstuffs.
7. Maintains a property register book of all food service equipment.
8. Enforces supply economy.
9. Directs inventory procedures for dining equipment and supplies.
10. Promotes efficiency and operation of the district's dining operation.
11. Establishes and supervises inservice training for food service employees.
12. Supervises the food service personnel program.
13. Supervision of the food service sanitation program.
14. Supervision of the food service safety program.
15. Overall responsibility for the annual master menu.
16. Responsible for food service evaluation.
17. Seeks to improve the district's food service operation through innovation, new equipment, new procedures, new methods of food preparation and labor saving procedures.

The board of education and the superintendent must allow the Director of Cafeteria Services the authority that is needed to operate a highly successful program. He/she (the Director of Cafeteria Services) must be given latitude to apply innovative procedures which can allow more economy and efficiency in service.

Safety and Sanitary Procedures

Safety and sanitation are features that cannot be overstressed. Adherence to safety procedures lessens the likelihood of accidents taking place. Preventive procedures can well weigh on the side of the school administration in possible tort liability situations.

Safety practices should be promoted regarding the following areas:

1. Keeping all poisons and flammable mixtures out of the food preparation area.
2. Cleaning the floors to clear them of slippery substances and unauthorized items.
3. Establishment of incoming and outgoing routes in order to prevent collisions and falls.
4. Establishment of proper procedures to prevent scaldings and burns from cooking utensils, stoves, dishwashers and steam tables.
5. Establishment of proper procedures in the handling of knives, slicing and cutting machines. Also installation and use of safety guards on all automated and manual cutting devices.

6. Making sure that all fire extinguishers are in working order and are periodically inspected.
7. Keeping water away from electrical appliances and electrical cords.
8. Make sure all electrical switch boxes are closed during operations. All switch boxes should be secured during off-duty hours.
9. Daily removal of grease collection in exhaust systems, grease pans, cooking ranges and other areas in order to prevent possible fire hazards.
10. Prompt clean up all spillages on floors, counters or other areas.
11. The wearing of gloves is necessary when working with wooden crates, metals, etc.
12. The wearing of thermal gloves is necessary when working with hot articles.
13. Cutting off power on all electrical appliances when not in use.
14. Shut down of all natural gas appliances when not in use.
15. Shut down of master power switch (except refrigeration and freezing units) at the end of the working day.
16. Purchase and use of "walk in" refrigeration and freezing storage spaces that can be opened and closed internally.
17. Strict adherence to procedures constructed to prevent food spoilage and food poisoning.

Sanitary measures like safety measures also cannot be overstressed. Improper sanitation practices can lead to mass illnesses or even deaths. Contamination of foodstuffs can come about by:

1. Faulty or improper procedures of personal hygiene by food service personnel. There is a need for:
   a. Pre-employment and annual medical examinations
   b. Hair net procedures
   c. Hand washing procedures
   d. Daily inspection of all food service personnel
   e. Daily wearing of a clean service uniform
2. Proper sanitization and cleaning of food processing and storage equipment.
3. Daily removal of all garbage and cleaning plus disinfecting of waste receptacles.
4. Use of first in first out procedure in order to keep food inventory at maximum freshness.
5. Daily cleaning and disinfecting of complete food service area.
6. Daily sanitization of all dishes, eating and cooking utensils.
7. Extermination of bacteria, insects, rodents and fungus through healthfully accepted procedures.

All supervisory and working personnel must adhere to safety and sanitary policies established by the state and local health departments, the board of education and the Director of Cafeteria Services. Those supervisors and working personnel that do not see fit to enforce or practice these policies should be released from the employ of the food service division. Noncompliance to sanitary and safety policies can place the school district and its employees in a precarious position concerning possible tort liability.

Personnel Requirements of the Food Service Operation

Those subordinate supervisory and working personnel employed in the school district's food service program should be charged with specific responsibilities. School districts maintaining a centralized food service program will have supervisory personnel and food service workers located in a central location. Decentralized supervisors and workers will be situated at school buildings located throughout the district, possibly having a greater number of total employees than the centralized organization. Personnel that should be found in either a decentralized or centralized kitchen operation are:

1. The cafeteria manager (decentralized) or food center manager (centralized). This individual bears the overall responsibility of his/her specific food preparation center (centralized or decentralized). The cafeteria of food center manager is not only responsible for food preparation, safety and sanitary procedures, but also for personnel matters in his/her zone of operation. The main duties performed by the cafeteria or food center manager are:
   a. Preparation of the cooks' menu duties from the master menu.
   b. Prepares weekly or monthly announcements concerning the monthly or weekly menu for presentation to students, parents and mass media units (such as local newspapers, local radio and television stations).
   c. Supervision of the entire preparation, cooking and serving process.
   d. Inspection of the prepared ready-to-serve meal.
   e. Takes care of all fiscal and record keeping matters related to the food service operation.
   f. Supervises portion control.
   g. Projects daily headcount. Uses past records and current eating population in projections.
   h. Records pupil attitudes (positive and negative) to each menu. This data can be used in future meal preparations and will help to eliminate waste and shortages.

   i. Supervises proper storage of unprepared food.

   j. Supervises proper storage of leftovers and their disposition.

   k. Coordinates with and keeps the central office Director of Cafeteria Services abreast of his/her unit's operation.

   l. Daily inspection regarding cleanliness and personal hygiene of subordinate personnel.

   m. Plans procedures for the cooking unit's personnel.

   n. Coordinates daily with the cooking unit staff regarding status of overall operation.

   o. Supervises and enforces the cooking unit's safety and sanitation program.

   p. Oversees the security of the kitchen unit.

   q. Supervises the flow of the serving line (applicable to the decentralized unit).

   r. Inspects and determines the layout of the serving area (applicable to the decentralized unit).

   s. Checks the operating status of all food service equipment.

   t. Checks the availability of all food service supplies.

2. First Class Cooks

    Cooks that have five or more years of experience should be classified as first class cooks. These individuals have the responsibility of preparation and supervision of the entire daily menu. First class cooks will also assign preparation and cooking duties of the daily menu to subordinate food service personnel. The first class cook evaluates the preparation, the cooking process, the finished menu and the consumer response to the daily menu.

3. Second Class Cooks

    Second class cooks are those individuals with less than five years experience as cooks. The second class cook is actively involved in food preparation and cooking process. The following of recipes, cooking procedures and the daily menu are the second class cook's duties. He/she also supervises the work of the subordinate cook's helper. The second class cook will evaluate food preparation, the cooking process and the work of the cook's helper.

4. The Cook's Helper

    The cook's helper position should be at entry level for personnel coming into the employ of the school food service program. A period of three years work as a cook's helper should be required before promotion to second class cook. The cook's helper will be supervised by both the first and second class cooks. His/her duties will consist mainly of food preparation such as inspecting, sorting, washing, paring, etc. Additional duties should be in the storage and inventory of foodstuff items, plus the cleaning and care of the various items of kitchen equipment.

5. Baker

The title of baker applies to the cook that has the special talent of preparing pastry items such as:

   a. Breads
   b. Rolls
   c. Cakes
   d. Pies
   e. Cookies
   f. Puff pastries
   g. Puddings and fillings

The baking process should be separate from the daily cooking preparation. Supervision of the baking process should be assigned to the cafeteria or food service manager.

The daily preparation of bakery products should start very early in the day. The bakers and the baker's helpers could operate on a 12 midnight to 8:00 a.m. shift. This would allow for the preparation of the daily pastry requirement for the breakfast and lunch meals. Time would also be allowed for cleaning chores after completion of the baking process.

Bakers would be responsible for the overall daily preparation of bakery products. The senior baker would be responsible for determining the daily needs (of ingredients for the baking process) and the supervision of the overall baking operation. He/she (the senior baker) should also determine baking personnel duties and assignments.

6. Baker's Helper

The baker's helper should assist the bakers in the mixing process, weighing and shaping of various types of dough, pan preparation, oven loading and supervision, pudding and filling preparation, storage room duties, and the cleaning plus servicing of the bakers' equipment.

Types of Food Service Facilities

Public school food service offers two types of facilities for breakfast and lunch programs. They are:

1. The decentralized kitchen
2. The centralized kitchen

The decentralized kitchen set-up which is found in many schools throughout the nation involves the kitchen facility located within the individual school building. The building level cafeteria manager will administer food service, food preparation, and personnel for that particular building.

Some primary advantages of the decentralized kitchen are:

1. Close coordination between the cafeteria manager and the building level administrator.
2. Close coordination between the cafeteria manager and the student body as it related to evaluation of food offerings and participation in menu planning.
3. Close coordination between the food service manager and the small building level food service staff.
4. Easier adjustment to portion control problems.
5. Close supervision of safety and sanitary procedures.

Some primary disadvantages of the decentralized kitchen are:

1. High labor costs due to the need of more personnel requirements than the centralized system.
2. Increased equipment costs due to more units needed to cover each school building in the system.
3. Increased costs for energy used in food preparation at each individual school.
4. More opportunity for waste.

The centralized kitchen unit provides for the preparation of breakfast and lunch meals at a centrally located facility or regionalized facilities. Foods are then transported to each school building in the school district.

Some advantages of the centralized food service operation are:

1. Reduced labor costs
2. Reduced energy cost and consumption
3. Reduced equipment costs
4. Greater overall efficiency and economy in food processing and preparation.

Some primary disadvantages for the centralized kitchen are:

1. Increased costs due to food delivery (to individual schools) and delivery personnel.
2. Increased problems in sanitation due to delivery and additional handling of food.
3. Increased cost due to the purchase of thermal equipment and thermal insulated vehicles for food transportation.
4. Portion control problems and adjustments.
5. Nonadherence to menu adjustments.
6. Nonadherence to ethnic or religious food serving situations (in individual school settings).

7. Effects of inclement weather and traffic problems to the delivery process and the individual school serving schedule.

The selection of the decentralized or centralized food operation is left to the discretion of the Director of Cafeteria Services, the superintendent, and the local board of education. Detailed planning is needed to determine the type of kitchen operation that best meets the district's needs. Also, efficiency and economy must be considered in such a decision. The decision to place the entire school district under a decentralized or centralized plan should not be taken until the evaluation of a pilot program has been undertaken.

PLANNING AND FOOD PREPARATION

Food Purchasing Practices

Federal, state and local policies and procedures must be adhered to in the food purchasing procedure. There is a need for specifications in the purchasing of the various food classifications. Specifications are important in regards to quality, nutrition, serving portions, taste and appearance. Classifications of the various food items to be purchased are:

1. Meat, poultry and seafoods
2. Fresh and frozen vegetables
3. Rice and paste products
4. Condiments
5. Dairy products
6. Flour and milling products
7. Spices
8. Fresh and frozen fruits
9. Canned products
10. Frozen meats, poultry, and seafood

Foods are perishable and there must be carefully projected figures regarding probable headcounts and intensity of consumption. In reference to the annual master menu, purchases may be further broken down into quarterly, monthly, weekly and daily periods of time (according to perishability).

Purchasing in the food service operation considers not only foodstuffs, but working supplies and equipment. Board of education and state bidding laws may have considerable effect upon the purchasing process in this area. Standardization and specifications could well apply here.

Consideration must be taken concerning the perishability of foods and the schedule under which they are purchased. The classification used here could be as follows:

1. High risk foods
   a. Fresh and frozen seafoods
   b. Fresh meats
   c. Fresh fruits
   d. Fresh vegetables
   e. Fresh poultry
2. Medium risk foods
   a. Frozen fruits, vegetables and meats
   b. Dried fruits, vegetables and meats
3. Low risk foods
   a. Canned fruits, vegetables and meats
   b. Staple items

Purchasing schedules should be determined according to (1) time of need as required by the master menu and (2) perishability. Before the actual bidding and purchasing of various food items, there is a need to test the quality of the items offered by food jobbers. Evaluation of the food items can help to determine if the school district should offer the particular food item for consumption.

Preparation, Serving and General Classification of Foods

The planning of the master menu should be one year in advance. The Director of Cafeteria Service and the menu planning committee should have the master menu ready before the beginning of the new fiscal year. The projected purchasing schedule should also be planned before the beginning of the fiscal year. The master menu must provide foods and preparation processes that offer the proper nutritional requirements. Daily preparation by cooks and bakers will require:

1. Starting time for the cooking or baking operation
2. Estimate of time consumption required for daily meal preparation and bakery production
3. Selection of proper recipes
4. Estimated portions to be served
5. Estimated size of portions to be served
6. Preparation of serving area
7. Method of serving to be used

Foods to be served throughout the academic year should be generally classified as follows:

1. Bakery items
   a. Breads

    b. Dinner rolls
    c. Puff pastries
    d. Cakes
    e. Cookies
    f. Pies
    g. Breakfast rolls
2. Beverages
3. Salads
4. Vegetables
5. Meat
6. Poultry
7. Seafood products
8. Soups
9. Paste products
10. Dairy products
11. Appetizers
12. Condiments
13. Seasonings
14. Ice creams, sherbets, yogurt, frozen or chilled desserts

Food Service Projections

Food service operations in the nation's school has brought forth problems of student waste of food; student refusal of standard meal preparations; increased costs of individual meal offerings; presentation of the breakfast program; contracting of food service operations; and the introduction of meals and beverages contrary to past nutritional policies. We could add factors such as union organization of food service employees and the inflationary bloating of food prices as the primary causes of increased costs.

The above-mentioned items will have a great effect on the school food service program in future years. There is also the possibility of less student demand for food services due to decreasing enrollments and less attraction to food offerings by children. The future could hold drastic changes in school operated food services. Fiscal demands, because of increased costs and the public clamor for decreased spending of public funds, could well cause drastic changes in food service operations. Public pressure on boards of education, state legislatures and the United States Congress could well effect governmental support for school feeding programs.

THE FISCAL ASPECTS OF THE SCHOOL LUNCH PROGRAM

School food service will involve a considerable amount of time that must be devoted to the task of financial management. Segments that make up a part of the financial management of the food service program are:

1. The food service budget
2. Payroll preparation for food service personnel
3. Foodstuffs purchasing
4. Equipment purchasing
5. Supply purchasing
6. Average daily individual meal preparations.
7. Actual daily meals purchases
8. Actual daily free meals served to impoverished children
9. Cafeteria cash register receipts
10. Books of account
11. Food service forms and records.

Methods of accounting and record form style and demands are guided by local, state, and federal requirements. Keeping an almost constant vigil upon the food service financial scene is a necessary task by food service administrative and supervisory personnel.

There is also a demand for a cost analysis study of the food service operation at the individual school and of the overall school district. The primary aim of the school district cafeteria program is to serve a nutritious and attractive meal at minimum cost. The almost constant rise in food prices plus the increases in equipment, supplies and labor make for a difficult procedure to hold meal costs down.

Procedures which should be carried out in regard to the fiscal portion of the food service program are:

1. Calculation of the mean figure for daily servings (for both breakfast and lunch) at individual schools and the school district as a whole.

2. Completion of accounting for daily cash receipts.

3. Completion of accounting for daily free meals.

4. Arrange for daily pickup or administrative delivery of cash receipts to a local bank.

5. Keep accurate record of cash disbursements (by check) for purchases and food brokers.

Reports for the food service operation will vary somewhat from state to state and from district to district. Some of the basic reports that may be found at the local school district level are:

1. Master menu cost form.
2. Requisition forms for purchases of foodstuffs.
3. Requisition forms for equipment and supply items.
4. Food inventory sheets for individual schools, food preparation center, and food storage centers.
5. Milk accounting form.
6. Daily total food purchases.
7. Free meal distribution.
8. Total head counts for individual school and school district.
9. Periodic total food service report (breakfast, lunch, milk, and other programs) for state and federal units.
10. Payroll and wage reports for food service employees.

Summary

School systems are becoming more involved in the serving of food to its student population. Within the past two decades some school districts have added a breakfast offering to the lunch effort. Any mass feeding operation calls for the need of proper administration by qualified personnel. In order that administrative directive be carried out, there must be adequate board of education policy.

The top central office administrator of a school food service program is the Director of Cafeteria Service. This individual must oversee the entire food service program in areas such as food purchases, food preparation, record keeping, financial management, personnel, and other food service logistical needs.

Food preparation practices in school districts are either:

1. Centralized or regionalized
2. Decentralized

Centralized or regionalized food preparation centers allow for massive processing and cooking of foods which are then shipped in thermal containers and vehicles to individual schools for serving.

Decentralized food preparation units are located within individual schools where the serving process is also undertaken. Regardless of the school districts' selection of meal preparation, safety and sanitary procedures must be adhered to. A food preparation unit opens the door to many types of dangers regarding safety and sanitation. Procedures to combat the negative aspects of these conditions should be formulated as policy; enforced by administrative and supervisory personnel; and adhered to by food service employees.

REFERENCES

CHAPTER I FOOTNOTES

[1] *United States Government Financial Accounting Classification and Standard Terminology for Local and State School Systems, Publication No. 73-118000.* Washington, D.C.: United States Department of Health, Education and Welfare, 1973, p. 194.
[2] Ibid.
[3] Ibid.

CHAPTER II FOOTNOTES

[1] *Collegiate-Webster's Ninth New Collegiate Dictionary.* Springfield, Massachusetts: G. & C. Merriam Company, 1983, p. 117.

CHAPTER III FOOTNOTES

[1] Alexander, Kern et al. *Public School Law: Cases and Materials.* St. Paul, Minnesota: West Publishing Co., 1969, p. 35.
[2] Ibid.
[3] United States v. Butler, 297 U.S. 1, 56 S Ct. 312 (1936).
[4] Helvering v. Davis, 301 U.S. 619, 57 S. Ct. 904 (1937).

CHAPTER IV FOOTNOTES

[1] *Collegiate-Webster's Ninth New Collegiate Dictionary.* Springfield, Massachusetts: G. & C. Merriam Company, 1983, p. 330.
[2] Ibid., p. 266.

CHAPTER V FOOTNOTES

[1] *The World Book Encyclopedia.* Chicago, Illinois: World Book, Inc., Volume 17, 1984, p. 4.

CHAPTER VII FOOTNOTES

[1] *The Random House College Dictionary.* New York: Random House, Inc., 1984, p. 10.
[2] *Tennessee Internal School Financial Management Manual.* Nashville: Tennessee State Department of Health, Education and Welfare, 1977, Section 11, pp. 185–197.

CHAPTER X FOOTNOTES

[1]United States Government, *Financial Accounting Classifications and Standard Terminology for Local and State School Systems.* Washington, D.C.: United States Department of Education, 1973, p. 194.

[2]Ibid., p. 194.

CHAPTER XI FOOTNOTES

[1]Wood v. Strickland, 95 S. Ct. 992 (Ark., 1975).

BIBLIOGRAPHY

Ackerman, Kenneth B. *Warehousing: A Guide for Both Users and Operators*, 1st ed. Washington, D.C.: Traffic Service Corp., 1977.

Adizes, Ichak. *How to Solve the Mismanagement Crisis.* Homewood, Illinois: Dow Jones—Irwin, 1979.

Alexander, Kern. *School Law.* St. Paul, Minnesota: West Publishing Co., 1980.

Alexander, Kern, and Jordan, K. F. *Constitutional Reform of School Finance.* Lexington, Massachusetts: Lexington Books, 1973.

Alexander, Kern et al. *Public School Law: Cases and Materials.* St. Paul, Minnesota: West Publishing Co., 1969.

American Association of School Administrators. *To Re-create a School Building: "Surplus" Space, Energy, and Other Challenges.* Arlington, Virginia: American Association of School Administrators, 1976.

Amey, Lloyd R. *Budget Planning and Control Systems.* Marshfield, Massachusetts: Pitman Publishing, 1979.

Anthony, William P. *Participative Management.* Reading, Massachusetts: Addison-Wesley Publishing Co., 1978.

Anthony, Robert N., and Reece, James S. *Accounting Principles*, 4th ed. Homewood, Illinois: R. D. Irwin, 1979.

Archer, Stephen H., et al. *Financial Management: An Introduction.* New York: Wiley, 1979.

Arkin, Herbert. *Handbook for Auditing and Accounting,* 2d ed. New York: McGraw-Hill, 1974.

Athearn, James L. *Risk and Insurance.* St. Paul: West Publishing Co., 1977.

Bakalis, Michael J. *A Strategy for Excellence: Reaching for New Standards in Education.* Hamden, Connecticut: Linnet Books, 1974.

Baker, Joseph J., and Peters, Jon S. *School Maintenance and Operation.* Danville, Illinois: The Interstate Press, 1963.

Baldridge, Victor, Deal, T. E., and Ancell, Mary Z., Editors. *Managing Change in Educational Organizations.* Berkeley, California: McCutchan Corp., 1975.

Ballou, Ronald H. *Business Logistics Management.* Englewood Cliffs, New Jersey: Prentice-Hall, Inc., 1973.

Banghart, F. W., and Trull, Albert. *Educational Planning.* New York: Macmillan, 1973.

Baron, George, Editor. *The Politics of School Government.* New York: Pergamon, 1981.

Barnes, Ronald E. *Learning Systems for the Future.* Bloomington, Indiana: Phi Delta Kappa Educational Foundation, 1972.

Barr, Rebecca, et al. *How Schools Work.* Chicago: University of Chicago Press, 1983.

Baxter, Carolyn, O'Leary, P. J., and Westoby, Adam, Editors. *Economics and Educational Policy.* New York: Longman, 1977.

Becker, Selwyn W., and Neuhouser, Duncan. *The Efficient Organization.* New York: Elsevier, 1975.

Benjamin, James J., et al. *Financial Accounting.* Dallas: Business Publications, 1975.

Bierman, Harold, and Drebin, A. R. *Financial Accounting: An Introduction,* 3d ed. Philadelphia: Saunders, 1978.

Bliss, Sam W. *Zero-Base Budgeting: A Management Tool for School Districts.* Chicago: Research Corporation of the Association of School Business Officials, 1978.

Brigham, Eugene F. *Financial Management: Theory and Practice,* 2d ed. Hinsdale, Illinois: Dryden Press, 1979.

Brooks, Kenneth W., et al. *From Program to Educational Facilities.* Lexington, Kentucky: Center for Professional Development, College of Education, University of Kentucky, 1980.

Brown, J. Douglas. *The Human Nature of Organizations.* New York: AMACOM, A Division of American Management Associations, 1973.

Burke, W. Warner, Editor. *The Cutting Edge, Current Theory and Practice in Organization Development.* LaJolla, California: University Associates, 1978.

Burrup, Percy B. *Financing Education in a Climate of Change,* 2d ed. Boston: Allyn & Bacon, 1977.

Bushnell, David S., and Rappaport, Donald, Editors. New York: Harcourt, Brace and Jovanovich, 1971.

Candoli, I. Carl, et al. *School Business Administration: A Planning Approach,* 3d ed. Boston: Allyn & Bacon, 1984.

Casey, Leo M. *School Business Administration.* New York: Center for Applied Research in Education, 1966.

Castetter, W. J. *The Personnel Function in Educational Administration,* 3d ed. New York: Macmillan, 1981.

Clubb, Jerome M., and Traugott, Michael W. *Using Computers.* Washington, D.C.: Division of Educational Affairs, American Political Science Association, 1978.

Cobb, Joseph J. *An Introduction to Educational Law for Administrators and Teachers.* Springfield, Illinois: Charles C. Thomas, Publisher, 1981.

Collegiate — Webster's Ninth New Collegiate Dictionary. Springfield, Massachusetts: G & C Merriam Company, 1983.

Conner, James E., and McVity, Richard L. *Educational Program Planning and Evaluation Handbook: A Systems Approach.* Washington, D.C.: National Support Services, 1974.

Constantin, J. A. *Principles of Logistics Management.* New York: Appleton-Century-Crofts, 1966.

Correa, Hector, Editor. *Analytical Models in Educational Planning and Administration.* New York: D. McKay Co., 1975.

Corwin, Ronald G., and Edelfelt, Roy A. *Perspectives on Organizations: The School as a Social Organization.* Washington, D.C.: American Association of Colleges for Teacher Education, Association of Teacher Educators, 1977.

Coyle, John J., and Bardi, Edward J. *The Management of Business Logistics,* 3d ed. St. Paul: West Publishing Co., 1984.

Dalin, Per. *Limits to Educational Change.* New York: St. Martin's Press, 1978.

David, Thomas G., and Wright, Benjamin, D., Editors. *Learning Environments.* Chicago: University of Chicago Press, 1975.

Delon, Floyd G. *School Officials and the Courts.* Arlington, Virginia: Educational Research Service, Inc., 1979.

DeRoche, Edward F., and Kaiser, J. T. *Complete Guide to Administering School Services.* West Nyack, New York: Parker Publishing Co., 1980.

Dow, Clista. *Lunchroom Waste: A Study of "How Much and How Come."* Mansfield Center, Connecticut: Creative Learning Press, 1978.

Educational Facilities Laboratories. *The Economy of Energy Conservation in Educational Facilities: A Report from the Educational Facilities Laboratories — Revised,* 2d ed. New York: Educational Facilities Laboratories, 1978.

England, Wilbur B., and Leenders, Michiel R. *Purchasing and Materials Management,* 6th ed. Homewood, Illinois: R. D. Irwin, 1975.

Erickson, Kenneth A., and Gmelch, Walter H. *School Management Teams: Their Structure, Function, and Operation.* Arlington, Virginia: Educational Research Service, 1977.

Farmer, Ernest M. *Pupil Transportation: The Essentials of Program Service.* Danville, Illinois: Interstate Printers & Publishers, 1975.

Fawcett, Claude W. *School Personnel Systems.* Lexington, Massachusetts: Lexington Books, 1979.

Fetyko, David F. *Financial Accounting: Concepts and Principles.* Boston, Massachusetts: Kent Publishing Co., 1980.

Fife, Dennis W. *Computer Software Management: A Primer for Project Management and Quality Control.* Washington, D.C.: U.S. Department of Commerce, National Bureau of Standards, 1977.

Flamholtz, Eric. *Human Resource Accounting.* Encino, California: Dickenson Publishing Co., Inc., 1974.

Frederick, Franz J. *Guide to Microcomputers.* Washington, D.C.: Association for Educational Communications and Technology, 1980.

Frederick, Len. *Fast Food Gets an "A" in School Lunch.* Boston: Cahness Books International, 1977.

French, Wendell L. *The Personnel Management Process: Human Resources Administration and Development,* 4th ed. Boston: Houghton Mifflin Co., 1978.

Garms, Walter I., et al. *School Finance: The Economics and Politics of Public Education.* Englewood Cliffs, New Jersey, 1978.

Gee, E. Gordon, and Sperry, David J. *Education Law and the Public Schools: A Compendum.* Boston: Allyn & Bacon, 1978.

Gellerman, Saul W. *The Management of Human Resources.* Hinsdale, Illinois: Dryden Press, 1976.

Getzels, J. W., et al. *Educational Administration as a Social Process: Theory Research and Practice.* New York: Harper & Row, 1969.

Gland, James R., and Wildey, Carl A. *Custodial Management Practices in the Public Schools.* Chicago: Research Corp. of the Association of School Business Officials, 1975.

Golembiewski, Robert T. *Public Budgeting and Finance: Readings in Theory and Practice,* 2d ed. Itasca, Illinois: F. E. Peacock Publishers, 1975.

Gonder, Peggy. *How Schools Can Save $: Problems and Solutions.* Arlington, Virginia: American Association of School Administrators, 1980.

Granof, Michael H. *Financial Accounting: Principles and Issues.* Englewood Cliffs, New Jersey: Prentice-Hall, 1977.

Greene, Mark R. *Risk and Insurance,* 4th ed. Cincinnati: South Western Publishing Co., 1977.

Grossman, Alvin. *Data Processing for Educators.* Chicago: Educational Methods, 1965.

Guthrie, James W., Editor. *School Finance Policies and Practices: The 1980's, A Decade of Conflict.* Cambridge, Massachusetts: Ballinger Publishing Co., 1980.

Hallack, Jacques. *Planning the Location of Schools: An Instrument of Educational Policy.* Paris: UNESCO International Institute for Educational Planning, 1977.

Hanson, Mark E. *Educational Administration and Organizational Behavior.* Boston: Allyn & Bacon, 1979.

Hawkins, Harold L. *Appraisal Guide for School Facilities,* 2d ed. Midland, Michigan: Pendell, 1977.

Helvering v. Davis, 301 U.S. 619, 57 S. Ct. 904 (1937).

Herman, Jerry J., and Hirsekow, Robert. *Administrator's Guide to School Construction, Remodeling and Maintenance.* West Nyack, New York: Parker Publishing Co., 1975.

Hill, Frederick W., and Colmey, James W. *School Business Administration in the Smaller Community.* Minneapolis: T. S. Denison, 1964.

Hobbs, James B., and Moore, Carl L. *Financial Accounting: Concepts, Valuation, Analysis,* 2d ed. Cincinnati: South-Western Publishing Co., 1979.

Hodel, Ross A. *A Guide to Operational Facility Planning.* Ph.D. Thesis: The Ohio State University, 1977.

Homonoff, Richard, and Mullins, David W. *Cash Management: An Inventory Control Limit Approach.* Lexington, Massachusetts: Lexington Books, 1975.

Houck, Lewis D. *A Practical Guide to Budgetary and Management Control Systems: A Functional and Performance Evaluation Approach.* Lexington, Massachusetts: Lexington Books, 1979.

Hoy, Wayne K., and Miskel, Cecil G. *Educational Administration: Theory, Research and Practice,* 1st ed. New York: Random House, 1978.

Hudgins, H. C., and Vacca, Richard S. *Law and Education: Contemporary Issues and Court Decisions.* Charlottesville, Virginia: Michie Co., 1979.

Jenson, Theodore J., and Clark, David L. *Educational Administration.* New York: Center for Applied Research in Education, 1964.

Johnson, James A., et al. *Introduction to the Foundations of American Education,* 3d ed. Boston: Allyn & Bacon, 1976.

Jones, J. William. *Budget-Finance Campaigns: You Can't Afford to Lose (National School Public Relations Association).* Arlington, Virginia: National School Public Relations Association, 1977.

Jones, Phillip E. *Comparative Education: Purpose and Method.* St. Lucia: University of Queensland Press, 1971.

Jordan, Kenneth F. *School Business Administration.* New York: Ronald Press Co., 1969.

Kaufman, Roger A. *Education System Planning.* Englewood Cliffs, New Jersey: Prentice-Hall, 1972.

Kimbrough, Ralph B., and Nunnery, Michael Y. *Educational Administration: An Introduction.* New York: Macmillan, 1976.

Kinder, J. *Decision Making in Public Education.* Austin, Texas: MESA Publications, 1978.

Kirp, D. L., and Yudof, M. G. *Educational Policy and the Law.* Berkeley, California: McCutchan Publishing Corp., 1974.

Knirk, Frederick G. *Designing Productive Learning Environments.* Englewood Cliffs, N.J.: Educational Technology Publications, 1979.

Kotschevar, Lendal H., and Terrell, Margaret E. *Food Service Planning: Layout and Equipment.* New York: Wiley, 1961.

Landy, Frank J., and Trumbo, Don A. *Psychology of Work Behavior,* rev. ed. Homewood, Illinois: Dorsey Press, 1980.

Lapati, Americo D. *Education and the Federal Government: A Historical Record.* New York: Mason-Charter, 1975.

Lee, Lamar, and Dobler, Donald W. *Purchasing and Materials Management,* 3d ed. New York: McGraw-Hill, 1977.

Leggett, Stanton, et al. *Planning Flexible Learning Places.* New York: McGraw-Hill Book Co., 1977.

Linn, Henry H. *School Business Administration.* New York: Ronald Press, 1956.

Martin, James. *Computer Data-Base Organization,* 2d ed. Englewood Cliffs, New Jersey: Prentice-Hall, 1977.

McCarty, Donald James, and Ramsey, Charles E. *The School Managers: Power and Conflict in American Public Education.* Westport, Connecticut: Greenwood Publishing Corp., 1971.

McConaughy, David. *Readings in Business Logistics.* Homewood, Illinois: Richard D. Irwin, Inc., 1969.

McGhehez, M. A., Editor. *Contemporary Issues in Education.* Topeka, Kansas: National Organization on Legal Problems of Education, 1979.

McGhehez, M. A., Editor. *School Law in a Contemporary Society.* Topeka, Kansas: National Organization on Legal Problems of Education, 1980.

Mehr, Robert I., and Cammack, Emerson. *Principles of Insurance,* 6th ed. Homewood, Illinois: R. D. Irwin, 1976.

Meyers, John L., and Donaho, Melvin W. *Get the Right Person for the Job.* Englewood Cliffs, New Jersey: Prentice-Hall, Inc., 1979.

Milstein, Mike M., and Belasco, James A., Editors. *Educational Administration and the Behavioral Sciences: A Systems Perspective.* Boston: Allyn & Bacon, 1973.

Mitchell, Herbert S. *School Accounting for Financial Management.* Danville, Illinois: The Interstate, 1964.

Mixon, Shirley R. *Handbook of Data Processing Administration, Operations and Procedures.* New York: AMACOM, A Division of American Management Associations, 1976.

Montgomery, John D. *Alternatives and Decisions in Educational Planning.* Paris: International Institute for Educational Planning, 1976.

Moran, Kay Don. *The Legal Aspects of School Communications.* Topeka, Kansas: National Organization on Legal Problems in Education, 1980.

Morphet, Edgar L., et al. *Educational Organization and Administration: Concepts, Practices and Issues.* Englewood Cliffs, New Jersey: Prentice-Hall, 1974.

Mossman, F. H., et al. *Logistics System Analysis.* Washington, D.C.: University Press of American, 1977.

Neale, Daniel C. *Strategies for School Improvement: Cooperative Planning and Organization Development.* Boston: Allyn & Bacon, 1981.

Nelson, D. L., and Purdy, William M. *School Business Administration.* Lexington, Massachusetts: Heath Books, 1971.

Nolte, M. Chester. *Duties and Liabilities of School Administrators.* West Nyack, New York: Parker Publishing Company, 1973.

Ohio Division of School Finance. *The Administration of School Plant Maintenance and Operations in Ohio.* Columbus, Ohio: Ohio State Department of Education, Ohio Division of School Finance and the Ohio Association of School Business Officials, 1971.

O'Neil, Robert M. *Classrooms in the Crossfire: The Rights and Interests of Students, Parents, Teachers, Administrators, Librarians, and the Community.* Bloomington, Indiana: Indiana University Press, 1981.

Orlicky, Joseph. *Material Requirements Planning: The New Way of Life in Production and Inventory Management.* New York: McGraw-Hill, 1975.

Ornstein, A. C., and Miller, Steven I., Editors. *Policy Issues in Education.* Lexington, Massachusetts: Lexington Books, 1976.

Owens, Robert G. *Organizational Behavior in Education,* 2d ed. Englewood Cliffs, New Jersey, 1981.

Owens, Robert G., and Steinhoff, Carl R. *Administering Change in Schools.* Englewood Cliffs, New Jersey: Prentice-Hall, 1976.

Payne, A., and Hutchings, P. A. *Computer Software for Schools.* London: Pitman, 1980.

Perry, Charles R., et al. *The Labor Relations Climate and Management Rights in Urban School Systems, Report No. 11: The Case of Philadelphia.* Philadelphia: Industrial Research Unit, The Wharton School, University of Pennsylvania.

Perryman, John N. *The School Administrator and the Food Service Program.* Washington, D.C.: National Association of School Principals, 1972.

Petit, Thomas A. *Fundamentals of Management Coordination: Supervisors, Middle Managers, and Executives.* New York: Wiley, 1975.

Plossl, George W., and Welch, W. Evert. *The Role of Top Management in the Control of Inventory.* Reston, Virginia: Reston Publishing Co., 1979.

Plowman, E. G. *Elements of Business Logistics.* Stanford, California: Stanford University Press, 1964.

Powers, Thomas F. *Introduction to Management in the Hospitality Industry.* New York: Wiley, 1979.

Pulliam, John D., and Bowman, J. R. *Educational Futurism in Pursuance of Survival.* Norman, Oklahoma: University of Oklahoma Press, 1974.

Rebell, Michael A., and Block, Arthur R. *Educational Policy Making and the Courts: An Empirical Study of Judicial Activism.* Chicago: University of Chicago Press, 1982.

Riegel, Robert, et al. *Insurance Principles and Practices: Property and Liability,* 6th ed. Englewood Cliffs, New Jersey: Prentice-Hall, 1976.

Rubin, Louis, Editor. *The Future of Education: Perspectives on Tomorrow's Schooling.* Boston: Allyn & Bacon, 1975.

Sanders, Donald H., and Birkin, Stanley J. *Computers and Management: In a Changing Society,* 3d ed. New York: McGraw-Hill, 1980.

Sanders, Susan, et al. *The Computer in Educational Decision Making: An Introduction and Guide for School Administrators (Northwest Regional Education Laboratory).* Portland, Oregon, and Hanover, New Hampshire: Time Share, 1978.

Sanford, Aubrey C., and Braccy, Hyler J., 2d ed. Columbus, Ohio: Merrill, 1977.

Sergiovanni, Thomas J., and Carver, Fred D. *The New School Executive: A Theory of Administration,* 2d ed. New York: Harper & Row, 1980.

Sergiovanni, Thomas J., et al. *Educational Governance and Administration.* Englewood Cliffs, New Jersey: Prentice-Hall, 1980.

Shelly, Gary B., and Cashman, Thomas J. *Introduction to Computers and Data Processing.* Fullerton, California: Anaheim Publishing Company, 1980.

Sippl, C. J., and Sippl, R. J. *Computer Dictionary and Handbook,* 3d ed. Indianapolis: H. W. Sams, 1980.

Sleeman, Phillip, and Rockwell, D. M., Editors. *Designing Learning Environments.* New York: Longman, 1981.

Spiva, Ulysses V., Editor. *Leadership Plus Administration in School Management: Selected Readings.* Sherman Oaks, California: Banner Books International, 1978.

State of Tennessee. *Tennessee Internal School Financial Management Manual.* Nashville, Tennessee: Tennessee State Department of Education, 1977.

Steiner, George A., and Miner, John B. *Management Policy and Strategy.* New York: Macmillan, 1977.

Stoops, Emery, et al. *Handbook of Educational Administration: A Guide for the Practitioner,* 2d ed. Boston: Allyn & Bacon, 1981.

Swieringa, Robert J., and Moncur, Robert H. *Some Effects of Participative Budgeting on Managerial Behavior.* New York: National Association of Accountants, 1975.

Swinth, Robert L. *Organizational Systems for Management: Designing, Planning, and Implementation.* Columbus, Ohio: Grid, Inc., 1974.

Tanner, C. Kenneth, and Williams, Earl J. *Educational Planning and Decision-Making: A View through the Organizational Process.* Lexington, Massachusetts: Lexington Books, 1981.

The Random House College Dictionary. New York: Random House, Inc., 1984.

The World Book Encyclopedia. Chicago, Illinois: World Book, Inc., 1984.

Thompson, John T. *Policymaking in American Public Education: A Framework for Analysis.* Englewood Cliffs, New Jersey: Prentice-Hall, 1976.

Thomas, Norman C. *Education in National Politics.* New York: David McKay Co., 1975.

United States v. Butler, 297 U.S. 1, 56 S. Ct. 312 (1936).

United States Government. *Financial Accounting Classification and Standard Terminology for local and State School Systems.* Publication No. 73–118000. Washington, D.C.: United States Department of Health, Education and Welfare, 1973.

Van Horne, James C. *Financial Management and Policy,* 5th ed. Englewood Cliffs, New Jersey: Prentice-Hall, 1980.

Van Meter, Eddy J., Editor. *The Educational Organization Development Handbook.* Manhattan, Kansas: Educational Administration Development Associates, 1975.

Vaughan, B. W. *Planning in Education.* New York: Cambridge University Press, 1978.

Ware, Martha L., and Remmlein, Madaline K. *School Law,* 4th ed. Danville, Illinois: Interstate Printers, 1979.

Weir, Stanley M. *Order Selection: A Focal Point for Developing Warehouse Machine/Systems.* New York: American Management Association, Purchasing Division, 1968.

Westing, John H., et al. *Purchasing Management: Materials in Motion,* 4th ed. New York: Wiley, 1976.

Wiles, David K. *Energy, Winter and Schools: Crisis and Decision Theory.* Lexington, Massachusetts: Lexington Books, 1979.

Wiles, David K., et al. *Practical Politics for School Administrators.* Boston: Allyn & Bacon, 1981.

Williams, Chester A., and Heins, Richard M. *Risk Management and Insurance,* 3d ed. New York: McGraw-Hill, 1976.

Wilson, Frank C. *Short-Term Financial Management: How to Improve Financial Results Now?* Homewood, Illinois: Dow Jones-Irwin, 1975.

Wilson, L. Craig. *School Leadership Today: Strategies for the Educator.* Boston: Allyn & Bacon, 1978.

Wilson, Richard M. S. *Financial Control: A Systems Approach.* New York: McGraw-Hill, 1974.

Wood v. Strickland, 95 S. Ct. 992 (Ark., 1975).

Yourdan, Edward. *Managing the Structured Techniques,* 2d ed. New York: Yourdan Press, 1979.

Zaltman, Gerald, et al. *Dynamic Educational Change: Models, Strategies, and Management.* New York: Free Press, 1977.

Zeisel, John. *Stopping School Property Damage: Design and Administrative Guidelines to Reduce School Vandalism.* Arlington, Virginia: American Association of School Administrators; New York: Educational Facilities Laboratories, 1976.

Zirkel, Perry A., and Bargerstock, Charles T. *The Law on Reduction—In-Force: A Summary of Legislation and Litigation.* Arlington, Virginia: Educational Research Service, 1980.

NAME INDEX

SUBJECT INDEX